A Preface to Theology

W. Clark Gilpin

A PREFACE TO THEOLOGY

For Steve Peterson —
with gratitude for your
commitment to
theological scholarship
in the Protestant
tradition.

Clark Gilpin

THE UNIVERSITY OF CHICAGO PRESS
CHICAGO & LONDON

W. Clark Gilpin is a historian of American Christianity and the dean
of the University of Chicago Divinity School.

The University of Chicago Press, Chicago 60637
The University of Chicago Press, Ltd., London
© 1996 by The University of Chicago
All rights reserved. Published 1996
Printed in the United States of America
05   04   03   02   01   00   99   98   97   96   1   2   3   4   5

ISBN: 0-226-29399-8 (cloth)
ISBN: 0-226-29400-5 (paper)

Library of Congress Cataloging-in-Publicaton Data

Gilpin, W. Clark.
  A preface to theology / W. Clark Gilpin.
    p.   cm.
  Includes bibliographical references and index.
  ISBN 0-226-29399-8 (cloth).—ISBN 0-226-29400-5 (pbk.)
    1. Theology—Study and teaching—United States—History.
  I. Title.
  BV4030.G55   1996
  207'.73—dc20   96-10871
                                                     CIP

Parts of chapter 1 appeared originally as "The Seminary Ideal in American Protestant Ministerial Education, 1700–1808" in *Theological Education* 20 (Spring 1984).
Reprinted by permission. Parts of chapter 4 appeared originally as "The Theological
Schools" in J. Carroll and W. C. Roof, *Beyond Establishment* (Louisville: Westmin-
ster/John Knox Press, 1993), pp. 188–204. Reprinted by permission.

⊚ The paper used in this publication meets the minimum requirements of the
American National Standard for Information Sciences—Permanence of Paper for
Printed Library Materials, ANSI Z39.48–1984.

CONTENTS

ACKNOWLEDGMENTS

My questions about the history and character of the academic study of theology in America began with an unusual committee assignment—unusual because unusually interesting. The committee in question was the Issues Research Advisory Committee, created in 1985 by the Association of Theological Schools in the United States and Canada. The committee had been formed to promote research and stimulate conversation on the governing concepts, presuppositions, and fundamental purposes of theological education in North America. Members of the committee reflected a wide range of academic disciplines, institutional affiliations, and religious and theological predispositions. Meetings invariably subordinated procedural details to substantive discussion of the state and possibilities of contemporary theological inquiry. It is with pleasure and deep gratitude that I acknowledge the intellectual benefits of my association from 1985 to 1990 with Leon Pacala, then president of ATS, and with the members of the committee: Joseph C. Hough (chair), James H. Evans,

Millard J. Erickson, Francis S. Fiorenza, Franklin I. Gamwell, David H. Kelsey, Robert P. Meye, Robert J. Schreiter, Peter Slater, Marjorie H. Suchocki, Barbara G. Wheeler, and Charles M. Wood.

Chapter 1 is built on research that was largely conducted as a Samuel Foster Haven Fellow at the American Antiquarian Society, Worcester, Massachusetts, and an earlier version appeared in *Theological Education*. An earlier version of chapter 4 appeared in *Beyond Establishment: Protestant Identity in a Post-Protestant Age*, edited by Jackson Carroll and Wade Clark Roof for Westminster/John Knox Press.

Finally, my colleagues at the University of Chicago Divinity School have strongly influenced my outlook on the issues discussed in the following pages. In particular, I thank B. A. Gerrish, Paul Griffiths, Martin E. Marty, Richard E. Rosengarten, and David Tracy for reading and commenting on the manuscript.

The modern man who has ceased to believe, without ceasing to be credulous, hangs, as it were, between heaven and earth, and is at rest nowhere. There is no theory of the meaning and value of events which he is compelled to accept, but he is none the less compelled to accept the events. There is no moral authority to which he must turn now, but there is coercion in opinions, fashions and fads. There is for him no inevitable purpose in the universe, but there are elaborate necessities, physical, political, economic. He does not feel himself to be an actor in a great and dramatic destiny, but he is subject to the massive powers of our civilization, forced to adopt their pace, bound to their routine, entangled in their conflicts. He can believe what he chooses about this civilization. He cannot, however, escape the compulsion of modern events. . . . Events are there, and they overpower him. But they do not convince him that they have that dignity which inheres in that which is necessary and in the nature of things.

Walter Lippmann, *A Preface to Morals*, pp. 9–10

INTRODUCTION

WHAT DO THEOLOGIANS DO?

This book interprets the academic study of theology in America from the eighteenth century to the present. It borrows its interpretive clue (and the impetus for its title) from Walter Lippmann's pointed inquiry of 1929, *A Preface to Morals*. In a famous phrase, Lippmann declared that "the acids of modernity" had dissolved the conception of a governing purpose to the universe, from which human ethical conduct had traditionally derived its meaning and its dignity. Lippmann saw that the articulation of this universal governance had been the customary activity of theologians, and its dissolution left, among many questions, the question "What do theologians do?" This book is *A Preface to Theology* in the sense that it will explore how Lippmann's "acids" not only dissolved a traditional conceptual framework but also deeply etched a distinctive pattern of intellectual problems into the academic study of theology in America. I have written during a decade of widespread perplexity about the human importance of humanistic scholarship, when a strikingly large number of books have inquired into the history and purposes of particular academic disciplines, analyzing such fields as sociology, history, and English as well as professional education in medicine and law.[1] But no educational endeavors have been more vigorously investigated in the past decade than the academic study of religion and graduate professional education for ministry. Nearly a dozen recent books and scores of articles have appraised the nature and purposes of divinity schools, departments of religious studies, and theological seminaries.[2] The writing is notable for its tone of discontent, suggesting that scholars become interested in the history of their disciplines because they are uncertain or skeptical about the contemporary purposes of the enterprise. It is writing that asks for, proposes, and demands change. Inquiry into the history of an academic discipline is prompted, it would seem, by the desire to uncover, assess, and reconstruct the discipline's governing principles and assumptions.

This climate of perplexed discontent is provocatively interpreted in a book by Russell Jacoby, entitled *The Last Intellectuals*. Jacoby laments the retreat of academics from larger social domains in order to write solely for the "insular societies" of their scholarly disciplines. In so doing, Jacoby declares, they have forsaken an earlier tradition of American intellectuals who wrote to "address a general and educated audience." The consequence, he concludes, is the "impoverishment of public culture."[3] One way of interpreting current discontent over the purposes of scholarship is, therefore, to say that scholars, perhaps especially scholars of religion, have lost sight of their public. Uncertainty or disagreement about the public to whom and for whom they are accountable leaves scholars uncertain or disagreed about the point and significance of the scholarly enterprise itself. Not only is public culture impoverished by insular scholarship but scholarship itself is impoverished by the eclipse of its public commitments. Inquiries into the history of disciplines become, in this intellectual context, efforts to retrieve, or reconstitute, or reconceive the purposes and the publics of scholarly work.

Prompted by perplexity about intellectual purposes and publics, this book aims to achieve some self-critical understanding of the conditions for an American theological scholarship in the Protestant tradition that would be responsible to a threefold public in the churches, the academic community, and civil society. It approaches this contemporary objective indirectly, by investigating historically the social roles of Protestant theologians and the educational institutions in which they pursued their scholarship and teaching.[4] Baldly stated, the question is: What do theologians do? I have put that question to a long series of Protestant theologians, beginning with the New England Puritan Cotton Mather, who in 1726 wrote the first American book on how to study theology. Thus far, the theologians have all "answered" that they are scholars and teachers. But, not surprisingly, the aims and methods of their scholarship and their goals for the students whom they teach have varied dramatically according to the time and place in which they spoke.

To ask *what theologians do* is, of course, to invite an answer that emphasizes context and social role to a degree that might not be the case if one were to ask *what theology is*. My argument unfolds on the hypothesis that we will misunderstand the ideas of a particular era about the nature of theology as an academic discipline unless we also understand those ideas as statements about the roles of theologians and theological schools in American society. Definitions of theology have not arisen in abstraction, I suggest, but in relation to institutions of theological scholarship and vocations of theological scholars that are diverse and changing over time. In short, I propose to find out what theology is by asking what theologians do.

In colonial America, for example, theological scholarship was in the hands of the Protestant pastor, and students were educated in theology by apprenticeship with a more experienced minister. Theological seminaries did not come into existence until the beginning of the nineteenth century, and their character was substantially influenced at the end of the nineteenth century by the development of divinity schools connected with modern research universities and in the twentieth century by the creation of departments of religious studies uninvolved with ministerial education. The social context of theological scholarship gradually shifted from church and parsonage to school and office. The customary employments of the theologian shifted from pulpit to classroom. Ministerial tutors, engaged in the theological formation of apprentice pastors, were replaced by theological professors, responsible for the mastery and extension of a particular field of scholarship. The primary professional organization became the academic society rather than the ministerial association. In this process of becoming a specialized academic enterprise, theology itself changed, being differently oriented toward its audiences, investigating different problems, and employing different methods of scholarship in those investigations. The interaction between the changing intellectual practice of the theologian and the definition of theology will be the central subject matter of this book.

Theologians, of course, have not been unaware of such changes and have responded by reflecting on their own scholarly and educational purposes, producing across three centuries an extensive *literature on the rationale for theological study*. These diverse expositions of "the idea of a theological school," ranging from manuals of advice for theological students to polemics against the theological curriculum to reflective essays on the theologian's vocation, collectively interpret the human import and social consequences of the intellectual work done by theologians.[5] It is literature that expresses the considered judgment of theologians on the governing purposes of their work and argues for its continuing importance to their ecclesial, academic, and national publics. In focusing my attention on this collection of literature, I have not undertaken to survey the history of Protestant theological education in America. Although, along the way, I will say some things about the historical development of theological schools, their faculty, students, and curriculum, I will do so only to the extent that institutional forms illuminate presuppositions about the proper cultural work of disciplined theological inquiry. Nor, certainly, am I attempting a general history of Protestant theology in America. For one thing, that task would lead my narrative far beyond schools, scholars, and scholarship into other important settings of theological reflection, the preparation of sermons, the composition of worship and hymnody, tracts on religious reform, the writing of imaginative literature, corporate Bible study, and so on. For another, the point of this essay is to interpret the "architecture" of theological inquiry, to suggest how particular cultural problems have shaped what theologians do, not to sketch the history of substantive theological doctrines or theological systems. Nor, given my interest in context, am I suggesting a generalization about what theologians have done in all times and in all places. Instead, I am proposing that a characteristic orientation toward the vocation of theological scholarship has developed in American Protestantism, an orientation that has drawn out and emphasized features shared with the wider Christian theological tradition in order to meet the exigencies of "the American circumstance."

When I refer to an encounter between the wider Christian theological tradition and the exigencies of "the American circumstance," I mean, in its broadest contours, the transition from theology done in the context of nationally established churches to theology done in the context of religious pluralism and the separation of church and state. Traditional Christian theology always sought in one way or another to speak about all reality in relation to its ultimate source or ground—to speak about belief in a God who was "maker of heaven and earth." In the course of the sixteenth-century Reformation, in which the Western church splintered into Roman Catholic and various Protestant churches, this Christian speech about humanity's ultimate environment was codified in a diverse series of creeds and confessions, each one becoming the uniform standard of truth for a particular national church. Not only did each Protestant national church thus specify its distinct beliefs, but each also assumed, first, that the well-being of any society depended on such a body of commonly shared religious beliefs about human destiny and conduct and, second, that the inculcation of these shared beliefs must be guaranteed by the coercive power of the state.[6] When representatives of these state churches migrated to North America in the seventeenth and eighteenth centuries, they gradually and often grudgingly faced the questions of whether these multiple versions of truth could peacefully intermingle within a single territory and, if so, whether the resultant society could survive and its citizens flourish without the cohesive influence of common religious belief. The American "experiment" with religious freedom unfolded from the halting recognition that the churches could persist, grow, and exert their several influences on national life by persuasive appeal and the voluntary commitment of their members, without recourse to the legal sanctions of the state.[7]

The transition from state church to pluralism came to completion between the American Revolution and approximately 1840. This proved to be critical for the shaping of American theological scholarship, since during this period the religious pluralism of America was largely limited to the churches of Reformed Christianity, that is, the confessional tradition that began among the Swiss with Ulrich Zwingli and John Calvin and was appropriated by the Dutch, English, Scottish, and some of the German churches. As one recent interpreter has observed, the broad tradition of Reformed Christianity—including Puritan Congregationalists, Presbyterians, Methodists, Baptists, Episcopalians, and the Continental Reformed churches—comprised approximately 90 percent of American Christians at the time of the American Revolution. As late as 1865, this collection of Reformed churches still represented about 60 percent of American Christians and exerted cultural, political, and economic influence commensurate with that majority status.[8] Hence, during the decades when formal theological reflection in America began to reshape its institutional forms in order to address the cultural issues of pluralism, toleration, and the separation of church and state, it did so with intellectual resources derived largely from the Reformed tradition. As my narrative will indicate, both these cultural issues and the Reformed bias toward them persisted in American theological scholarship down to the 1960s and perhaps beyond.

In order to delineate the purposes of theological scholarship within this "American circumstance," each of the following chapters will investigate the rationales that particular theologians have given for their aims as educators and scholars in order to discover their assumptions about the social task of theology itself. Chapter 1, "The Fruition of the Seminary Ideal," focuses on the century from the 1720s to the 1820s. It assesses the ways in which inherited patterns of theological study presupposed a society in which church, nation, and school were organically coordinate elements of a single whole. Education was conceived to be "all of a piece," and its goals were comprehensively summarized as "piety, civility, and learning." The social task ascribed to the theologian was to inculcate these virtues in behalf of a morally ordered and intellectually coherent society. But by the time the first Protestant seminaries were founded, beginning with Andover in 1808, the inherited congruities of church, nation, and school—of piety, civility, and learning—no longer existed, and the work of the theologian required a new rationale. Political theory, for example, now developed in substantial independence from explicitly religious presuppositions, and churches promulgated their beliefs without formal help or hindrance from the state. The theological work of articulating the interdependence of all life could no longer *proceed from* the assumed interdependence of social institutions; rather, the theological problem lay precisely in *arguing toward* such a social interdependence. As a consequence of this institutional dispersal, I will argue, later historical efforts to state the rationale for theological study in America became efforts to order or prioritize the contending communal loyalties of theologians: loyalties to the church, the nation, and higher education. These rationales have attempted to define the norms, methods, and tasks of the theologian in such a way as to delineate and harmonize the contributions of theology to the life of the church, the academy, and the society at large. In so doing, they have not simply explained theology to "outsiders" but also self-critically explored the theologians' own vocation, questioning whether and in what way theology was a subject worthy of intellectual labor.

The next three chapters chronologically pursue this search for the idea of a theological school. Chapter 2, "Scholarship and the Culture of Protestantism," examines the period from approximately 1830 to 1880, when the seminary theologians defined their work as "theological science," pursued in behalf of a national culture. Chapter 3, "The Case for Theology in the University," focuses on the decades from 1880 to 1930, when theologians debated the task of theology in terms of its contribution to the modern research university. Chapter 4, "Intellectual Center of the Church's Life," compares two major studies of theological education directed by William Adams Brown and H. Richard Niebuhr in order to interpret the relation of theological scholarship to the church in the period from 1930 to 1960.

The chronological organization of these three chapters is, at another level, also a thematic organization. As their titles suggest, the three are concerned, in turn, with the relation of the academic study of theology to the American nation, to the university, and to the church. By combining chronological and thematic treatment, I am not, however, suggesting a straightforward progression in which theologians of one era focus on a particular audience and subsequent theologians set that audience aside in order to address another. Instead, each of these publics presents a recurrent set of issues to theologians of every generation. The enterprise of relating theology to university education, for example, which I illustrate from the period 1880 to 1930, presented comparable issues both before and afterward, down to our present situation. Furthermore, theology is distinctive among the scholarly disciplines for attempting to speak to and from these three distinct publics.[9] But the same speech may not equally address all three. A mode of theology that augments the internal life of a particular denomination may be less effectively deployed to interpret the wider religious life of the nation. For this reason, theologians have especially concerned themselves with systematic questions of the connections among these publics and the coherence of a theology that attempts to interpret each and all. The thematic organization of the following chapters, therefore, explores what happens when these systematic connections among the three publics are differently balanced or articulated. On the basis of this historical and thematic inquiry into the relation of theologians and theological schools to their publics, I have then attempted in the final chapter to assess the contemporary situation of theological scholarship. Hence, chapter 5, "The Background of Possibilities," deals chronologically with the years since 1960 and thematically with the question of the academic theologian's appropriate responsibilities to nation, university, and church.

Throughout, I have stressed that multiple perspectives on the aims of theological study have existed in every era and that the "nature" of theology at a particular moment is to be found less in some regnant consensus about specific doctrines than in certain characteristic issues that shape theological debate. Indeed, since these characteristic issues most often came as the intellectual inheritance from a previous generation of scholars, theological debate has usually been intergenerational, contesting earlier thinkers and arguing with contemporaries about how those previous positions should be received or revised. Given my emphasis on debate, I shall not argue that the theological educators discussed below were somehow "typical" of their times in the proposals they made for the appropriate relation between theology and its publics. Indeed, in each case, their answers were only partly representative and sometimes "creatively out of step" with the general direction of development.[10] However, by adopting particular perspectives, it is possible to delineate the contested issues during a given period or between periods and to suggest how thinkers interior to an age went about the activity of identifying, formulating, and resolving theological problems. It allows us to enter the dialogue, so to speak, and to feel the force of argument and counter-argument regarding the formation of students, the unity of the curriculum, or the integrity of faculty members as citizens, scholars, and church leaders.

And yet, this is obviously not simply a case of "adopting" historical perspectives, since underlying all of them is my own prior vantage point as a theological educator of the late twentieth century seeking some leverage on the immediately impending task. The questions I have posed to these earlier theologian-educators are my own questions; I have sought to recognize that they would "hear" these questions with the nuances and connotations of their times and not mine; I have sought to respect the integrity of the "answers" they give. Historical dialogue in these respects shares the hazards and hopes of conversation with contemporary acquaintances.

What remains in this introduction is the task of identifying the general issues that have arisen in each era as theologians have sought to situate their work in relation to church, academy, and nation. Before launching into the more detailed discussion of the ensuing chapters, I will preview specific features of *American* society that have given a distinct disposition to Protestant theological scholarship conducted here. I will sketch how the transition to *modern* American society that occurred in the two and one-half centuries traversed by this narrative raised a constitutive theological problem that informs what theologians do. And I will suggest why the history of theology as an academic discipline has importance not only for theological scholars but also for church members, for citizens concerned for the health of civil society, and for the theologians' colleagues in the wider scholarly community.

The Communal Contexts of Theological Study

H. Richard Niebuhr began his well-known analysis of theological education, *The Purpose of the Church and Its Ministry* (1956), by emphasizing the interconnection of schooling and society. "Education," he wrote, "is so closely connected with the life of a community that queries about the aims of teaching and learning cannot be answered unless ideas about the character and purposes of the society in which it is carried on are clarified first of all."[11] But, for Niebuhr and other Protestant thinkers who have assessed theological education in North America, the task of establishing its communal context has been obviously complicated by the multiplicity of communities—communities concrete and abstract, tangible and ideal—to which theological schools have understood themselves to be related. The denominations, the church universal, religion, the clerical profession, North American higher education, the nation, and what, two hundred years earlier, Jonathan Edwards had called "the universal system of being in general" have all laid their various and sometimes conflicting claims upon the loyalties of divinity schools, their students, and their faculties. How were these communities to be defined? Which of them should take priority in establishing the aims of theological scholarship? And, could the relationships among these communities be interpreted in such a way as to advance the coherence of theology itself?

Niebuhr's answer to the general question of the theological seminaries' communal context was, broadly speaking, the same answer American Protestant theologians had given for more than two centuries: "The community in which they work is the Church; the objectives they pursue are those of the Church."[12] But, as Niebuhr well knew, this answer contained numerous ambiguities, especially when one proceeded from broad affirmations to the specific issues of founding an institution, appointing a faculty, or designing a curriculum. Most obvious was the question of the relation between church and denomination. It was the churches, the denominations of Protestantism, who at the beginning of the nineteenth century had founded the theological schools. It was they who supported the schools financially. And, it was into these churches that graduates of the schools proceeded as ministers. Over the course of American history, the responsibilities of the seminary to the church universal and to the particular denominational manifestations of that wider community have by no means been clearly or easily adjudicated. The plurality of churches has thus raised a series of complex questions of loyalty or accountability for theological schools, and these questions have had major consequences for Protestant theological study, both in terms of its institutional form and its intellectual purposes.

This is especially true because the churches, from the founding of Harvard College in 1636, have been convinced that the moral and intellectual stature of their leadership represented perhaps the single most crucial ingredient in their future prosperity. As the seedbed of leadership, the seminary has not only had a profound *practical role* in preparing the church's future ministers but also a powerful *symbolic role* in expressing the church's present values. The seminary has given institutional focus to questions about what is worthy of being handed on—what beliefs, what moral commitments, what liturgical patterns, and what social vision. For this reason, historical perspective on the religious and cultural purposes of theology is indispensable to contemporary Christians seeking to make informed decisions both about ministerial education and, more generally, about the role of systematic theological reflection in the on-going life of churches.

But, the traditional identification of the church as the ordering community of theological education does not provide any simple or single resolution of the responsibilities of theological schools to the nation or to other institutions of higher education. The literature of theological education abounds in references to "theological education *in America*" or to "the education of *American ministers.*" These references imply more than a merely convenient geographic delimitation of the subject. Rather, they raise questions about the extent to which the national ethos has shaped—or ought to shape— the character and purposes of theological education. And, since it is "the advancement of theological *education*" that this literature addresses, it must also be asked in what ways institutions created to pursue the educative purposes of the church are nonetheless to be held accountable in their methods and standards to more general educational criteria in the society. In these ways the theological school has given institutional focus to questions about the relation between the church and the nation's general intellectual culture. To put the matter in a slightly different way, theologians, by virtue of their location on the boundary between the church and higher education, speak from two of the most important components of the voluntary domain of American public life that, in common parlance, is often distinguished from government and the economic sector and identified as society's "third sector." At least since Alexis de Tocqueville this voluntary, non-profit sector has been regarded as a crucial contributor to the shaping of the civil society that extends beyond the formally organized state and provides a crucial arena for public discussion about the collective values of the society. Given the sharp disagreement in contemporary America about the appropriate place of explicit religious convictions in political debate and civic life, informed judgments about "religion and politics" will benefit from historical understanding of the diverse ways theologians have contributed to discourse in this "third sector" concerning the interconnections of religion, national identity, and education.[13]

Thus far, I have characterized the shaping of Protestant theological study in America primarily in terms of the *external pressures* brought to bear by its environing communities. This is only one side of the story. In addition, an *internal dynamic* has also propelled transformation. This has been the case because theological schools— like other schools in American society—have been understood to play a double social role. They have been conceived, in almost equal degree, as purveyors of inherited values and as institutions of innovation, free inquiry, and reform. This dual role, as institutions of tradition and as institutions of innovation, has generated tensions within the schools and between the schools and their communities, tensions that have made periodic reassessments, renewals, and revisions familiar features of the seminary landscape. To speak generally, the internal dynamic of theological education raises questions about what might be called "the ethics of change." It forces theologians concerned about the cultural purposes of their work to consider, for example, why they evaluate the scholarly achievements of previous generations in the way that they do, what they would preserve and what they would jettison; to consider the adequacy of their descriptive premises about the present and its problems; to consider the direction of intended change and the arguments for preferring it over other alternatives.

Given these multiple allegiances and the complex lines of accountability that they entail, it is not surprising that theologians and theological schools have been challenged from several quarters to define and defend their purposes and methods. Nor is it surprising that, in the course of responding, different schools and different scholars have weighted their communal loyalties differently and articulated significantly different conceptions of the proper purpose of academic theology with respect to church, nation, and academy. Further, given what I have termed the "external" and "internal" dynamics for change, these various conceptions have undergone major revision over the course of American history. In sum, questions concerning the multiple communal loyalties of theological study are the hardy perennials of debate among American theologians. Shifting patterns and perceptions of ecclesial, political, and educational life have exerted pressures that have altered not only the modes of theological training but also, I will argue, the definition of theology itself.

The Perplexity of Theologians

The condition underlying questions about the multiple loyalties of theological study to church, nation, and academy has been the modern historical shift in understanding the nature of social institutions. In *Religion and the Rise of Capitalism* (1926), the economic historian R. H. Tawney described this change by stating that "modern social theory, like modern political theory develops only when society is given a naturalistic instead of a religious explanation, and a capital fact which presides at the birth of both is the change in the conception held of the nature and functions of a church."[14] The development of academic theology in America has coincided with the development of naturalistic explanations for state, economy, school, and family. Rather than reflecting divinely instituted orders of creation, these institutions, it is generally assumed, have taken form from the contingent influences of strictly human fears, interests, and aspirations. Hence, the historic task of the theologian to offer a comprehensive interpretation of the transcending presuppositions of social life has had to take account not simply of the multiplicity of social institutions but also of the fact that many participants in these institutions interpret them without any explicitly religious reference.

As part of this changing conception of social institutions the church, too, has received "a naturalistic instead of a religious explanation." In the twentieth century, especially, this naturalistic interpretation has argued that churches, like all human institutions, reflect the class, ethnic, and gender biases of their participants. From this perspective, the teachings and practices of the church are less the universal and authoritative guides for the conduct of life than they are the historically contingent expression of life as it has actually been conducted—for good and for ill—by particular social groups. The communal loyalties of theological scholarship therefore appear problematic not only because of their multiplicity nor even because these theological loyalties adhere to institutions not themselves theologically understood. The communal loyalties of theological scholarship appear problematic because of the tension between universal norm and historical bias. For the purposes of this study, the consequence of these developments in modern social theory is that the theologian works out the aims and methods of theological scholarship in relation to multiple communities of affiliation by raising critical questions about the ethical and religious adequacy of the norms embedded in the institutional structures of the communities themselves.

It is partly in light of these theological questions about human communal life that the title of this book echoes Walter Lippmann's *A Preface to Morals.* There, Lippmann identified his audience as "those who are perplexed by the consequences of their own irreligion,"[15] meaning by religion the conviction that all human strivings and destinies derive their final worth from an inexorable purpose that sustains and directs all that is. In no small measure, irreligion has taken modern form as the incapacity to attribute anything other than a "naturalistic explanation" to the social institutions we inhabit. For this reason, perplexity about irreligion, Lippmann argued, stood prefatory to all efforts at ethical engagement with modernity, because "the acids of modernity" had eaten away the framework of meaning that supported the customs and institutions of society.

> The modern man who has ceased to believe, without ceasing to be credulous, hangs, as it were, between heaven and earth, and is at rest nowhere. There is no theory of the meaning and value of events which he is compelled to accept, but he is none the less compelled to accept the events. There is no moral authority to which he must turn now, but there is coercion in opinions, fashions and fads. There is for him no inevitable purpose in the universe, but there are elaborate necessities, physical, political, economic. He does not feel himself to be an actor in a great and dramatic destiny, but he is subject to the massive powers of our civilization, forced to adopt their pace, bound to their routine, entangled in their conflicts. He can believe what he chooses about this civilization. He cannot, however, escape the compulsion of modern events. . . . Events are there, and they overpower him. But they do not convince him that they have that dignity which inheres in that which is necessary and in the nature of things.[16]

This developing crisis with respect to the enduring moral coherence of social life and institutions has been, this book will argue, the enduring problem of American Protestant theology. The enterprise of Protestant theological scholarship in America from the eighteenth century to the twentieth has been propelled by this perplexity over irreligion, an irreligion with respect to church, nation, and school that the theologians often espied in "the world" but more often, and increasingly, encountered as "their own." The vocation of perplexity over human institutions and our allegiances to them thus represents the continuity running through the changes examined in the following chapters. Consideration of the intellectual and ethical consequences of this perplexed condition is what theologians do.

Over the years, this perplexity about human institutions has perennially intertwined with questions about God and the self. In one sense, this is not at all surprising. Calvin, after all, had opened his *Institutes of the Christian Religion* (1559) with the famous observation that "nearly all the wisdom we possess" consists of "the knowledge of God and of ourselves." And, although these two parts of wisdom are "joined by many bonds, which one precedes and brings forth the other is not easy to discern." In the history of American theological scholarship, I wish to propose, reconsiderations of God and of the self were "brought forth" by religious pluralism and the naturalistic explanation of human institutions: reconsideration of the self because of the felt dispersal of identity in disparate responses to contending, largely independent, and seemingly incommensurate communities of accountability; reconsideration of God as the single object of loyalty "beyond the many" that articulated corporate life and unified our disparate strivings.

Thus, I hope to show that the vocational perplexity of contemporary theologians is a genuinely theological perplexity that is thoroughly implicated in its specific cultural context. It is theological because it pursues the coherence of self and society by questioning the wholeness of all that is. It is contextual because it asks whether personal experience and social experience contain clues to their ultimate source or ground. This route of the theologians through perplexity into the interpretation of American experience has, in turn, contributed to the broader stream of American thought, and its parabolic employment by Henry David Thoreau prefigures the conclusions of this book. In the chapter of *Walden* entitled "The Village,"[17] Thoreau recounted the pathfinding prowess of his late-night journeys of return from town to pond, passing, as he boasted, between two pines "not more than eighteen inches apart, in the midst of the woods, invariably, in the darkest night." Sufficient familiarity with daytime landmarks enabled the confident passage through an occasional nocturnal pilgrimage. And yet, Thoreau turned to observe, "it is a surprising and memorable, as well as valuable experience, to be lost in the woods at any time."

> Not till we are completely lost, or turned round . . . do we appreciate the vastness and strangeness of nature. . . . Not till we are lost, in other words not till we have lost the world, do we begin to find ourselves, and realize where we are and the infinite extent of our relations.

Invariably to know the way was, somehow, its own lostness because it prevented appreciation for "the vastness and strangeness of nature." Unthinking confidence in feet on beaten paths ironically obscured real knowledge of "where we are and the infinite extent of our relations." To suggest how the potential for having "lost the world" was interwoven with the seeming familiarity of everyday life, Thoreau told of two, fishing late at Walden Pond, whose feet he set on the path home as night fell. Despite the initial assistance, they roamed through the rain-soaked woods, until dawn disclosed they had been circling "close by their own premises" all along. In contemplating the necessity of being lost to the process of finding, Thoreau challenged any routine activity by which days transpire, perhaps expire, in busy-ness. More specifically, his parable invites intellectual discovery to take the form of theological inquiry, that is, inquiry proceeding from the hypothesis that serious and critical appraisal of "where we are" entails reflection on "the infinite extent of our relations."

*So many faiths, so many loyalties, are offered to the modern man that
at last none seems to him wholly inevitable and fixed in the order of
the universe. The existence of many churches in one community
weakens the foundation of all of them.*

Walter Lippmann, *A Preface to Morals*, p. 76

ONE

THE FRUITION OF THE SEMINARY IDEAL,
1720–1830

Protestant educators in colonial America assumed what had long
been assumed in Western culture, that education was the comprehensive formation of character. It was *paideia*. It inculcated the virtues that fitted a student for responsible public life. In the case of
collegiate education, formation led toward one of the learned professions or one of the various stations of government and commerce to
which "men of substance" stood obligated. And, among those offices,
particular attention was directed toward the ministry of the church.

During the seventeenth and eighteenth centuries, metaphorical use of the term *seminary* to designate a school not only expressed
this formative aim of education but also intimated the school's
broader cultural importance and responsibilities. These educational
connotations of *seminary* depended on the term's horticultural reference to a plot of ground in which seedlings were cultivated for later
transplanting. Education was gardening. The 1584 statutes of Emmanuel College, Cambridge, for example, observed that "it is an ancient institution in the Church, and a tradition from the earliest

times, that schools and colleges be founded for the education of young men in all piety and good learning and especially Holy Writ and theology, that being thus instructed they may thereafter teach true and pure religion, refute all errors and heresies and by the shining example of a blameless life excite all men to virtue." Hence, in order to spread Christ's gospel, "there were decked out in his church, as it were in the garden of paradise, some seed-plots of those most noble plants of theology and right good learning, from which such as had grown to maturity might be transplanted to all parts of the Church, that she, being watered by their labours and increased by the gift of God, might come at last to a most flourishing and blessed estate."[1]

As the Cambridge statutes illustrate, the seminary metaphor portrayed two mutually supportive environments, the smaller a sheltered and more nurturing version of the larger. School and church were distinguishable, but coordinate, realms of society, espousing shared values and a shared intellectual outlook. In this image of education, as historian Sidney Mead has summarized it, "learning as such was all of a piece."[2] The college was the custodian of true religion, communicating it faithfully to each generation and thereby preserving the church from error, in order that it might ultimately arrive at "a most flourishing and blessed estate." The college was a fountain of virtuous learning, from which flowed pure waters that sustained society in both its present welfare and its future prospects. The seminary metaphor presupposed that the fundamental institutions of society—church, state, and school—had established a working agreement on the virtues of an educated person: piety, civility, and learning. That is, *seminary* conveyed an ideal picture not only of the relation between church and school but also of the relation between religion and liberal learning in the life of the student being tutored for civic responsibility. The student was a microcosm, and the personal virtues instilled by education were analogous to the principal social institutions.

In its role as educator of clergy, the college was the school of the prophets, and its faculty stood in the tradition of the prophetic office of Christ. Teaching was, in other words, an office of the church and, especially in the Reformed traditions that dominated formal education in the colonies, a specialized form of the ministry.[3] The college, its faculty, and its students held in trust a cultural tradition whose charter was the Christian religion. Prompted by this custodial responsibility, a long line of Protestant educators would have subscribed to Increase Mather's dictum of 1702 that, unless authentic piety directed learning, the college would become "a seminary of degenerate plants, who will with their foolish hands pull down those houses which their fathers have been building for the name of the Lord in this wilderness."[4] Less figuratively put, the common good depended on the devotion of society's leaders to inherited religious principle.

But, although the educational assumptions encapsulated in the seminary ideal weathered the transit of European civilization to colonial America, they were thoroughly transformed in their new intellectual and social environment. These transformations were already beginning in the seventeenth century, because it was the *Puritan* form of the seminary ideal that first significantly shaped the rationale for theological studies in America. The Puritan movement had, from the first, numbered the reform of ministerial education among its leading purposes and understood colleges not only as institutions of social continuity but also as *institutions of social renovation*, instruments of the Puritan drive to establish the holy commonwealth. In their zeal for educational reform the Puritans emphasized a long tradition, reflected in the Emmanuel College statutes, of interpreting the religious significance of higher learning in relation to the garden of paradise. Faith and reason had been at one before the Fall, and now, in a fragmentary and emblematic way, the university prefigured their ultimate reunion. Thus, in the Puritan version of the seminary metaphor, latent tensions between the ideals of social reform and social stability were inherent to the school's relations to church and to nation. The metaphor suggested that Christian scholarship was a providential agent of cultural transformation, and the Puritan rhetoric of renovation and millennial hope became, thereby, integral to the meanings of education in America. In 1663, for example, Jonathan Mitchell composed a "model" for Harvard College in which he argued that the Protestant Reformation had arisen in conjunction with a general revival of learning at the hands of Erasmus and Luther, because all of the arts and sciences were necessary for "understanding and improving" the Bible. "It is no new thing," Mitchell reminded his reader, "for a reforming people to need excitation to the maintenance of learning, without which all their endeavors after reformation will soon come to nothing." Biblical prophecies foretold the role of learning in the restoration of paradise, and Mitchell speculated that "when the Lord would destroy Antichrist and spread the light of the gospel in these latter days," an angel would be seen descending from heaven carrying an open book, and men would become "devourers of books."[5]

This vision of a renovated society had its parallel in Puritan theories of the self, and their educational theory aimed for the renovation of *persons* as well as *institutions*, by insisting that Christian character was not simply the product of formation but of reformation, the fruit of the mighty act of God in conversion. This affirmation, that authentic knowledge of God and of the self in relation to God came only as a gift of divine grace, provoked a host of questions about the proper relation of civic virtue and academic study to authentic piety. If piety was a gift of God, what did education contribute to it? If Christian faith was the foundation of virtue, could non-Christians be responsible citizens? Puritan religion forced reconsideration, in other words, of the inherited triad of educational virtues: piety, civility, and learning.

From approximately 1720 to 1830, these Puritan transformations of the seminary ideal were joined by broader social and intellectual movements that dissolved the inherited connections among church, nation, and school—among piety, civility, and learning—and recombined them in a new pattern invested with new cultural meaning. In the course of these decades, denominations gradually consolidated, expanded competitively into new geographic regions, and reoriented themselves toward one another and away from parent churches in Europe. The organic relations of church and state were disestablished, and the geographic parish was replaced by the congregation based on voluntary membership. Colleges redirected their purposes in ways that reflected the intellectual impact of the Enlightenment, that enlarged their educational commitment to professions other than ministry, and that altered their relationships to the churches. These changes gradually modified both the conception of the ministry and the practical life of the minister because they encouraged measurement of ministerial authority by the pragmatic criterion of power to persuade, that is, the power to build and support religious institutions by voluntary lay participation and financial contribution.[6] This new religious landscape dominated by denominational pluralism, voluntary church affiliation, and the ministry of persuasion changed the social background of theology and thereby redefined the work of theologians.

Despite these far-reaching challenges, inherited educational assumptions retained their influence, and when, beginning in 1808, the Protestant denominations established schools intended specifically for ministerial training, they chose to name them *seminaries*. But the actual seminaries of the early American republic existed within a religious, political, and educational environment far removed from that presupposed by the seminary ideal. Indeed, the founding of theological seminaries marked the intellectual dissolution of the seminary ideal. This chapter sketches the history of that dissolution and proposes that it generated the central intellectual problem for Protestant theologians in America.

Reading Divinity in New England

For the period 1720 to 1830 as a whole, the most common method of formal theological study, utilized at one time or another in all the major denominations, was a ministerial apprenticeship known as *reading divinity*. The arrangement was a simple one; a local pastor, or perhaps a college president or professor of divinity, would tutor one or more theological students, leading them through a course of studies and overseeing the exercise of their practical talents in the churches. Not infrequently, the apprentice would reside with his instructor during his studies, and the instructor, in turn, often informally sponsored the candidate during examination for ordination. The outward structure of this apprenticeship remained remarkably constant across decades, denominational lines, and geographic regions. Study typically proceeded in a catechetical progression through a text in systematic divinity, the instructor propounding theological questions to which the student responded with essays for the tutor's criticism and comment. As with college education in the era, formal disputation and extensive memorization were employed to hone mental discipline. Meanwhile, students gained confidence in their practical skills by preaching or offering prayer in private religious gatherings and advanced from these duties to assisting in public worship or supplying vacant pulpits. In this educational model, theological reflection was *a catechetical inquiry:* appropriating an authoritative theological tradition, considering its systematic structure with a view to its harmonious exposition, and applying its teachings to faith and conduct. Reading divinity was a churchly enterprise, conducted by ministers and aimed at the formation of ministers for civic religious leadership.

But, for understanding the historical significance of reading divinity, these similarities of form and purpose across time, regions, and denominations must be balanced against important differences. This is the case because the very flexibility and simplicity of reading divinity permitted it to be detached from its intellectual context in the seminary ideal and to function in ways disruptive of that ideal. Between 1720 and 1830, the varied employments and eventual collapse of reading divinity became a barometer of the social and cultural pressures that were transforming the seminary ideal of theological study.

In the early decades of the eighteenth century, opportunities were scarce for the formal study of theology in America, indeed, for formal study related to any of the professions. Prior to 1750, among ministers, lawyers, and physicians the only professional groups offering both formal and in-service training in British North America were the Congregational and Presbyterian clergy.[7] And, in the first three decades of the eighteenth century, systematic academic preparation for the ministry was occurring only in New England. In 1726, for example, the year that Cotton Mather published his manual for Congregational theological students, *Manuductio ad Ministerium,* there were no native colonials among the Anglican clergy of Virginia. Parishes there depended on the bishop of London to recruit their ministers, most of whom were English or Scottish, with degrees from Oxford, Cambridge, Edinburgh, or Glasgow.[8] Thus, the institutions and purposes of Protestant theological study first developed in

New England in the years leading up to the publication of Mather's manual of advice, roughly the first quarter of the eighteenth century.

Among New England Congregationalists in this period, reading divinity with a clerical tutor became a reasonably well-defined rite of passage for the ministerial candidate.[9] Based on seventeenth-century English and colonial precedents, the practice culminated a comparatively elaborate educational system that led the student through hornbook and catechism to the more formal classical studies of Latin school and college. Public culture presupposed theology, and collegiate education included the Bible and works of systematic theology by William Ames (1576–1633) or Johannes Wollebius (1586–1629). The common educational experience at Harvard or at Yale made the college "as much a cultural and political institution as an academic one,"[10] and, as the eighteenth century proceeded, commencement ceremonies increasingly became prominent public rituals.[11]

After earning bachelor's degrees, ministerial candidates sought out theological tutors and, for an indeterminate period ranging from a few months to more than a year, pursued a more or less systematic course of reading, perhaps taught school, were licensed to preach, and engaged in pulpit supply. Reading divinity was only loosely related to the Master of Arts degree,[12] and, to the extent that uniformity emerged in theological study, it derived less from specifically academic requirements than from the expectations of the ordained clergy. In 1705, for example, Massachusetts clergy proposed that local ministerial associations examine candidates and advised congregations that it would be "counted an offence" for them to engage a preacher without an association's "testimonial" to his fitness for the work. The ministers of the association were to examine the student's character, the principles which motivated his desire to enter the ministry, his adherence to the Westminster Confession, and his knowledge of the "three learned languages" and the "sciences commonly taught in the academical education." In 1726 Cotton Mather reported that "several associations" were following this examination procedure; it persisted with little alteration for the remainder of the century.[13] These ecclesiastical expectations established the routine—curriculum would be too strong a term—of theological studies.

Time spent reading divinity overlapped the time of candidacy with the congregation in which the student would eventually settle. After the call to a church, the prospect of ordination itself spurred further study and reflection on ministerial duty. Candidates regularly attended one another's ordinations, and clergy employed the ordination sermon to set forth the character and work of the pastor. Ordination inducted the theological student into a form of local public office in which lifetime tenure was the ideal. In conformity with this ideal, long pastorates of thirty and forty years were common. At the opening of the century, the vast majority of Connecticut and Massachusetts towns contained only one orthodox church; public taxes supported the minister's salary and maintained the meeting-house; attendance at worship was compulsory. To be sure, changes of great consequence were occurring in this system of religious establishment, and 40 percent of the region's approximately 260 towns would be multiparish communities by 1750. But despite these important changes, the ministerial office embodied ordered continuity in communal life. "The clergyman," writes historian Donald M. Scott, "was both the keeper and purveyor of the public culture, the body of fundamental precepts and values that defined the social community, and an enforcer of the personal values and decorum that sustained it."[14]

The *covenant theology* provided the classic articulation of this public role by constructing a theory of church and society around the idea that God, since the time of the biblical patriarchs, had dealt with humanity through a series of binding agreements or covenants. The Bible, it was supposed, set forth a single covenantal narrative of history in its entirety, from beginning to end, from Genesis to Revelation. Hence, the biblical narrative, in history and in prophecy, encompassed every age, including the present one, within a single cumulative and complex pattern of meaning. When subjected to scrupulous and pious investigation, the Bible and human experience therefore rendered reciprocal interpretations of one another, even though the final consummation of this narrative was hidden from human sight.[15]

Within this cosmic drama, *covenant* was a metaphor that interactively connected the self and social institutions. For the individual, the covenant of redemption was the means by which saving grace was given to the elect, and the Puritans emphasized the personal appropriation of this covenant in the conversion experience. The true form of the church was a congregation bound together by a signed covenant to worship God and obey the divine will. And, since the law of God extended to all persons, the congregation of "visible saints" stood at the center of a social compact that established the moral standards for the entire community. The work of the ministry presupposed these personal, ecclesiastical, and political dimensions of the covenant theology, which were clearly reflected in the two classic types of New England sermons: the Sunday sermons directed toward the salvation of souls and the "occasional" sermons preached on election days, fast and thanksgiving days, and similar public occasions as expositions of social, economic, and political duty.[16] Reading divinity prepared the student for the task of interpreting human existence, personal and public, within the covenantal history of divine providence.

In sum, New England Congregationalism during the opening decades of the eighteenth century incorporated the practice of reading divinity in an extensive professional initiation, an initiation in which college, clergy, and congregation all had their necessary parts to play and for which the covenant theology provided an intellectual framework. The need for guidance through the formal and informal elements of this education gave rise to a literary tradition of handbooks and letters of advice for the ministerial candidate. Bibliographic guides to theological study circulated in manuscript at least as early as the 1680s and, throughout the colonial period, primarily recommended authors from the Puritan tradition or the more systematically inclined Dutch Reformed.[17] Among these introductory pieces Cotton Mather's *Manuductio ad Ministerium* was the most fulsome American example. Drawing on more than forty years experience in the ministry of Boston's Second Congregational Church, Mather's "directions" arrayed a panoply of student duties and pastoral activities, proceeding through collegiate studies to the study of theology proper, offering instructions for preaching and pastoral visits, appealing for the union of Protestants, and concluding with advice on the maintenance of bodily health.

Mather understood education in terms of its contribution to

the supreme goal of human existence, life lived to the glory of God. Any other, inferior aim of education—worldly comfort or public advancement—would reduce the student to the level of the "beasts that perish. . . . A little more hair, and crawling on all four, and what the difference!"[18] From this perspective, the distinguishing mark of the human creature was the capacity for self-conscious pursuit of purposes, and genuine wisdom was to pursue a purpose ultimately good, true, and beautiful. By virtue of its all-comprehending aim— saving knowledge of God—the study of divinity properly directed all other academic pursuits. To underscore the ultimate end of education, Mather therefore opened his treatise by imploring the student to ponder human frailty:

> Do this, that you may do nothing like living in vain. Place yourself in the circumstances of a dying person; your breath failing, your throat rattling, your eyes with a dim cloud, and your hands with a damp sweat upon them, and your weeping friends no longer able to retain you with them. And then entertain such sentiments of this world, and of the work to be done in this world, that such a view must needs inspire you withal. Such a numbering of your days, I hope, will compel you to apply your heart unto wisdom.[19]

The student who thus contemplated his life in light of his death would elevate the self above the impassioned subjectivity of the dying self, Mather hoped, in order to view and appraise life in its ultimate frame of reference.

Having graphically depicted the religious background of all education, Mather turned to theological studies themselves. Here, he followed a common pattern of organization, used earlier in the century by Samuel Willard (1640–1707), the minister of Old South Church, Boston, in his *Brief Directions to a Young Scholar Designing the Ministry*. Both Willard and Mather *assumed* the truth of Scripture and assigned theology the tasks of elucidating, defending, and applying the revealed text's true meaning. They therefore divided theology into four parts: the study of the Bible, systematic theology, polemics, and casuistry.[20] As Willard explained, although "all theological truths be contained in the word of God, yet they are not there digested into a methodical system, but it is to be gathered from thence." On this assumption, the first task in theological study was, in Willard's words, to become "soundly principled" in systematic theology in order to establish an orthodox framework for biblical exegesis and thereby to avoid being "led about by every wind of doctrine."[21]

But, although theology began with catechetical instruction in orthodox doctrine, its final objective was something more profound. The essence of theology, Mather argued, was saving wisdom, the "new heart" enlightened by grace directing the steps of the person who would "live unto God." In adopting this definition of theology, Mather employed an aphorism that was common property through the length and breadth of the Puritan tradition. A century earlier, William Ames had said that "theology is the doctrine or teaching of living to God," and Jonathan Edwards would state in 1739 that theology was "the doctrine of living to God by Christ."[22] As Edward Farley has recently argued, theology in this sense was fundamentally a disposition of the soul, "an actual, individual cognition of God and things related to God."[23] The goal of theological study was the actual life of piety, and Mather urged students to recognize that contrition, "with ardent and constant cries to the gracious God, who giveth wisdom to them that ask it of him, is the way to come into *the experience of a principle infused from above* into you, that shall be indeed Christ formed in you." Apart from this infused spiritual principle "all intellectual accomplishments and embellishments . . . are but gilded vanities."[24]

Mather underscored his view that saving wisdom was the ultimate goal of theological study by presenting biblical studies in the form of a devotional exercise. Elaborating advice from the Lutheran pietist Philipp Jakob Spener (1635–1705), Mather asserted that the Holy Spirit, when inspiring the authors of the Bible, "produced in their hearts those motions of piety, which were agreeable and answerable to the matter then flowing from their pens." This spiritual attribute of the inspired text dictated the manner in which it should be studied.

> Now, do you lay one sentence, and then another, and so a third, of your Bible before you. Find out which of these affections is obvious and evident, in the sentence under consid-

eration. Try, strive, do your best, that the same affections may
stir, yea, flame in your soul. Be restless, till you find your
soul harmonizing and symphonizing with what the Holy
Spirit of God raised in his amanuensis at the time of his writing. Be not at rest, until you find your heart-strings quaver
at the touch upon the heart of your writer, as being brought
into an unison with it, and the two souls go up in a flame
together.[25]

Apart from the desire to know God, nothing of consequence could
be learned. Theological knowledge ascended to its divine object by
the affective power of pious desire.

Despite the fact that Mather distinguished between saving wisdom and merely doctrinal knowledge of Christian truth, he by no
means followed the radical wing of the Puritan movement that had
earlier used this distinction to discount the contribution that "human learning" in theology made to the pilgrim's progress toward
salvation. Contrary to such views, Mather and his colleagues among
the educated clergy assumed not only that orthodox doctrine was a
necessary condition for experiential wisdom, but also that the Christian vocation of "living to God" included an intellectual dimension
that could be clarified and strengthened by serious study. The learned
ministry was the means that God had appointed to teach divine truth
with power to enlighten the soul. Theological learning could not replace the Christian sagacity wrought in conversion, but it could enable the minister to discern counterfeit doctrine and to apply the
faith to the varied spiritual conundrums of soul and society.

To meet these practical demands of parish ministry, the third
and fourth components of theological study were polemics and casuistry. *Polemics* derived its prominence in theological studies from
the combat over doctrinal differences that was one legacy of the
sixteenth-century Reformation. It rested on the assumption that the
welfare of society required religious consensus, because false ideas
tended to incite immoral or disruptive behavior. Accordingly, courses
of reading in divinity often included controversial tracts and examples from heterodox authors (although not so early in the student's career as to occasion an inadvertent misstep into error). *Casu-*

istry sought to resolve the concrete cases of conscience that arose in the course of parish ministry by applying general rules of religion to specific situations or to cases in which there appeared to be a conflict of duties. Both polemics and casuistry assumed that, if theology was ultimately "saving wisdom," it was also a "practical wisdom" to be applied fittingly in particular circumstances.

Cotton Mather's father, Increase, described this process of practical application with respect to *the minister's social responsibility* in a sermon entitled *David Serving His Generation* (1698). The teachings of God were unchanging, said the elder Mather, but each age and place was susceptible to certain "errors" and "scandals" rather than others. The immutable truths were manifold, but God had made it the lot of a particular church to uphold some more than others. Theology must address the spiritual condition of its own historical situation: "In order to [serve] our generation, we should consider what are the special sins of the age wherein we live, and endeavor the reformation of them; and what are the more peculiar truths and duties of the times, so as to fall in with them."[26]

The *pastoral guidance of individuals* required a similar aptitude for the application of general principles to particular circumstances. In 1714, for example, the influential Northampton minister Solomon Stoddard, grandfather of Jonathan Edwards, wrote *A Guide to Christ*, which went through several editions in the first half of the eighteenth century. This brief tract on pastoral care answered a request from some younger ministers who desired specific advice on "directing souls that are under the work of conversion." Two things, said Stoddard, were especially important to the task of spiritual direction. First, ministers must have experienced conversion themselves or else they would be "blind guides," who misled in the very act of seeking to direct. Second, since there was "great variety in the workings of the spirit, and in the workings of men's hearts under the convictions of the spirit," the minister should not assume that everyone's religious experience would be like his own but should solicit advice from ministers more "seasoned in the care of souls."[27]

In their observations on preaching and pastoral care, both Increase Mather and Solomon Stoddard took for granted the unified, harmonious, and unchanging character of Christian truth. The task in preaching was to select from that gospel armory the doctrine or moral principle that would meet the present need. Pastoral care presupposed a specific understanding of fallen human nature that dictated a determinate "morphology of conversion"[28]: the humiliation of pride in human works, repentance, and the gift of faith. Within this structure the dealings between God and the soul might take innumerable particular forms, but these were variations on the general "human condition" definitively portrayed in the biblical revelation.

For the Mathers and Stoddard, then, devout study of divinity and the practical work of the ministry had the same objective: the inculcation of saving wisdom. Reading divinity was reading *with* the tutor, an interlocutor who was not merely imparting information but conducting a catechetical, transformative dialogue intended to change the student's mental attitude, disposition, point of view. The classic tutorial pattern of education understood the tradition being transmitted to be itself transformative of the student, and this transformative purpose of catechetical inquiry remained the theological core of ministry. The theology thus catechetically appropriated was likewise the theology to be preached. In the introspective passages of the minister's diary, the word of truth was directed inward as the measure of the pastor's self; in the work of ministry it was directed outward as the truth of judgment and comfort for church and society. Not surprisingly, Mather advised the fledgling minister that a theologically balanced sermon series could be achieved by proceeding week by week through a system of divinity, the same catechetical format that the theological tutors employed in directing their pupils. Indeed, the structure of theological study (exegesis, systematic and polemical theology, and casuistry) was formally parallel to the classic structure of a Puritan sermon (exposition of the biblical text, abstraction of true doctrine from the text, and application to life or "uses"). The minister's preaching, like his own devotional study of the Bible, sought to stir the affections by the spirit of truth: "Try, as much as with good judgment you can, to set the truths on fire . . . and let them come flaming out of your hand with excitations, to some devotion and affection of godliness, into the hearts of those whom they are addressed unto."[29] Preaching, prayer, catechizing, pastoral visits, and even the lending of books should all set forth "the whole body of divinity," steer past doctrinal error, and apply the word to the consciences of those who sought full membership in the church or had strayed from its discipline.[30] God used the minister as a principal means of grace to communicate knowledge of divine things to the people: "Be a star, to lead men unto their savior, and stop not until you see them there."[31]

These practical religious purposes formed the theological habit of mind. But, like the star of Mather's metaphor, they were not stationary. His idealized presentation of the symmetries between theological study and the pastoral office obscured religious and educational changes that events in the 1720s had brought pointedly to Mather's own attention and that would influence ministerial education through the remainder of the century. Controversy over these changes circled around the central objective of the seminary ideal: *student formation* or, more precisely, the student's catechetical transformation.

Mather presumed that ministerial training included the classical languages and liberal arts, presuming, as well, that such knowledge distinguished the minister from "uncultivated" humanity.[32] Classical learning fitted the student for the social office of the ministry, for membership in an intellectual elite responsible for transmitting a cohesive cultural tradition. But, a proper liberal education must remain the instrument of piety, and suspicions about orthodoxy and student discipline at Harvard therefore led Mather and the Board of Overseers to conduct a "visitation" in 1723. In preparation, Mather composed a strident manuscript, listing twelve "important points, relating to the education at Harvard College, needful to be inquired into." These "inquiries" registered complaints that would become commonplaces in American Protestantism's long debate over the relation of piety and learning. Did the students "spend their time well," Mather asked, or instead were not "their shelves filled with books which may truly be called Satan's Library?" Were the tutors recommending "erroneous and dangerous" theological texts? Did they ever "confer with their pupils, about their interior state and labor as men in earnest with them for their conversion to God?" Mather doubted that the answers to such questions would be reassuring, and he sadly concluded with the query "whether the most of those excellent young ministers, who are the gift of Christ, in the service of our churches, will not upon inquiry declare, that before they came to be what they are, they found it necessary to lay aside the learning which they brought from the college with them?"[33]

As Mather's inquiries illustrate, the catechetical dialogue between tutor and student was intended to transmit the specific configuration of beliefs, spiritual disciplines, code of behavior, and pattern of worship and polity that constituted the established religious culture of New England. In the 1720s, *religious pluralism* confused this process of transmission. Changes in religious climate, it might be said, disrupted the "transplanting" of students from seminary to society. Specifically, Rector Timothy Cutler and the Yale tutors had shocked New England Congregationalists in 1722 by "defecting" to Anglicanism, and Cutler subsequently made an unsuccessful effort to claim a seat on Harvard's Board of Overseers. The presence of lay and ordained Anglicans within New England's leadership revealed, in Mather's view, a fateful falling away from the founding vision. But the Anglican presence was only one part of an increasing pluralism in the first third of the eighteenth century. The major dissenting groups, Baptists, Quakers, and Anglicans, had successfully agitated for toleration from the Puritan establishments and won the right to hold public worship. By the 1720s and 1730s, Massachusetts and Connecticut further relented to the dissenters by freeing them from the obligation to support the Congregational establishment through the ministerial tax.[34] The implications of religious toleration and Protestant pluralism for the proper nurture of ministerial students remained largely unresolved at the time Mather wrote; he and his contemporaries were uncertain how different Protestant pieties could be harnessed to advance a common civility. Although Mather himself corresponded widely with European and British divines, had attended the ordination of a Baptist minister, and had advocated Protestant union for a generation, "polemics" remained a living part of his theology. In the same years that his *Manuductio ad Ministerium* called theological students to participate in the mission of transatlantic, interdenominational Protestantism, his inquiries about education at Harvard berated the tutors for failing to "establish" students in the Congregational way, which was the "distinguishing interest and beauty of the churches in this country."

The gift in 1721 by Thomas Hollis, a London Baptist, creating a professorship in divinity at Harvard, marked another change in this decade with significant ramifications for ideals of student formation. The Hollis gift encouraged interdenominational education by stipulating that both the professorship and related student scholarships would be open to Presbyterians and Baptists as well as Congregationalists. More importantly, Hollis had investigated *the duties of professors of divinity* in Scotland and the Netherlands. On this basis, he proposed that, unlike the college tutor who led a class of students through its entire course of studies, the Hollis Professor would be responsible for a specific subject matter, including yearlong lecture series in systematic theology and polemics for students who had completed at least two years in the college.[35] Establishment of this and subsequent professorships in divinity initiated major changes in the academic study of theology, by transforming the college teacher from tutor to professor and by heightening the distinction between preparatory liberal education and specific work in divinity.

Student formation also involved definite *presuppositions about human nature*, presuppositions expressed in Mather's fear that the Harvard tutors were not earnestly conferring with students about their conversions. This fear, in no small measure, reflected a challenge to the Puritan theory of the human predicament posed by what Norman Fiering has aptly termed "the first American Enlightenment," that is, the influence in the New England colleges of English Latitudinarian thought, especially through the published sermons of Archbishop John Tillotson (1630–94).[36] Tillotson's sermons declared that reasoned investigation could discover in nature and human nature a promulgation of divine law independent of, but consonant with, scriptural revelation. Humanity's natural endowment of moral principle could be used by reason to overcome the passions and advance toward the virtuous life and, thereby, toward virtue's eternal reward. "The practice of virtue and goodness," Tillotson declared, was not only "the absolute and indispensable condition of our future happiness in another world" but also "the certain and infallible means of attaining it."[37] Since Tillotson's elevated view of human reason and its powers sharply contrasted with the Puritan insistence on the necessity of conversion, the two perspectives assigned differing roles to education in the advancement of piety and civic virtue, a difference in educational theory that foreshadowed debates later in the century.

Finally, by 1726 when Cotton Mather published *Manuductio ad Ministerium,* the emphasis that he, Solomon Stoddard, and their contemporaries placed on preaching directed toward conversion was acquiring a significance for ministerial formation that they could not foresee.[38] The population of British North America was rapidly expanding in the 1720s, and clerical representatives of *an international evangelical piety* began to make their religious presence felt. In 1726 among the Dutch Reformed of central New Jersey, Theodore J. Frelinghuysen began preaching that conversion was the essential condition of authentic Christianity. Also in 1726, William Tennent began his ministry among the Scots-Irish Presbyterians in Neshaminy, Pennsylvania, where he later opened a "log college" aimed at ministerial education of a revivalistic bent. In the same year, Jonathan Edwards was completing his work as tutor at Yale and preparing to join the ministry of Solomon Stoddard at Northampton, where eight years later Edwards led a religious revival that received international publicity. Together these various religious stirrings prepared the colonies for the arrival in 1740 of the itinerant English preacher George Whitefield, whose sermons were the catalyst for a "Great Awakening" that crossed denominational and colonial borders.[39]

As this synopsis suggests, Protestant pluralism, tendencies toward the separation of theological studies from collegiate education, contending theories of human nature, and nascent revivalism were rapidly altering the intellectual context of theological study in colonial New England. *Manuductio ad Ministerium* had been written at the last possible cultural moment in which its educational advice could plausibly be received. These alterations accelerated during the era of the Great Awakening, and the years from roughly 1740 to 1760 marked the transition to a new social environment for Protestant theology.

"The Moral Rectitude of the Heart of God"

In the context of Protestant pluralism, the Great Awakening raised pointed questions about the nature and consequences of affiliation with a religious community. Advocates of the Awakening asserted that religious revivals produced a wider social harmony through the communal power of the Spirit, and, indeed, their emphasis on personal piety did stimulate cooperation among revivalistic Protestants across denominational lines. Shared religious experience took precedent over traditional differences of doctrine and polity and molded an interdenominational solidarity of shared religious sentiment. In this sense, the theology of the revival transcended the theologies of the denominations. At the same time, however, the very rhetoric of "revival" and "awakening" conveyed the implicit judgment that congregations and ministers who remained untouched by religious fervor languished in a death-like stupor of unfaith. To this, there was a prompt rebuttal. Debate over the religious and moral efficacy of revivals soon separated contending clerical parties within the denominations, and, although the division between "new light" revivalists and their "old light" opponents does not fully describe these various parties, it nicely conveys the sharpness of the controversy.[40]

Since debate focused on the spiritual competence of the ministry, the standards and purposes of ministerial education quickly became controversial. Some among the revivalists offered offensive judgments that the educational attainments of specific ministers could not mask a lack of spiritual power. In rejoinder came the charge that revivalistic "enthusiasm" had overwhelmed reason and mistaken emotional whims for the voice of God. When contention over revival entered the colleges, turmoil erupted. Harvard and Yale issued formal repudiations of Whitefield's preaching, and at Yale Rector Thomas Clap expelled student zealots for criticizing their supposedly "graceless" tutors. Dissidents refused to return to the college and in 1742–43 studied with Timothy Allen in New London, Connecticut, at a revivalist seminary known as the Shepherd's Tent.[41]

The revivalists, it must be noted, did not assault education itself but rather insisted on the priority of piety among the aims of education. While scornfully attacking mere "human learning," they vigorously advocated and established new colleges, schools, and academies. William Tennent's "log college," for example, produced the most notable Presbyterian revivalists of the era and important leaders in founding the College of New Jersey (Princeton) in 1746. In turn, Princeton graduates not only established a host of Presbyterian academies along the expanding frontier of the later eighteenth century but also led higher education among the Baptists and Lutherans.

Still, the rhetoric of grace did elevate immediate illumination at the expense of study, and the revivalists did stretch to the breaking point the commonplace distinction between two forms of religious knowledge: doctrinal knowledge and "experimental" knowledge of the saving power of Christ. When the New York Presbyterian Ebenezer Pemberton preached at Yale College in 1741, for example, he insisted that knowledge of Christ was "not confined to the head but seated in the heart." This authentic knowledge was decidedly "not produced by the powers of human reason or the common methods of education and instruction, but is the effect of a divine illumination, a spiritual discovery of Christ to the Soul."[42] When the fate of the soul was at issue, it would be the height of folly to make "knowledge of the secrets of Nature" an end in itself.

> But O! what darkness and horror will surprise the secure and inconsiderate sinner, who has spent his time in the empty speculations of science falsely so called, and the idle amusements of the gay and fashionable world, when he comes to stand upon the awful confines of the grave, and finds himself just stepping into the amazing gulf of eternity? With what sorrow and regret will he reflect, upon those many hours he has wasted upon unprofitable vanities, while he has neglected, the one thing needful, the knowledge of Christ, and the way of salvation by him?[43]

Without spiritual knowledge, which redisposed the human heart toward God and the neighbor, all naturally acquired knowledge—including even theological knowledge—was misdirected and of no effect for salvation.

Historian Douglas Sloan has discerned in revivalist zeal for colleges a "subtle but important shift" from a conservative to a more dynamic view of education.[44] In effect, the Awakening revivified the earlier Puritan conviction that the school was an agent of social transformation. Just as conversion laid the foundation for the proper use of learning by the individual student, so, according to the revivalists, evangelical Christian piety undergirded any college that hoped to exert a redemptive influence on public life. Personal transformation was the condition for an educational reformation that, in turn, molded leaders for a wider reform of society, a reform that some regarded as "a precondition of the millennium."[45] For a century and more, this belief that personal rebirth was the means to social reform would encourage college revivals and prompt Protestant ministers to pursue careers that combined the college presidency with the work of the evangelist.

But the revivalists were not alone in taking the dynamic view that colleges had a transformative task in society. American thinkers who participated in what Henry May has called "the moderate Enlightenment"[46] likewise had transformative hopes but based them on a contrasting view of education. Whereas the evangelicals believed that virtue was the fruit of divine grace, thinkers of the moderate Enlightenment argued that a natural human capacity—conscience or the moral sense—enabled humans to distinguish between right and wrong and was the basis of ethics, including Christian ethics. Therefore, education could appeal to human nature in order to bring about the moral uplift of the individual, and, perhaps, the society as well.

At mid-century, the College of Philadelphia became the educational center for varied expressions of this moderate Enlightenment. In one version, Benjamin Franklin argued that moral action ensued from reason's control of desire; hence, virtuous behavior could, in an incremental, progressive way, be made habitual by reasoned self-discipline. Franklin's ethical theory attributed moral progress to the gradual modification of external behavior, and he rejected the revivalist argument that spiritual conversion was the necessary precondition to virtue.[47] Another and more common strategy for linking ethics to education was followed by the college provost, William Smith, and his colleague the Presbyterian educator Francis Alison. Representing Presbyterians who desired ministerial training untainted by revivalism, Alison had approached Smith with the idea of raising a fund to support students who would take their degrees at the College of Philadelphia and at the same time read divinity with Robert Cross, the minister of First Presbyterian Church in the city.[48] Although the scheme failed to materialize, Alison and Smith briefly found common cause in the elevation of moral philosophy as the capstone of collegiate education.

Adopting the Enlightenment view that the principles of Christianity were implicit in nature, Smith concluded that religion transcended denominational differences and could be taught in congruity with science and philosophy, since the governing principles of all alike could be discovered through the empirical investigation of nature and human life.[49] Productive citizenship required justice and honesty as well as mathematics and logic, and religion promoted the social welfare by cultivating such virtues. Alison elaborated the same perspective by introducing the thought of Francis Hutcheson (1694–1746), professor of moral philosophy at Glasgow. Hutcheson had based ethics in benevolent affections guided by an intuitive moral sense that was intrinsic to human nature. This proposal not only made the capacity to distinguish right from wrong a common capacity of humanity but also made the foundations of ethics accessible by an empirical inquiry into human nature and society. Following Hutcheson's lead, Alison asserted that moral philosophy should occupy a more central place in education than had been customary, since it was the branch of knowledge that could defend a rational Christianity, explicate human rights, and persuasively present the moral duties all persons owed to God, to neighbor, and to self.[50] In these ways, the moderate Enlightenment argued that the essentials of religion, prior to the doctrinal particularities of the denominations, could be discovered in the universe through natural philosophy and in humanity through moral philosophy. "Enlightened" Protestant thinkers proposed to build moral character on this God-given endowment of benevolent affections. Not revival but education was the foundation of civic virtue.

As these divergent notions of the relation of religion to education and citizenship unfolded, each in its own way diminished the importance of confessional uniformity for the operation of colleges, by emphasizing that either a conversion experience or a common moral sense constituted the core of true religion and that this common core transcended denominational orthodoxies. Whether established on revivalist or Enlightenment theories of education, therefore, American colleges of the mid-century decades explicitly opened their doors to students of all denominations. In this new interdenominational educational context, the religious concert of church and college that had been presupposed by Cotton Mather could no longer be sustained, and it was a skirmish in retreat when Rector Thomas Clap of Yale declared in 1754 that the "original end" of Yale was "to educate ministers in our own way." For Clap, the college was an extension of New England Congregationalism; indeed, colleges were "religious societies of a superior nature" to local congregations, since congregations edified "the common people" whereas colleges trained a ministerial elite. This consideration made it imperative that colleges have "all their religious instructions, worship, and ordinances . . . under their own regulation," including the authority to nominate their own ministers. Students would be allowed to attend worship beyond the college only with the college's express permission; otherwise, Clap warned, "there may be as many kinds of religious worship at college as there are different opinions of parents."[51] But Clap's appeal for religious uniformity came too late. The "different opinions of parents" reflected the Protestant pluralism of the wider society, and the possibility of using the college to instill a denominationally specific tradition of piety was rapidly becoming a thing of the past.

This educational context of both denominational pluralism and contrasting interpretations of the relation of religion to education prompted minister-educators to seek a common ground on which the churches could cooperate in forming citizens and inculcating a common culture. They found it in the emphasis that both revivalism and the Common Sense philosophy placed on the affections as the animating source of moral action. The relation of the mental faculties (intellect, emotion, and will) to specifically religious experience became the philosophical terrain in which theologians sought to establish a new configuration of piety, civility, and learning that was viable in the context of Protestant pluralism. Since revivalism and the Common Sense philosophy not only shared an emphasis on the affections but also differed significantly in their appraisal of human nature, their combination had inherent difficulties. Nevertheless, because it held the promise of providing a plausible intellectual framework for relating religious experience to moral action, efforts to achieve this combination soon dominated the attention of the theologians and would continue to do so until the middle of the nineteenth century.[52]

By 1760, the task of realigning piety, civility, and learning to accommodate Protestant pluralism had led many religious thinkers to relinquish the inherited truism that public welfare required religious uniformity. In that year Ezra Stiles, minister in Newport, Rhode Island, and later president of Yale, articulated the new, favorable interpretation of diversity in an address to the Congregational clergy of Rhode Island. Not established religious uniformity, Stiles declared, but rather "the precious jewel of religious liberty" would guarantee social harmony and advance the best interests of religion in America. Providence itself had planted America with a variety of Protestant churches that counterbalanced one another, and Stiles forecast that "their temporary collisions, like the action of acids and alkalies after a short ebullition, will subside in harmony and union, not by the destruction of either, but in the friendly cohabitation of all."[53] Stiles still took pride in the relative "purity" of Congregationalism, but, embracing the new pluralist formula for social harmony, he had no doubt that persons could "become good and holy in all communions" and emphatically separated himself from the bigotry that restricted salvation to one's own church. Charitable disquisition among Protestants of various theological persuasions marked the line of advance toward the future when "resplendent and all-prevailing Truth will terminate the whole in universal harmony."[54] Stiles had crisply stated what would, over the next seventy years, become the prevailing perspective on plural Protestantism in America. No one of the Protestant communions could claim that it alone was the true church or that the well-being of society depended on the membership of all its Christian citizens in a single church. The *denominations* of Protestantism were, within limits, acknowledged as diverse expressions of the one church and shared the commitment to establish a common Christian truth in America through the powers of persuasion rather than coercion.[55]

The career of Jonathan Edwards, the most profound religious thinker of colonial America, well illustrates the work of the minister-theologian in the transitional era inaugurated by the Great Awakening. Edwards had been educated in the same New England context in which Cotton Mather had written *Manuductio ad Ministerium,* having earned his B. A. at Yale in 1720, read divinity there, briefly held a pastorate in New York, and returned to Yale as one of the college tutors from 1724 to 1726. At Northampton, where he shared the ministry of his grandfather Solomon Stoddard and then succeeded him, Edwards became one of the leading preachers of the Great Awakening and, in its aftermath, reflected on its religious and theological meaning in his famous *Treatise concerning Religious Affections* (1746). Controversies over the standards for church membership led to his dismissal from the Northampton church in 1750. Taking up duties at the small parish of Stockbridge, he became a tutor to theological students and devoted his intellectual energies to a series of treatises that reinterpreted classic doctrines of the Puritan tradition in a critical engagement with the central ideas of the Enlightenment about human nature and the foundations of ethics. Called in 1758 to the presidency of the College of New Jersey at Princeton, he died that same year from the effects of a smallpox vaccination.

For Edwards the theological controversies during the era of the Great Awakening posed a single, comprehensive question: "What is the nature of true religion?"[56] His major writings on the freedom of the will, original sin, and the religious affections responded to various facets of this general question, and his sermons of the 1730s, prior to the arrival of Whitefield in New England, had already disclosed the perspective of his response. In those early sermons he enunciated a position in continuity with the preceding generation of New England's minister-theologians who had posed a classic query about the efficacy of preaching, namely, how was it possible that human exposition of Scripture communicated the word of God in its transformative power? Human reasoning, Edwards answered, may accumulate extensive knowledge, but, if it did not include knowledge of the ultimate purpose and final cause of personal existence, for the sake of which the person "had more understanding given him than the beasts; then . . . his faculty of reason is in vain; he might as well have been a beast, as a man with this knowledge." And, since "the last end" of human existence was God, knowledge of "divine science" was infinitely more important than "all other sciences whatever." But in actual fact, Edwards continued, this knowledge of God was not naturally accessible: "Such are our circumstances now in our fallen state, that nothing which is needful for us to know concerning God, is manifest by the light of nature in the manner in which it is necessary for us to know it." Only the word of God revealed in Scripture taught the knowledge that ultimately constituted all human existence worthy of the name. Further, this knowledge was not simply *information* drawn from the Bible. The theologian must distinguish between speculative and practical knowledge of divinity. The former, Edwards observed, "remains only in the head," whereas the latter "consists in the sense of the heart." Although saving wisdom could not, indeed, exist without some naturally acquired body of information, it was not simply the result of that knowledge. Theological information derived its value from the sense of the heart. To be sure, God employed the Bible "to convey to the mind the subject matter of this saving instruction," but the written word was not properly the cause of that "true sense of the divine excellency of the things revealed in the word of God," an apprehension which was "a divine and supernatural light, immediately imparted to the soul by the Spirit of God."[57]

Edwards found this distinction between doctrinal knowledge and the sense of the heart confirmed by the memory of his own religious experience. About 1739 he wrote an autobiographic "personal narrative," in order to retrace his change from one form of knowing to the other. There, Edwards recalled that since childhood he had been "full of objections" against the "horrible doctrine" of God's sovereignty "in choosing whom he would to eternal life, and rejecting whom he pleased; leaving them eternally to perish, and be everlastingly tormented in hell." But the time came when Edwards's "reason apprehended the justice and reasonableness" of this fearsome doctrine, and he afterward raised no *intellectual* objections against it. Intellectual acquiescence to the divine sovereignty proved to be, however, quite different from "another kind of sense of God's sovereignty," in which this doctrine "appeared, an exceeding pleasant, bright and sweet doctrine to me." Reoriented by this "new sense" of divine things Edwards came not simply to accept the inescapable facts of existence but to embrace their "beauty and excellency." Lured by the divine beauty, the cadence of his religious transformation quickened after he completed his collegiate education and began considering his calling to ministry. "Inward, sweet delight in God and divine things" gradually increased during the two years that Edwards read divinity following graduation from Yale, and he felt it "in a much higher degree" when he began preaching in New York in 1722. In this new affective disposition toward God, Edwards knew the world differently than before: "The appearance of everything was altered: there seemed to be, as it were, a calm, sweet cast, or appearance of divine glory, in almost every thing . . . in the sun, moon, and stars; in the clouds, and blue sky; in the grass, flowers, trees; in the water, and all nature; which used greatly to fix my mind."[58]

Thus Edwards interpreted true theological knowledge as the affective knowledge of God on the part of the unified self, and he understood this affective disposition to be a supernatural gift of divine grace rather than an acquired body of information or an inherent moral sense. Illumined by the Spirit, natural human powers exercised a new apprehension of the divine glory, but the divine light itself remained supernatural and not at the disposal of human agency. This disposition of the knowing self, "the sense of the heart," was an infused habit of grace, abiding and dependable, sustaining the human faculties yet without becoming a natural principle.[59]

In one aspect, this new sense of the divine sovereignty expressed itself in worshipful contemplation. "The soul of a true Christian," he wrote regarding his spiritual disciplines while preaching in New York, "appeared like such a little white flower, as we see in the spring of the year: low and humble on the ground, opening its bosom, to receive the pleasant beams of the sun's glory." But in another aspect of his piety, Edwards was motivated by "great longings for the advancement of Christ's kingdom in the world" and scoured the newspapers for reports that cast some "favorable aspect" on this interest. In this dialectic of repose before the absolute and loyalty to the cause of God, Edwards composed a covenant in January 1723, before returning home to receive his M.A. and begin work as a tutor at Yale, "engaging to fight with all my might, against the world, the flesh and the devil, to the end of my life."[60] Aesthetic insight into the harmony of the whole, so it seemed, emboldened moral engagement with the exigencies of life. God was present and available *not only as compassion* for the sinner *but as power* for the enactment of the divine will.[61]

But if the transformative appropriation of Christian doctrine was the core narrative of personal life, it could also and equally become a narrative of society, as Edwards demonstrated in his account of the Northampton revival, *A Faithful Narrative of the Surprising Works of God* (1737). In this long public letter describing the "harvest" of souls that occurred in 1734 and 1735, Edwards told the cumulative story of a community that, although well-schooled in the formal teachings of the Christian tradition, now came to make religion its "principal business." Personal "humiliation before the sovereign disposer of life and death" and the inward firm persuasion of the divine glory manifested themselves in transformed social relationships, resolving the rancor of "parties" within the town and promoting a new harmony. But personal and social narratives of transformation were themselves encompassed by a far larger narrative, and, in 1739 on the eve of the Great Awakening, Edwards placed them within the framework of universal history in the series of sermons later published as *A History of the Work of Redemption*. Time and again, Edwards proclaimed, God had acted extraordinarily to bring about "a new thing" in the providential history of humanity, and this progressive revelation of the divine purposes was, in all its variety, a single grand scheme tending toward a single end. The individual soul and the town of Northampton, alike, were set within the cosmic drama of God's purpose; apart from God their particular narratives were "meaningless and might as well not have been."[62] As historian Michael J. Crawford has effectively argued, this portrayal of a revival of religion had its roots in the covenant theology. *Revival* referred not simply to the conversions of numerous unassociated individuals but meant rather "the transformation by grace of a community, a group of people bound together as a single moral entity."[63] The tangible fruit of the sense of the heart wrought by revival was a new social harmony; divinely inspired benevolence toward one's fellows became the affective principle of affiliation.

But in observing the course of everyday life, Edwards saw that human affections rarely produced such harmony within the self or within society. The emotions were indeed "the springs of life that set men agoing in all their pursuits: these are the things that put men forward, and carry 'em along, in all their worldly business." But, they attached themselves to many and conflicting objects. Although God had given humans affections in order that they might be subservient to the chief end of human life—"the business of religion"—it must still be acknowledged that human "affections are much more exercised and engaged in other matters, than in religion!"[64] If the affections were "the springs" of all human action, by what standards could one judge the truth of this affective knowledge of the world or the ethical adequacy of the objects of affection? When did seemingly religious emotion mask selfishness, or apparent benevolence arise from avarice? When did the contending objects of emotional attachment pit the self against itself? Confronted with such questions about true virtue, Edwards concluded that they could properly be answered only in terms of his overarching question of the nature of true religion, since it was religion that taught of an all-comprehending love, which ordered contending temporal desires. He therefore sought to assert a theological ethic against the idea of a natural moral sense, which American religious thinkers were borrowing from Francis Hutcheson and the Scottish Common Sense philosophers. Love to God, Edwards argued, was not only the essence of personal redemption but also the genesis of any adequate and genuine regard for "the public welfare" or "the public good." He most fully explored this proposition in two treatises written near the end of his life and published in 1765 by his student Samuel Hopkins, *The Nature of True Virtue* and the *Dissertation concerning the End for Which God Created the World.*

True virtue consisted not simply in benevolent disposition toward "our fellow-creatures," said Edwards, but more precisely in "benevolence to being in general."[65] This comprehensive benevolence he contrasted with love toward any more limited group, any "private circle or system of beings, which are but a small part of the whole."[66] And, since God "is the head of a universal system of existence," true virtue was finally nothing other than the consent to the divine will and the adoration of divine beauty that had been the gifts of conversion. "Beauty does not consist in discord and dissent, but in consent and agreement. And if every intelligent being is some way related to being in general, and is a part of the universal system of existence; and so stands in connection with the whole; what can its general and true beauty be, but its union and consent with the great whole?"[67] Virtuous benevolence expressed this disposition toward "the great whole" by seeking the good of every individual being in ways consistent with the highest good of being in general. Affective concord with the universal system of existence, according to Edwards, was reflected in a secondary way throughout nature and society, from the symmetry of inanimate objects or the harmony of sounds to the order of society's members in their appointed offices and stations.[68]

This ethic of universal benevolence had the social purpose of governing the passions, challenging their attachment to narrow communities, directing them toward more comprehensive objects, and thereby consolidating a coherent and cumulative set of social loyalties. In the emerging context of pluralism and voluntary affiliation, this regulative function of universal benevolence was directly related to the problem of choosing among multiple objects of affection or motives to action that pulled in contrary directions. The ideal was a society bound together by willing consent among persons of good will, a public benevolence that had its source in true religion and whose social harmonies were properly upheld, if always imperfectly displayed, in the church. The ultimate norm for the affective unity of a society was the comprehensive scope of its benevolence. In this sense, *universal benevolence* was also *disinterested benevolence*, willing the common good rather than pursuing the good for particular interests or parties. The ethical conduct of the public was appraised not simply by relations among the "private circle" of its own members but, ultimately, by its most comprehensive ethical disposition. It was a transvaluation of values that elevated mundane attachments to family or to nation by ordering them toward an ultimate attachment to the divine purpose. Public faith, it might be said, took distinctive shape by the imaginative envisionment of the ultimate public: the city of God, the kingdom of God, the divine republic, the universal system of existence. Allegiances to families, villages, churches, and governments were evaluated in terms of their consonance with the ultimate public, the wholeness of all that is. Indeed, within this vision of the ideal public, the sovereign God acted the part of ultimate citizen who by "the disposition of his heart" displayed a "love of the public" that was indistinguishable from love of himself as the source of all things, "because God's being, as it were, comprehends all." God's love ordered a universal commonwealth by the bonds of voluntary affiliation. Creation, in such a vision, was finally held in harmony by the ethical and affective ties of divine respect and consent: "the moral rectitude of the heart of God."[69]

From Theological Tutors to Theological Seminaries

Edwards was the great representative of mid-century theological inquiry: the congregational pastor reflecting, from the perspective of a specific theological tradition, on the ultimate frame of reference for his ministry and educating ministers in this pastoral context. He and his contemporaries had pursued theological study in the course of daily pastoral work, and, like the classic sermon, such study culminated in "uses," the application of theological teaching to concrete, daily experience. Theological discourse aimed to transform persons and societies, and, in order to stir and to shape the wholehearted loyalty of their auditors, the preacher-theologians enfolded the immediate affiliations of family, congregation, and township in the wider circle of the divine government of creation. This theological response to pluralism and voluntary affiliation decisively influenced the direction of later religious thought in America, by its emphasis on the interpretation of concrete experiences, its favoring of tracts for the times and occasional pieces rather that systematic works, its propensity for narratives of transformation, and its interpretation of experience in light of a transcendent reference. But this era of cultural transition had three unforeseen consequences for the practice of reading divinity with a pastoral theologian, consequences that raised serious problems for the seminary ideal of cultivating a comprehensive cultural synthesis.

First, although Edwards had oriented theology toward "the

universal system of existence" in order to challenge inordinate attachment to a "private circle," his most immediate and tangible legacy was, ironically, a particular school of thought: the "New Divinity" theologians who represented a distinctive doctrinal interpretation of New England Congregationalism and who aggressively advanced this interpretation through their work as theological tutors. The most famous of these New Divinity tutors, Joseph Bellamy in Bethlehem, Connecticut, and Nathanael Emmons in Franklin, Massachusetts, each educated as many as one hundred ministerial students in their homes over the course of long ministries. And, from the era of the American Revolution to the early decades of the nineteenth century, the New Divinity had its analogues in other communions, as groups of scholarly pastors sprang up within each denomination, giving specific interpretations to the inherited theological traditions of the churches.

Since ministerial education was understood on all sides to play a formative role in perpetuating a church's tradition and establishing its direction of development, the work of these theological tutors was politically sensitive, and Congregationalists, Presbyterians, and Lutherans struggled to secure the ecclesiastical accountability of their tutors and to discourage competing versions of denominational orthodoxy. But efforts at regulation did little to prevent controversy or stop accusations that tutors influenced—indeed, corrupted—students with their personal theological biases. The revivalistic influence of William Tennent's "log college" had earlier been a factor in the split between New Side and Old Side Presbyterians; no small number of Congregational clergy chaffed at the way New Divinity pastors dominated private theological instruction; among the Lutherans Frederick Quitman of the New York Ministerium was regarded as a "rationalist" who ignored Lutheran distinctives and threatened the confessional orthodoxy of his students. Reading divinity was becoming a decidedly mixed blessing that not only instilled denominational traditions but also disrupted consensus by attaching the theological student to a particular party within the denomination. The net effect of these internal denominational controversies was the elaboration of characteristic teachings—and disputes about them—as "markers" of denominational identity. Theology surveyed the intellectual territory of denominational life and drew the boundaries between the denomination and other groups. But this pivotal role in constructing denominational identity in the context of Protestant pluralism simultaneously made theology a less effective instrument for interpreting the shared life of citizens as economic, intellectual, and political actors in the wider public realm.

Second, despite these controversies, the denominations were increasingly drawn to the use of theological tutors by the felt need to provide what colleges seemed no longer able to insure: the ecclesiastical context of ministerial formation. Colleges were enrolling students from different denominations; the professions of law and medicine were competing successfully with ministry for the vocational attentions of graduates; the natural sciences were expanding and the formal study of divinity by undergraduates was diminishing; the gradual transformation of the teacher from the tutor, responsible for the instruction of an entire class of students, to the professor, responsible for a particular area of study (the languages, sciences, moral philosophy, or divinity), was reducing the traditional role of the educator in the religious formation of students. These difficulties were compounded for denominations such as the Lutheran and German Reformed, who had strong traditions of a learned ministry but had not yet established their own colleges. They found themselves caught between their desire to maintain historic educational standards and their dissatisfaction with the ineffectiveness of recently immigrated ministers trained in European universities. In an effort to attune their ministry to the emerging American society in which their parishioners participated, the German Reformed argued in the 1780s that immigrant pastors had difficulty adjusting to American customs, that English schools might suppress German language and nationality to the disadvantage of religion, and that establishing their own school was therefore "the safest and surest way to provide our churches with honest and tried young men, well acquainted, from their youth, with the customs of the country."[70] But as an interim device until such colleges could be established, denominations experimented with reading divinity as a way of mediating between American colleges and their own confessional traditions. During the Revolution, for example, the Lutherans sought to make a professorship of Oriental and German languages at the College of Philadelphia a vehicle for Lutheran ministerial education. In the 1780s and 1790s they attempted, unsuccessfully, to act on a clause in the King's College charter that permitted the formation of self-sustaining, denominational chairs of theology.[71] In all such experiments, the desideratum was supplementing the college curriculum with a given denominational tradition of theology.

Meanwhile, college presidents and professors searched in natural theology and moral philosophy for a common moral ground to the culture, thereby moving religious and ethical instruction yet further away from piety that was denominationally specific. Although religious instruction was by no means discontinued, religious and curricular pluralism did mean that the college less tangibly embodied the culture and spiritual disciplines of a particular denomination. The Alford Professorship created at Harvard in 1789, for example, contained in its academic purview the topics of natural religion, moral philosophy, and civil polity. Its charter stipulated its purpose "to demonstrate the existence of a Deity or First Cause, to prove and illustrate his essential attributes, both natural and moral, to evince and explain his providence and government . . . to deduce and enforce the obligations which man is under to his Maker . . . together with the most important duties of social life, resulting from the several relations which men mutually bear to each other."[72] Clearly, such a professorship aimed to instill a common religious foundation for citizenship, but its charter left unclear the relation between that natural theology and the discrete confessional traditions of the churches, leaving also unclear the import of confessional theology for civic life.

Third, the denominations resorted to theological tutors in an effort to keep pace with the geographic expansion of the churches, and, on the eve of the Revolution, Presbyterian and Congregational clergy were corresponding about the need for new educational strategies that enlisted ministerial candidates to "form our new scattered places into a church state" and trained them "for keeping school and preaching both."[73] One such strategy, Presbyterian academies on the "frontier" of denominational expansion, exhibited a spare simplicity in comparison to colleges of New England, New York, or eastern

Pennsylvania. When, for example, Archibald Alexander, later a faculty member at Princeton Theological Seminary, obtained his license to preach in 1791, the respected Virginia educator William Graham had directed his entire formal training, the counterpart of preparatory, collegiate, and theological studies.[74] Barton Warren Stone, subsequently the principal leader of the Christian movement in Kentucky, completed his studies in 1793 at David Caldwell's academy in Guilford, North Carolina. Having decided for the ministry, he began to read divinity under the direction of the Orange Presbytery and Reverend William Hodge; Stone later recalled that until that time he "had never read any books on theology but the Bible."[75] Lacking both the educational context of the college and a settled ecclesiastical context, William Graham in Virginia and David Caldwell in North Carolina taught in settings of denominational pluralism, protracted revival meetings, and itinerancy. The educational experiences of their students, Archibald Alexander and Barton Stone, were strongly influenced by encounters with clergy and laity of other denominations, and both young men embarked upon preaching excursions over several counties immediately after they received their licenses.[76] Although New England students regularly traveled to fill vacant pulpits, Archibald Alexander's education during the era of Southern revivals, 1788–95, was literally peripatetic. In 1790, Alexander rode to hear one Nash LeGrand preach at "the forks of Jackson's River and the Cow Pasture":

> The people seldom heard a sermon; being so strung along the narrow valleys, that they can never form self-supporting congregations, but must always depend on itinerants, or the transient visits of ministers from a distance. In such regions it is pleasing to see the ardour with which the mountain people flock to the place of meeting; issuing from every hollow of the neighboring hills, on horseback and on foot.[77]

Reading divinity in such settings was far distant from what had been the prevailing understanding seventy-five years earlier in Cotton Mather's New England: the culmination of a college education by residential study with the pastor of a unified, geographic parish.

Congregational, Presbyterian, and Lutheran deployments of

theological tutors at the end of the eighteenth century made it clear that *reading divinity was no longer a single institution* but rather the collective name for a variety of educational tasks capable of being performed by individual persons and intended to insure ecclesiastical guidance for ministerial candidates. Simple and flexible, tutorial education eased the distribution of schooling from home and congregation to more specialized institutions: schools, colleges, and lending libraries. This elaboration of educational forms progressed at different rates for different regions, denominations, and ethnic groups. But, when ministers with European educations could no longer be recruited, when colleges could not be founded, or when ministerial students had no books, the theological tutor emerged to "fill in the missing pieces." As nursery of denominational identity, as mediator between the churches and the changing colleges, or as surrogate college, reading divinity had become a buffer. It cushioned challenges to the seminary ideal. At the same time, however, its very flexibility disrupted the seminary ideal, first, by heightening the distinction between collegiate education and ministerial preparation and, second, by heightening the distinction between denominational theology and broader intellectual issues of national life. Although reading divinity offered attractive interim strategies, its dependence on the initiative of individual tutors made it too ephemeral to resolve the deeper issues of ministerial accountability to church, nation, and academy.

When, therefore, theological tutors failed to maintain academic standards, proved susceptible to disruptive church politics, or appeared too partisan to appraise the moral health of the commonweal, the establishment of seminaries as consolidating institutions rapidly gained favor and proceeded with amazing rapidity. From the founding of Andover Seminary in 1808 by the Congregationalists to the mid–1820s, some fifteen schools came into being, representing the Congregationalists, Baptists, Episcopalians, Presbyterians, Dutch Reformed, German Reformed, and Lutherans. In the same years the American Education Society, a voluntary philanthropic organization heavily populated with Congregationalists and Presbyterians, began providing interdenominational scholarship support and using this financial leverage to pressure schools toward the standard of a three-year graduate program of ministerial education. By approximately 1830 the AES was providing $75 to $100 in annual scholarship aid to more than 1000 students at some two dozen seminaries and thereby widely extending the influence of its curricular standards.[78]

The fact that social and theological changes had made the seminary ideal difficult to approximate by no means deterred the minister-theologians from calling their schools *seminaries*. To the contrary, precisely the dispersal of the inherited institutional contexts and the triad of civic virtues that had supported the old ideal now made the theologians all the more insistent that their new institutions must invigorate the hope for a comprehensive and coherent religious culture. With that intent Jedidiah Morse reinvoked the seminary metaphor at the opening of Andover Seminary in 1808: "May the Church, which is here established and placed under the joint care of the Professors, become as a well watered, skillfully cultivated, and plentifully furnished, nursery for our American Churches; from whence shall be successively transplanted *Trees of Righteousness; Plants of renown,* which shall flourish and bear abundance of the fruits of holiness, *in the courts of our God.*"[79] The seminary was understood to be a fresh strategy for achieving a venerable goal, but Morse and his contemporaries did not see the extent to which the institution belied the ideal.

The founders of the early seminaries were motivated by a threefold objective: the supply of ministers who by virtue of a common education would share a common doctrinal stance, a commonality of affection for one another, and a common zeal for the evangelistic mission of the church. President Timothy Dwight of Yale, grandson of Jonathan Edwards and perhaps the most influential educator of the era, aptly summarized this motivation in his remarks at the opening of Andover Seminary, by contrasting the isolated and haphazard instruction provided by theological tutors to the environment that the student would enter at Andover.

> Here, being educated together, being of the same age, pupils of the same instructors, tenants of the same buildings, engaged in the same delightful pursuits, and actuated, as we may reasonably hope, by the same spirit, [students] can

hardly fail to *be of one accord, and of one mind.* The friendships formed in youth, are peculiarly intimate and endearing. . . . The friendships, formed here, will, it is believed,
spring from the best of all sources: evangelical virtue. . . .
They will, therefore, last through life; will have a powerful
influence on their character and conduct; will extend their
efficacy over every part of this land; and will affect, in the
happiest manner, all the moral and religious interests of
its inhabitants.[80]

Not only would the seminary, claimed its early advocates, instill religious and intellectual accord, but in their retrospective opinion the proliferation of private tutors "during the last half century"
was the principal reason that "errors and sects have been multiplied
beyond calculation." The ideal situation, wrote Eliphalet Pearson in
1807, would be a single seminary "to which candidates for the gospel
ministry in all parts of our country, and at whatever college educated,
may resort" for the "reciprocal interchange of the purest energies of
mind," and thereby "efface local and other prejudices."[81] The educational harmonization of the clergy was a theme repeated with ritual
regularity at seminary foundings and professorial inaugurations
throughout the first quarter of the nineteenth century. At his installation in 1826 at the Lutheran Seminary in Gettysburg, for example,
the Princeton-educated advocate of Protestant ecumenical federation
Samuel S. Schmucker declared that nothing would better promote
unanimity of views and harmony of feeling among ministers of the
church than the uniformity of education and common disciplines of
study that a seminary employed to "entwine together the cords of
social feeling, and make the ecclesiastical sympathies of students
flow in the same channel." Further, in order to perpetuate the seminary ideal of cloistered nurture in the new denominational environment, it appeared obvious to Schmucker, "theological seminaries,
like the Saviour whom they teach, should court retirement, [and]
small towns rather than cities ought to be their favorite seats."[82]
From seminary seclusion bands of graduates would proceed outward
in order to "extend their efficacy over every part of this land" and
"affect, in the happiest manner, all the moral and religious interests

of its inhabitants." The social "efficacy" of seminary-educated ministers was achieved through the dissemination of the "evangelical virtue" that had stamped their educations. The "disinterested benevolence" that harmonized diverse students in the seminary was, when spread abroad, the preservative of republican government, because it inclined diverse members of society to will the public good over private interest and advantage. Indeed, this educational mission took on millennial overtones, expressed in the hope that ministers so educated would effect a "universal renovation" through their evangelistic work and become thereby "benefactors to the nations of the millennium."[83]

But, of course, the harmonial rhetoric was ambiguous in its reference and at odds with the institutional realities. The seminaries did not so much solve the problems associated with reading divinity as give them institutional form. The American religious circumstance of denominational pluralism and voluntary affiliation had changed the work of theologians by changing their basic situation. In the context of pluralism, theologians had the task of cultivating and clarifying the distinctive, shared beliefs of the particular denominations. Theologians were leaders and shapers of voluntary communities, both congregations and denominations, which were in competition with comparable communities for members and influence. The seminary theologians, in this aspect of their work, focused on the internal harmony of the denomination. Indeed, the very success of the seminary as an institution tightened this focus during the first third of the nineteenth century, as denominations founded their own seminaries and expected their ministerial candidates to attend them. But, the seminary ideal—whether in its earlier or its latest form— had never envisioned churchly harmony in isolation but only as the religious foundation of a wider civic harmony. The formation of a coherent denominational identity within the sponsoring denomination did not directly contribute to establishing a coherent national identity in the context of religious pluralism. It remained unclear, as it had with the private theological tutors, how the seminary theologians could cooperatively interpret the nation's ethical and religious foundations. Attention to harmonies in one sphere of social responsibility was not necessarily conducive to harmony in another sphere.

This tendency toward the isolation of theology from civic discourse was heightened further because the founding of seminaries had the effect of segregating theology from general education. In the negotiations connected with the founding of Princeton Theological Seminary, for example, it was agreed that so long as the seminary remained at Princeton no professorship of theology would be established in the college, in effect a mutual agreement that "the seminary would not be a college, and that the college would not include the function of professional ministerial education."[84]

The complementary purposes of nation, school, and church had been the social presupposition of the seminary ideal. In that ideal the theological tasks of churchly formation and public voice had been intertwined, but now were in tension, even in conflict. The denominations promoted distinctive theological tenets, but the American polity of voluntary affiliation and the separation of church and state presupposed a toleration in which, in principle at least, all denominational beliefs were treated alike. The seminary theologians therefore continued the eighteenth-century search for a shared "core" of Protestant theology, and, not surprisingly, early discussions of the seminary curriculum gave considerable space to the connections and contradictions between natural theology and the revealed theology of the Christian tradition.[85] In part, such a core provided the practical basis for interdenominational influence in the culture. More fundamentally, however, the persuasive articulation of a common theological core buttressed the certainty of Christian theology against the unspoken erosion brought about by the availability of multiple denominational versions of revealed truth. As Walter Lippmann would write a century later, "so many faiths, so many loyalties, are offered to the modern man that at last none of them seems to him wholly inevitable and fixed in the order of the universe. The existence of many churches in one community weakens the foundation of all of them."[86]

Lippmann rightly attaches a religious urgency to the situation of multiple faiths. The search for a common "foundation" was the quest for certainty amidst unprecedented religious choices. He also rightly attaches a strong ethical dimension to this search, through his emphasis on the multiple loyalties of the modern circumstance.

The perennial problem of American theology had emerged as a problem in theological ethics: the problem of adjudicating competing responsibilities to the churches, the nation, and the schools. Hence, perhaps, the perennial lure of the ethics of Jonathan Edwards was its definition of true virtue as benevolence toward the universal system of being in general: God became the symbol for the ultimate community, the divine republic, that ordered loyalty to all more proximate communities.

Ethical codes cannot lay claim to unhesitating obedience when they
are based upon the opinions of a majority, or on the notions of wise
men, or on estimates of what is socially useful, or on an appeal to
patriotism. For they depend then on the force which happens to range
itself behind them at a particular moment; or on their convenience for
a moment. They are felt to be the outcome of human, and therefore
quite fallible, decisions. They are no necessary part of the
government of the universe.

Walter Lippmann, *A Preface to Morals*, p. 49

TWO

SCHOLARSHIP AND THE CULTURE OF
PROTESTANTISM, 1830–1880

By the 1840s, the theological seminary had emerged as a permanent
fixture of American religious and educational life, and a "second generation" of teachers was inheriting the leadership of these schools, a
generation that increasingly defined its vocation in terms of *the ideal
of scholarship*. The middle decades of the nineteenth century, from
approximately 1830 to 1880, marked the transformation of the seminary ideal by this newer ideal of scholarship, a transformation that
had major consequences both for the self-conception of the theological faculty and for the relation of theological scholarship to American public life.

As a school of the church, the nineteenth-century seminary
was answerable not simply to the church at large but especially to
the denomination that supported it. The school was an instrument
of denominational formation, and it played that formative role in a
double sense. First, it sought to form individual students by inculcating the particular configuration of beliefs, moral norms, and patterns
of worship and polity that made the denomination a recognizably

distinctive fellowship within the larger Christian tradition. Second, as custodian of this denominational lore, the theological school contributed significantly to the formation of the denomination itself, molding corporate practices and habits of mind by providing "expert" interpretation of the tradition. To be sure, the theological schools of the 1840s did not intend to be sectarian in their educational aims. They understood the Bible, theology, and church history as the legacy of the whole church. Nevertheless, exegesis, doctrine, and the historical development of Christianity all received interpretations that directly reflected the confessional standards, theological controversies, and spiritual disciplines of the parent church. Faculty members were recruited from the ordained ministry of the sponsoring denomination, and they pledged to uphold the denomination's doctrine and polity in pursuing their professional duties. In these ways a distinctive denominational culture permeated the theological school and its curriculum. The school's governing educational purposes included faithfully transmitting this culture in a way that shaped the religious identity of each student generation and of the denomination as a whole.

Elevation of the ideal of scholarship by no means diminished concern for the church. On the contrary, second-generation theological scholars considered the development of a distinctly academic theological community to be singularly important for the church at large and for their respective denominations. But the beginnings of the professionalization of theological scholarship did mean that a group of Protestant clergy claimed for themselves a specialized mission within the church, one that called for advanced training and scholarly resources. This specialized mission reshaped the theologian's catechetical concern for handing on a theological tradition by attaching to it the more strictly academic concern for the extension of knowledge within a specialized discipline. Given this dual educational responsibility, how should theological scholars contribute to denominational formation while also participating in an emerging community of scholars that crossed denominational lines? Could theological scholarship cultivate its inherited confessional forms and practical religious purposes yet also pursue specifically academic interests?

Edwards Amasa Park, a theologian in the Edwardsean tradition at Andover Seminary, meditated on this tension in an influential address entitled "The Theology of the Intellect and That of the Feelings" (1850). Park proposed that theology was deployed in relation to two different tasks and two different audiences, which affected its articulation of the Christian gospel. On one hand, *the theology of the intellect* strove to present a systematically consistent doctrinal position. Its natural habitat was the classroom or the public disputation. On the other hand, *the theology of the feelings* aimed at persuasively affecting the heart in order to bring about spiritual change, and, in pursuing this aim, it might well ignore the systematic consistency of one doctrine with another in the rhetorical effort to apply a particular teaching with transformative moral and religious power. Its environment was family nurture or the worshiping congregation. The theology of the intellect engaged in the broad progress of all the sciences and therefore changed over time as theological theories were refined or displaced. But the theology of the feelings appealed not to the successive attainments of higher learning but rather "to a broad and common nature which never becomes obsolete." It therefore "need not always accommodate itself to scientific changes" but may continue to use traditional formulations whose affective power was deeply "furrowed into the soul." Failure to distinguish between the theology of the intellect and the theology of the feelings was becoming, Park lamented, the source of needless confusion and controversy.[1] Academic differences of opinion need not, in short, impinge on the church's faith.

To considerable extent, Park had simply put to new purpose the old distinction between doctrinal knowledge and saving wisdom. But so stating the issue had the effect of institutionalizing a sharp contrast, which would have been unthinkable to pastoral theologians of the colonial period, between a mode of theology appropriate to the sanctuary and a mode appropriate to the academy. Given this contrast, what did the systematizing theology of the intellect *contribute* to the concrete religious faith expressed in pulpit and in pew?

At the same time that theological scholars struggled with the relation of their academic enterprise to the practical religious life of congregations and denominations, they also labored to connect academic theology to national educational purposes. The seminary stood within a larger educational constellation of colleges, museums, libraries, and literary societies that sought to cultivate both a national culture and citizens of republican virtue, alike grounded in the variegated forms of a generalized Protestantism.[2] But, while almost all Americans assumed that civic morality had a religious basis, theology itself appeared to many to be irrelevant—even detrimental—to the task of shaping the national character. Theology, it was said, undoubtedly had its place in bolstering denominations, but in the public realm it appeared contentious, sectarian, and divisive. This perception posed a problem for theological scholars, who understood themselves to be addressing denominational interests, to be sure, but contributing as well to wider Christian and national enterprises. What was the public utility of specifically *theological* scholarship in the advancement of national life?

Finally, the theologians associated closely with teachers in the American colleges, where a parallel development of scholarly ideals and academic disciplines was proceeding in history, classical philology, and the natural sciences. This collaboration encouraged American theologians to align themselves with an international academic community and to elevate the German university as the criterion for American intellectual life. Admiration for the German university paralleled growing interest in German philosophy and theology and signaled the gradual eclipse of the Scottish Common Sense tradition as the principal philosophical resource of American theology. But what did these changes mean for the academic status of theology? How should theological scholarship be related to scholarship in philosophy, philology, and history at a time when prominent practitioners in these fields of inquiry, especially in Europe, were demonstrating that they could be pursued independently of theological claims and assertions?

In adopting the ideal of scholarship, the second generation of seminary faculty had thus set itself a two-pronged agenda. First, it intended to craft a theological method that met fully the scientific criteria of nineteenth-century scholarship. Second, it argued what in America was a difficult case: the comprehensive religious and social utility of this emergent academic theology. Progress in these efforts depended on the new prominence of history in the theological curriculum, a discipline that had been peripheral to the study of theology during the preceding century. Disagreements over the nature of theology became so impassioned precisely because they took place within the agenda set by this shared ideal of scholarship.

The Social Utility of Theological Scholarship

In 1844 a "society of clergymen" presented in *Bibliotheca Sacra*, the journal of Andover Seminary, its collective opinion on the present state and future needs of theological scholarship in America. American theology, they found, had been produced almost entirely by clergy actively engaged in "the practical duties of ministry." While notable for its evangelical ardor and display of "native good sense," this indigenous theology by minister-theologians lacked comprehensive system and sufficient attention to philosophy and history, especially the history of doctrine. American Protestantism had entered a new era, one that called for the cultivation of "theological science." Achievement of this goal required a select few seminaries with faculties, student bodies, and libraries large enough to progress beyond denominational catechetics toward genuine scholarship. Unfortunately, more than 70 percent of the schools had three or fewer faculty, which meant that individual faculty members were responsible for so many different departments of study that they could treat none of them thoroughly. At the time, Andover had approximately 150 students and Princeton about 110, but among the two dozen American seminaries no other school had more than one hundred students, and most had fewer than forty. The authors believed that small size and modest resources encouraged provincialism and low standards. "Every seminary that is not plainly needed," they concluded, "is plainly a nuisance."[3]

As the "society of clergymen" recognized, the scholarly ideal required institutionalization. Authentic scholarship did not simply transmit information but framed questions for analysis and argumentation. This, in turn, required a strengthened sense of disciplinary fields: territories of research to be mastered and extended. Schools staked claim to the new ideal by establishing academic journals that, through book reviews, articles, and reprints of foreign scholarship, defined the scope and focus of a scholarly community and opened avenues of communication between it and the churches. The *Biblical Repertory and Princeton Review* (1829) and Andover's *Bibliotheca Sacra* (1844) disseminated the views of leading faculty at the largest theological schools, such as Edwards A. Park and Moses Stuart at Andover or Charles Hodge at Princeton. But smaller schools also entered the field of academic publication. The *Mercersburg Review* (1849), for example, provided a platform for two theologians at the seminary of the German Reformed Church, John Williamson Nevin and Philip Schaff, who assayed the American churches by standards sufficiently distinctive to be designated "the Mercersburg theology."

For these scholars the term *theological science* designated more than an approach to teaching and research; it was, in addition, the summary designation of a revised cultural role for theology, one that incorporated the doctrinal concerns of specific denominations in a comprehensive theological stance that would form and sanction a national religious culture. This mid-century interpretation of the task of theology presupposed the wider national rhetoric of education, which insisted that the survival and prosperity of a republic depended on educated citizens and on leaders, especially members of the learned professions, who brought religiously informed culture to an expanding nation. Despite denominational diversity, the churches and the schools they founded ought to imbue the emerging American civilization with a common, religiously grounded morality.

The portrayal of seminary-educated clergy as the authoritative custodians of the American cultural synthesis was not, of course, universally acknowledged by the American citizenry, else there would have been no cause to argue it so strenuously. Populist preachers among the Methodists, Baptists, and Disciples of Christ, who derived their authority from the church and the spirit, considered theological schools a detriment to authentic religious mission. Indeed, the ineffective seminary graduate, devoid of spiritual power, became one of the stock figures of derision in popular preaching: a "learned dunce" with no more religious vitality than the pale lettuce that grows under the shade of a peach tree.[4] Within the colleges and seminaries themselves, a parallel tension between piety and learning played itself out in controversies about campus revivals. For college and seminary presidents of an evangelistic bent, such as Charles G. Finney and Lyman Beecher, revivals in the colleges were essential to the welfare of society. Piety and liberal learning mutually reinforced one another; revivalism consecrated the student to the inherited teachings of a Christian civilization.[5] By the middle decades of the century, however, scholars began to look back with distaste on the campus revivals of their own youth, and the Mercersburg theologian John Williamson Nevin was not alone in objecting that revivals had only a circumstantial relation to the intellectual life of the schools, with the consequence that "the relation of religion to secular education is abstract and outward only—the two spheres having nothing to do with each other in fact."[6] In contrast to what they regarded as the merely external connection of revivalism to education, Nevin and his peers sought to describe and to cultivate an organic relation of piety to learning, and debate over the nature of Christian nurture represented an important dimension of the mid-century effort to define the pedagogical consequences of the scholarly ideal.

However defined, this mutual responsibility of religion and education for the guidance of the new nation and its citizens became the predominant theme in one of the minor literary genres of the era: fund-raising addresses to missionary and education societies. These addresses portrayed the theologically educated minister as an ambassador of Protestant culture and characterized colleges and seminaries as necessary institutions for extending this Protestant culture throughout the nation. Far from being aristocratic, so the argument went, these schools were preeminently republican institutions, "the intellectual manufactories and workshops of the nation," busily constructing a leadership elite from native ability rather than inherited privilege. Thus, Lyman Beecher, during his tenure as president of Lane Seminary in Cincinnati, declared that the colleges of a republic were "eminently the guardians of liberty and equality, and the great practical equalizers of society."[7] As such, they not only provided opportunity for individual advancement but also assured that the nation benefited from the talents of its most able citizens.

> They break up and diffuse among the people that monopoly of knowledge and mental power which despotic governments

accumulate for purposes of arbitrary rule, and bring to the children of the humblest families of the nation a full and fair opportunity of holding competition for learning, and honor, and wealth, with the children of the oldest and most affluent families—giving to the nation the select talents and powers of her entire population.[8]

In these colleges and seminaries the acquisition of "mental discipline" prepared "the governing minds of a community" to exercise a stabilizing influence on society. Without this discipline, society would be threatened with conflict and chaos: "Lawyers will jangle— physicians will quarrel—politicians will contend, and theologians dispute—and the public mind be darkened and distracted by the very orbs appointed to guide the day and rule the night."[9]

This image of educated clergy—pastors to "the public mind"—provided the central point for addresses delivered to the American Home Missionary Society by the Congregationalist Horace Bushnell in 1847 and the Presbyterian Albert Barnes in 1849. Each depicted the nation's destiny precariously balanced in the West, and Bushnell warned that, left to its own devices, a frontier situation soon descended into barbarism. "The power which is to determine the question, whether this land is to enjoy the blessings of liberty, civilization and Christianity, is indubitably now developing itself beyond the mountains," Barnes declared.[10] Only an alliance of learning and religion could insure the future. For both men, the educated minister brought morality, social order, and Protestant culture to the frontier, redeeming the land from Roman Catholicism, atheism, and barbarism. "We will not cease," Bushnell announced, "till a christian nation throws up its temples of worship on every hill and plain; till knowledge, virtue and religion, blending their dignity and their healthful power, have filled our great country with a manly and a happy race of people and the bands of a complete christian commonwealth are seen to span the continent."[11] The nation's very future called for the American Home Missionary Society and its counterparts to send forth into the western lands exemplary missionaries who combined piety with learning on behalf of civic unity. This ideal missionary, as Barnes portrayed him, is an educated man, having enjoyed the best advantages of our literary and theological seminaries. He is himself a friend of education, and will be a patron of colleges and schools. He is a man who will himself possess a library, if he can, and who will aim that there shall be a library in every neighborhood. He is a man who will be an advocate of temperance and a patron of every institution of benevolence. He is a man who will make his appeals to reason and the consciences of men, rather than to excited feelings.[12]

In 1850 W. G. T. Shedd, who would soon move from the University of Vermont to Union Theological Seminary, stated his views on the relation between this general educational responsibility to society and the specific enterprise of scholarship itself. How, he asked, could the specialized knowledge cultivated in the college also be diffused throughout society without, in the process of diffusion, rendering it merely superficial? The knowledge pursued in the academy, Shedd observed, was preeminently "an *organized* system" built on interconnected fundamental truths and first principles, and only portions of it were regularly used for the practical purposes of human commerce. Still, these separate practical applications of knowledge depended, as a tree on its roots, on the underlying organized system constantly extended and refined in the college. Hence, the desire to spread information should not be carried out "at the expense of that profound and scientific culture which must exist *somewhere,* in *some* portion of the community at least," in order to replenish "the common information of society."[13] For Shedd, the bridges connecting scientific to practical knowledge were members of the three learned professions, who understood the connection between systematic knowledge gained from their collegiate educations and the practical interests of society. Like Beecher, Shedd therefore argued that "scientific education" promoted the public welfare through the mediation of the professions: "It must be apparent even to the most superficial observer, that the removal and want of a physician, a lawyer, and clergyman in a particular town would work disastrously upon both its temporal and eternal interests."[14]

Typically, advocates for the public utility of theological science portrayed modern scholarship extending the domain of knowledge through specialized investigation and discovery. Edwards A. Park emphasized this theme in 1850 to the Society for the Promotion of Collegiate and Theological Education in the West, an organization of Presbyterians and Congregationalists created to raise funds for schools in the Mississippi Valley. Park shared the opinion of W. G. T. Shedd that the old model of the individual tutor-practitioner and his student apprentices could not advance disciplined, systematic investigation; it required, rather, the collaborative enterprise of communities of scholars. At a modern college or professional school, he stated, "investigating spirits" were brought together in a "division of labor" that enabled each to "concentrate on a single department, and thus pry into the laws which lie hidden from a cursory and divided view."

By emphasizing "new discovery," modern scholarship displayed a distinctly Protestant character, Park asserted, far different from "the Romish view" in which the main value of schools consisted in preserving the results of previous study. As this investigative, "Protestant" scholarship pursued new knowledge, the Christian faith had nothing to fear. Park, like many of his scholarly peers in the antebellum colleges, invoked the old commonplace that "the truths in the book of nature" and those in "the inspired volume" of Scripture would be found fully consonant as understanding of each progressed, because God was the source of both. Park was perhaps more sanguine than some in thinking that this implied only modest adjustments in the inherited theology, on the assumption that "the Puritan faith is so interwoven with the texture of science as to be ultimately confirmed or illustrated by every addition of our knowledge."[15]

Ideally, scholarship proceeded by dispassionate appraisal of "the facts," and this scientific impartiality was a mental discipline of notable social utility. Historical scholarship manifested this virtue in the highest degree, wrote Philip Schaff in 1849, since it presupposed that "the historian has freely surrendered himself to his object, brings it to a living reproduction in his spirit, and is concerned only to be a faithful mirror of what has taken place." Although this should not be taken to imply "the impossible task of laying aside all subjectivity, character, and religious interest," the fidelity of the historian

to the scholarly subject required that "he divest himself of all prejudices, of all party interests, in order to bring the truth . . . into the
light of day."[16] In particular, Schaff declared, the historian's view of
the church as a single, organic life was decisively important for cultivating this impartiality, since it did not look "through the colored
spectacles of a particular sect" but pursued unbiased investigation
"under the conviction that the boundless life of the Church can be
fully represented only through the collective Christianity of all periods, nations and persons, and with the persuasion that the truth finds
its best justification in the simple dispassionate exhibition of its own
historical course."[17]

In both seminaries and colleges at mid-century, scholars proposed to transcend sectarian debate and avoid the divorce of religious
belief from the academy by advancing a new understanding of religion based on historical scholarship, which could exert unifying intellectual influence in church and society. Out of enthusiasm for this
ideal, Noah Porter, future president of Yale, wrote from Berlin in
the early 1850s that he hoped to employ recent advances in German
theology in order to demonstrate to the American public how the
theologians of different Protestant denominations shared the same
underlying religious faith.[18] By 1850, as the mission to the West
combined with alarm for the future of the Union, Edwards A. Park
dared hope what was not to be, that the detached, comprehensive,
scholarly view of matters ideally taken in the college or professional
school might influence the course of national political debate. "Our
union under one government . . . is cemented by the spirit of our
universities," and this spirit said Park "is a considerate spirit not easily provoked by political strifes." In the gathering crisis over slavery,
the sectional political jealousy of "uninstructed men," Park argued,
"alienates those whom the comprehensive spirit of science binds together." The nation's "permanent seminaries of learning" established
the personal, affective bonds of loyalty that would sustain the nation,
because they fostered "life-long and endearing intimacies between
the physicians, statesmen, clergymen, teachers and authors of the
older and newer States, and thus imbue our various learned professions with one sentiment, and that a sentiment of fraternal regard to
each other, and of filial regard to our country—our whole country."[19]

Through such claims Park and his contemporaries fashioned theological science into the new form of the seminary ideal, attuned to the fact of Protestant pluralism but still aimed toward producing social harmony and cultural coherence through the influence of ministers educated for civic responsibility.

Theological Science

All such proposals for the social utility of theological science, to be academically persuasive, required an intellectual organization of theological inquiry consistent with the canons of nineteenth-century scholarship as a whole. American theologians met this need by adopting the theological encyclopedia of the German universities. As a genre of academic literature, the theological encyclopedia had developed in the latter part of the eighteenth century in order to delineate the relations among the fields that comprised theological study and to justify their place in the university. In appropriating the disciplinary structure of this literature, the Americans adopted a fourfold curriculum of biblical studies, systematic theology, church history, and practical theology that quickly became (and continues to be) the dominant pattern for theological studies in the United States. Especially notable was the prominence that the new organization gave to historical studies.

The new scheme was not without difficulties, however. According to Edward Farley, the mode of thinking expressed in the European theological encyclopedia constituted "a virtual cataclysm in the history of theological schools," because it marked the separation of the single inquiry of theology into a collection of discrete scholarly disciplines, each using methods derived from other parts of the academy.[20] Tutorial education oriented toward the catechetical transformation of the student was being dispersed into academic investigations aimed at advancing knowledge in discrete scholarly fields. This dispersal into distinct disciplines raised problems for the unity of theological study, because it left unclear how philological, historical, and philosophical investigations finally came to focus on unifying and shaping the self by reorienting it toward the one God. The most common resolution was to define the unity of the four theological disciplines functionally, in terms of their supposed pertinence to the adequate preparation of a student for the concrete tasks of ministry, what Farley calls "the clerical paradigm" of curricular unity. Brian A. Gerrish has made the same point with respect to one of the most famous and controversial texts on the theological encyclopedia, Friedrich Schleiermacher's *Brief Outline on the Study of Theology* (1811), which argued that theological study was held together by the single purpose of equipping leaders for the church. Without this practical aim, Schleiermacher thought (according to Gerrish), "all the various studies that go on in a theological faculty will fragment, or even dissipate into other parts of the academy."[21]

Since this effort to relate disparate academic fields to the practical preparation of clergy was the curricular analogue to American arguments for academic theology's social and religious utility, how was the fourfold curriculum of the theological encyclopedia translated into the American educational idiom? How were its unresolved questions with regard to the unity and purpose of theological study handled by American scholars who were fashioning a public role for "theological science?" Some answers can be inferred from "Theological Encyclopedia and Methodology," by Friedrich August Gottreu Tholuck (1799–1877), a transcription of unpublished lectures that Tholuck consented to have translated for an American audience by Edwards Amasa Park, who had studied with Tholuck at the University of Halle. Park's translation appeared in three successive issues of *Bibliotheca Sacra* during 1844, the same year in which the "society of clergymen" had published its thoughts on the American advancement of "theological science."

Tholuck himself was one of a company of German theologians who, since the 1830s, had sought to chart a churchly course for theology away from what they considered the deistic skepticism of the preceding generation of German intellectuals.[22] Philip Schaff, Mercersburg's Swiss immigrant theologian, had known Tholuck when Schaff was a student in Germany, and he sketched Tholuck's life for American Protestants in *Germany: Its Universities, Theology, and Religion* (1857), a book that traced the development of religious thought in Germany in order to counter the American tendency toward blanket condemnation of German "speculation."[23] In Schaff's portrait, Tholuck's career represented a model of scholarly piety easily recognizable by American evangelicals. Passing through skepticism in his student days, Tholuck had become a champion of evangelical Protestantism against Hegelian theological influences that threatened belief in a personal God. An idiosyncratic and somewhat irascible teacher, Tholuck was nevertheless deeply committed to his students and inventive in his teaching methods. He welcomed international students to Halle and influenced several leading American theologians who studied with him, including not only Park of Andover and Schaff of Mercersburg but also Edward Robinson and Henry Boynton Smith of Union Theological Seminary.

Tholuck organized Christian theology, "the science of the Christian religion," according to the fourfold encyclopedia: exegetical theology, systematic theology, historical theology, and practical theology. It was a science in the sense that it systematically exhibited "a class of ideas, which are so arranged as to form one whole, to be surveyed in one view, and which are susceptible of a division into distinct parts." The articulated unity of distinct disciplines was paramount in the definition of a science; indeed, he stated, "the opposite of a science is an aggregate."[24]

Biblical authority provided the foundational principles of the fourfold theological encyclopedia, and the disciplines were unified by the progression from the first division of study, exegetical theology, to the others, an approach illustrated by Tholuck's description of historical theology. In popular parlance, he observed, church history simply meant the chronicle of episodes from the church's origins to the present. But this did not suffice to make church history a science.

> Every scientific narrative of a course of events, must have one leading idea, which imparts unity to the whole. The idea of the kingdom of God, is the leading thought in the history of the church. . . . Now it is the province of Church-History to show the extent to which the Christian church, at different periods of her existence, has approximated to this state of ideal perfection. It is accordingly evident, that none but a theologian can write a narrative of the course of ecclesiastical events.[25]

In this definition of historical theology a biblical doctrine, the kingdom of God, unified church history by providing a theological and moral principle for judging the actual church's distance from its divinely revealed destiny. Theological study began with "Biblical Dogmatic Theology," which systematically arranged the Christian faith in a system of doctrinal topics "founded on the proof-texts of the Bible." But since, in the course of history, different groups united around different interpretations of the Bible, the one church had divided "into various branches which adopt different confessions of faith." Hence, a historical discipline, the "Dogmatic Theology of a Church," arose to engage in systematic exposition of the development of the theological views of "a particular ecclesiastical community." In turn, "Scientific Dogmatical Theology" was the enterprise of the scholar who "feels the imperative need of learning the logical necessity and the inward connection of all the propositions, which he believes to be correct" and who, therefore, wishes to "show the reasonableness of Christian truths, and the connection of one doctrine with another."[26] Through these disciplines, a systematically organized and historically determinate interpretation of the biblical revelation provided the normative point of view from which the historian appraised the history of the church.

In stating that only a theologian can properly narrate the church's history, Tholuck had two things in mind. First, in the structure of theological study, church history depended for its unifying point of view on the prior theological disciplines of exegesis and systematic theology. Thus, only a theologian, one conversant with the work of those two departments, could move beyond a mere chronology, an aggregation of historical facts, to present a systematically unified, scientific narrative. But, second and even more important, Tholuck believed that the proper interpretation of Christian history required Christian experience on the part of the interpreter. As he put it, the question was whether historical knowledge of the circumstances of the various biblical authors and of "the prevalent notions of their respective times" was sufficient for biblical interpretation. Tholuck answered that it was not: "When a pious man speaks, I cannot give the proper historical interpretation of his words, unless I know from my own experience what that is of which he speaks, and unless I interpret his expressions accordingly."[27] The study of theology required belief of the doctrines that were being studied. "It must be remembered," he stressed, "that the scientific apprehension of religious doctrines presupposes a religious experience. Without this moral qualification, it is impossible to obtain a true insight into theological dogmas."[28]

Although this point of view had obvious affinities with American Protestant piety, it left unresolved the "scientific" status of a work such as Edward Gibbon's *Decline and Fall of the Roman Empire*, which approached the history of Christianity from a point of view unified by skeptical rather than dogmatic principles. Hence, behind the historical study of Christianity lay the very basic question of the relation of revelation to that history. On this vexed issue Tholuck retreated to eighteenth-century apologetic strategies and claimed that historical evidence corroborated the supernatural authority of the Bible. Apologetics laid the "foundations of systematic theology" by weighing the historical evidence that the gospels represented the testimony of apostolic eyewitnesses to Jesus Christ performing miracles and possessing the gift of prophecy. This "historical and apologetic proof secures faith in the higher dignity of Christ, and also in the authority of the apostles, for it confirms their narratives."[29]

Since the pastor had the task of applying this authoritative, systematically organized doctrine to the present life of the church, Tholuck concluded his theological encyclopedia with practical theology, since "the ultimate use of all theoretical studies is, *to facilitate the discharge of practical duties;* and therefore it is in the highest degree desirable, to connect with these studies of a theologian some consideration of the active duties of a clergyman."[30] In this sense Tholuck presented what Farley has called "the clerical paradigm" for the unity of theology, in which the ultimate purpose of theology was practical and pastoral. But in Tholuck's encyclopedia this functional unity of theological studies was dependent on a prior, substantive unity derived from revealed truth.

Tholuck's conservative version of the theological encyclopedia, as refracted through Park's translation, had several appeals for Americans seeking to organize theological scholarship in ways that demonstrated both its academic status and its compatibility with the social and religious purposes of the Protestant denominations. Tholuck's twin pillars of revealed truth and religious experience translated easily into the evangelical piety of the American churches. His organization of church history around the motif of the kingdom of God attuned historical scholarship to American religious aspirations. His emphasis on the functional task of preparing ministerial leadership was, if anything, destined for even greater importance in the American religious environment of denominational pluralism and voluntary church membership, where the success of the minister was to be judged by the number of souls awakened and enlisted into congregational membership. Practical theology, when translated from theological encyclopedia into congregational life, was persuasive theology, theology that moved the heart, evoked commitment, and generated an active loyalty to the denomination and to interdenominational benevolent enterprises. Finally, the theological encyclopedia became in America the academic equivalent of denominationalism, a formal structure that recognized the rough parity of study at schools representing different denominations, that encouraged scholarly cooperation across denominational lines, and yet allowed each school to fill this formal curricular structure with its distinctive denominational traditions and approaches to ministerial formation. "Polemic divinity" was pushed to the margins of this new curriculum and replaced by the ostensibly more irenic discipline of church history. In all of these ways, the theological encyclopedia in America represented the effort to make the revealed doctrine of the church, the substance of evangelical preaching, into a subject for scientific scrutiny without diminishing its renovative influence on personal and social life.

Despite these appeals, the American encyclopedia proved unstable. The assertion that modern "theological science" was fully compatible with Protestant religious traditions would come under increasingly heavy siege by academic critics on one side and religious critics on the other. This was so primarily because the fourfold theological encyclopedia, despite the new prominence it gave to historical scholarship, obscured the relation of revelation to history. Whereas Protestants had traditionally employed the biblical narrative as the basic structure for human history, the problem inherited from the eighteenth century was the relation of this scriptural narrative to the independent narrative of the past provided by modern historical study. How, it might be asked, was the supernatural history of salvation, Edwards's "history of the work of redemption," related to Hume's "natural history of religion," in which religious beliefs were socially constructed from human fears and passions?

Earlier in the nineteenth century, Friedrich Schleiermacher had addressed the historical nature of religion in a more radical way than Tholuck, and, perhaps for that very reason, Schleiermacher's version of the theological encyclopedia had little currency in the American scene, even among scholars strongly influenced by his general theological position. In order to resolve the tension between the traditional salvation history and critical history, Schleiermacher had proposed that the Bible be studied by historical methods applicable to any other piece of literature and not be identified as a separate curricular field. Schleiermacher's encyclopedia therefore contained not four but three divisions: philosophical theology, historical theology, and practical theology. The functional unity of study, preparation for church leadership, was as prominent as in Tholuck's rendition, but the role of history in supplying the substantive unity of study was developed in a manner that reshaped theological reflection. The discipline of historical theology encompassed the entire development of the Christian religion, incorporating in its purview the Bible, the subsequent history of Christianity, and the dogmatic theology of the contemporary church. By this inquiry into the rise and development of Christianity, historical theology aimed to discern the historical essence of Christianity and to exhibit that essence as the substantive unity of theological studies. Whereas for Tholuck the history of the church was written by assessing its development in relation to unchanging norms enunciated in the Bible, Schleiermacher proposed to describe the church's organic development in order to disclose through that very description the distinctive and vital form that was coming to expression in the church's history. Theological studies, on Schleiermacher's reading, were historical in their entirety precisely because of the nature of their subject: the life of the church unfolding in history. Within this broad historical framework, dogmatic theology was the branch of historical theology that systematically presented the doctrine current at a given time. For Schleiermacher, one dealt with doctrines, "in the first instance, not by saying yea or nay to them, but by seeking to understand them functionally in the life of a particular religious community at a particular stage of its career."[31] Competent leadership of the church in the present, Schleiermacher concluded, took its temporal bearings by understanding this functional evolution of Christian life and teaching. Historical knowledge of the church, in sum, was the requisite knowledge for practical leadership of the church, built upon "the realization that this community, regarded as a whole, is a historical entity, and that its present condition can be adequately grasped only when it is viewed as a product of the past."[32]

Schleiermacher's proposal raised the critical question of the historical nature of Christianity as a religion. Although this question would prove inescapable in later decades, it was obscured in the initial elaboration of theological science by American scholars. They developed their rationale for the importance of theology to the nation and the denominations on the more conservative fourfold encyclopedia, which implicitly affirmed the supernatural authority of the Bible by separating biblical studies as a distinct discipline in the curriculum, thereby partially shielding it from the impact of historical consciousness. Indeed, leading American scholars such as Charles Hodge at Princeton or Bela Bates Edwards at Andover developed interpretations of "biblical science" that buttressed its supernatural inspiration and supported the belief that it was "not analogous to other books," because "it reveals truths which are to be believed, prescribes duties which are universally obligatory." They attacked "destructive criticism," whether German or American, that, by emphasizing ambiguities or double meanings in the text of Scripture and by substituting "theory for judicious investigation," undermined the permanence and clarity of true doctrine. In reaction Hodge, Edwards, and their peers employed "grammar and lexicography" to emphasize the univocal meaning of biblical texts as the basis for elaborating definite doctrinal propositions from them. The "fundamental importance of historical interpretation" rested, for them, on the fact that "history is the key to all fulfilled prophecy, and it supplies essential rules for the comprehension of those portions [of biblical prophecy] that remain unaccomplished."[33] To be sure, Schleiermacher's understanding of the organic development of the church influenced several American theologians, although even this was controversial enough. But, because the Americans separated Schleiermacher's historical organicism from his comprehensive understanding of the task and structure of theological study, the idea of history did not immediately disrupt the permanent deposit of truth they found accessible in Scripture.

The ways in which the German theological encyclopedia prompted a turn to history in American theological studies were clearly evident in programmatic essays on the nature of church history written by Philip Schaff and Henry Boynton Smith between 1849 and 1851. For both, church history became the most comprehensive of the four theological disciplines, and especially for Schaff the influence of Schleiermacher's organic understanding of the church received full emphasis. When Schaff wrote about "the progress of church history," he used the phrase with double intent. In the first instance, Schaff meant the disciplinary progress of church history toward scientific form, mere chronology giving way to the apprehension of history's organic wholeness, in which "the end is only the full evolution of the beginning." Scientific history was that history which investigated the church's living unity, "pervaded with a common blood," by elucidating its maturation through each successive epoch. In a second sense, "the progress of church history" was the historic progress of the church itself, understood now as "an organism, springing from the person of Jesus Christ, as the author and progenitor of the new humanity, extending itself outwardly and inwardly always more widely, engaged in perpetual conflict with sin and error from without and from within, moving forward through all sorts of difficulty and hindrance, and still surely tending always towards a definite end."[34]

But this progressive, organic development of the historical church was not, for Schaff and Smith, merely the story of one human institution among many. As Smith argued, the historian who sought "the true philosophy of human history" would never achieve this goal by examining temporal causation alone; the scholar who "reads history in the light of all its impregnable facts, to get from them its laws, will be led along to see that human motives and interests do not embrace the whole of it, but that it is also the sphere of a divine justice, and the theatre of a divine kingdom." Hence, the scholar would be led finally to see that the history of the church, "the record of the progress of the kingdom of God," interacted with all human activity and was "a part of universal history, containing its central and controlling elements."[35] Schaff, building on the same assumption, described the history of the church as "the gradual actualization of the plan of the kingdom of God in the life of humanity, the outward and inward development of the church; that is, her extension throughout the earth, and the introduction of the spirit of Christ into all spheres of human existence, the family, the State, arts, sciences, and morality, to form them into organs and expressions of this spirit, for the glory of God and the advancement of man to his proper perfection and happiness."[36]

This conviction that church history contained the clue to the final meaning of universal history, of course, afforded the Christian historian a privileged view. Schaff agreed with Tholuck that "the first condition of all knowledge is an active sympathy" with the object to be known. Only the philosopher understood philosophy and the poet poetry; likewise, the church historian "must live and move in the spirit of Christianity in order to do justice to his subject." But *to know church history was to know universal history* in a way inaccessible from other vantage points. "Since Christianity is the centre of the world's life and of truth itself, it unlocks also the sense of all other history. We cannot say then, that according to the same rule only a heathen can understand heathenism, only a Jew Judaism, and only a rationalist rationalism; for only from a higher position can we command a full view also of all below, and not the reverse."[37] For both Schaff and Smith, church history became the most comprehensive of the theological disciplines, the strongest case for the scientific character of theology as a whole, and the basis for relating theology to church and public life. At the same time, their emphasis on the immanence of God in the organic development of history preserved in a new form the traditional conviction that the Christian narrative encompassed and interpreted universal history.

This idealization of the educational contribution of theological science to American culture encountered three controversies that confounded theologians in the middle decades of the century and that, in fact, may serve as illustrations of continuing uncertainties in the theologian's cultural role. First, the longstanding tension between the school as an institution of continuity and social order and the school as an institution of social reform and innovation came to a climax in the debate over slavery, when advocacy of social transformation challenged the scholars' self-announced role of promoting social cohesion through dispassionate inquiry. Second, the ideal of scholarship itself received divergent interpretations, with quite different consequences for the scholar's social role. The educational ideal of transmitting a cultural heritage through scholarship was emphatically challenged in this generation by Ralph Waldo Emerson's image of the scholar as a social critic emboldened by the vision of an emerging new culture. Finally, these social tensions surrounding the ideal of scholarship interacted with the heightened historical consciousness in theological studies and prompted a reinvestigation of the nature of theological language that sought to overcome the divorce between "the theology of the intellect and that of the feelings."

Theological Study and Social Reform

As the Civil War approached, the hope that dispassionate theological science would contribute to harmonious social consensus clashed with the reform impulse of evangelical Protestantism. In the same years that theological education was an instrument for the extension of Yankee culture into the Middle West, it also became an institution of renewal, reform, and cultural innovation. These educational aims came into dramatic conflict over the antislavery movement in the theological schools. It was not a clash for which the schools, any more than the society as a whole, were morally and intellectually equipped. Free blacks in antebellum America were sometimes admitted to theological schools, but they seem to have been largely unaware of one another's presence scattered among the schools, and the denial of admission, for reasons of race, was by no means extraordinary.[38] Purposeful engagement in the theological education of African Americans would not begin until the establishment of the theological department of Howard University after the Civil War. The controversy in the theological schools thus centered on white Protestants, most famously at Lane Seminary in Cincinnati.

With Lyman Beecher's installation as its president in 1832, Lane Seminary began attracting substantial numbers of students, including several mature students, friends of the abolitionist Theodore Dwight Weld. During the 1833–34 academic year, the much-admired Weld began to proselytize on campus for the cause of abolition. Interest increased and in February 1834, Beecher granted a student petition to hold an extended public discussion. The "Lane Debate" ran over eighteen days, resembling, in the phrase of Gilbert Barnes, "a protracted meeting, a revival in benevolence."[39] The students, including several Southerners, developed a strong sense of personal guilt for the slave system, and, in the months following the debate, they sent delegates to the meeting of the American Anti-Slavery Society and began to work with the community of free blacks in Cincinnati. Supported by a gift from the Presbyterian philanthropist Arthur Tappan, they established a library, adult evening classes, Sunday schools, and a "freedom bureau" to assist free blacks in purchasing the liberty of relatives still in bondage.[40]

In the spring of 1834, President Beecher was in the East attending meetings of the national benevolent societies, when other college presidents and representatives in attendance conferred and formally resolved that student antislavery agitation be suppressed. Copies of the resolution were sent to colleges and theological schools throughout the nation, and the trustees of Lane Seminary responded by abolishing the students' antislavery society. That May, Theodore Dwight Weld wrote an open letter to James Hall, editor of the *Western Monthly Magazine,* who had denounced the Lane students as "political partisans." Weld countered Hall's criticism by asserting that the slavery issue was not simply political but also, and fundamentally, religious: "Why should not theological students investigate and discuss the sin of slavery?" For, in Weld's view, slaveholding was indeed *sin,* and therefore directly concerned those who were soon to be sent forth as "ambassadors for Christ—commissioned to cry aloud—to show the people their transgressions." Free discussion elicited truth, Weld continued, and if theological seminaries obstructed debate, "they will fall behind the age." Experience in discussing "subjects of great practical moment, such as slavery . . . is as important a part of the preparation for the ministry, as an acquaintance with the principles of interpretation or a knowledge of didactic theology." In sum, the theological student

> who would preach in the nineteenth century, must *know* the
> nineteenth century. No matter how deeply read in the history
> of the past, if not versed in the records of his own day, he is
> not fit to preach the gospel. If he would bless the church *now,*
> he must *know her now* . . . must scrutinize her condition—
> inspect her symptoms—ascertain the mode of previous treatment, and compare it with the prescriptions contained in
> God's book of directions, where the case is described.[41]

At the beginning of the next fall term, the trustees' policy was still in force, Beecher was not on the campus, and the antislavery students consequently left the school, reassembling in the spring of 1835 at Oberlin.[42]

As the turbulence at Lane Seminary indicated, theological debate about slavery could scarcely avoid issues of scriptural interpretation, since by the early 1830s abolitionists like Weld had begun to argue that slavery was not simply a political and moral evil but a sin. This argument, presenting a specifically theological justification for a radical political position, "linked the slavery question firmly to the biblical question since the proof of its sinfulness had to come from Scripture."[43] Both Unitarians such as William Ellery Channing and evangelical abolitionists such as Weld resolved this linkage, in their own ways, by appealing to broad principles of morality derived from Scripture. Thus, Channing argued that "textual difficulties could be avoided only by an appeal to the moral spirit or 'genius' of the whole, and not the simple letter of the text." Weld appealed to the general tenor of the Bible, by asserting that "the Ten Commandments themselves condemned slavery by implication, and the law of love, 'glowing on every page,' made the Bible not the 'sanctuary' of slavery but its 'sepulchre.'"[44]

Some among the theological scholars were persuaded. The youthful John Williamson Nevin, at the time professor of biblical literature at Western Theological Seminary in Allegheny, Pennsylvania, applauded the "wisely and temperately" stated principles of the Lane Seminary students and expressed hope that these would be "temperately considered," by the proponents of abolition, in order that "the friends of humanity will find themselves able to stand on common ground in regard to the great evil of slavery." In 1835, Nevin succinctly stated his own position: "Slavery is a sin as it exists in this country, and as such it ought to be abolished." In acquiescing to slavery as a supposedly necessary evil, the entire nation was implicated in guilt. The abolition movement was "among the noblest forms of benevolent action" precisely because it called attention to this national guilt in order to change the laws under which slavery persisted. "We glory then in being an abolitionist, and count it all honor to bear reproach for such a cause," Nevin wrote and predicted in conclusion that "it is the cause of God and will prevail."[45]

Other exegetes, like Moses Stuart of Andover, found themselves unable to reconcile abolition and biblical scholarship. The abolitionists' argument that slavery was a sin violated their understanding of the grammatical and historical meaning of the biblical text, since the institution of slavery appeared there uncondemned. The debate over slavery challenged the relationships among their commitment to Scripture as the authoritative expression of the divine will, their academic procedures of textual interpretation, and their hope that theological science would disseminate a harmonizing spirit throughout American society. Stuart, concerned in 1835 that agitation for immediate abolition would divide Andover as it had divided Lane, outlined an answer for students designed to steer an exegetical path between the interpretations of abolitionists on the one hand and proslavery apologists on the other. Although he granted that the principle of slavery was evil and that some slave laws were unchristian, Stuart argued that the abolitionists twisted the biblical text to their own interest when they called slavery sinful by its very nature, since scriptural passages could be adduced that spoke approvingly of the institution.

But this was an insufficient response to student reformers who asked how the Bible could give permission to slavery and still retain its religious and moral authority. Stuart resolved this dilemma by proposing that, just as Paul had tolerated slavery until the gospel could eliminate it, so modern Christians might in good conscience disagree about how long to tolerate slavery in American society and what steps should be taken to eradicate it, while still sharing the confidence that the gradual spread of Christian ethical principles would eventually destroy slavery. Stuart stated that his more "temperate" course, unlike the radical solution of abolitionism, was both more responsible exegesis and more prudent politics. He and the other members of the Andover faculty therefore persuaded the students to cease all organized agitation on the subject of slavery, on the grounds that it was threatening the basic purposes of their education by creating factional enmity, making them appear partisan on a complex ethical issue.

The debates at Lane and Andover illustrated the complex interweaving of two strands of Protestant theology in America: its drive toward the reform of persons and societies and its conviction that within Christian communities doctrinal consensus was a principal buttress of harmony. In the matter of slavery, however, white Christians derived opposing norms of conduct from the Bible, and congregations and denominations sundered. Events thus conspired to undermine the enterprise of building a unified national culture on the foundation of "theological science," and experience disproved the assertion that theological seminaries promoted professional harmony among the clergy. Although theological faculty could plausibly argue that reform activism itself was not an integral part of their professional function, they could not easily divorce reform from "impartial" transmission of the exegetical and doctrinal traditions of evangelical Protestantism, since those very traditions were unintelligible apart from the reformist ideal.[46]

The American Scholar

Professors did not have the field to themselves when it came to defining the public role of the scholar. Ministers, politicians, and public orators could and did address the academic community in ways that not only captured the attention of a wider public but also commanded scholarly respect and evoked response from the academicians. The most arresting contributor to this discussion of the public significance of scholarship was Ralph Waldo Emerson, whose Harvard Phi Beta Kappa address of 1837, "The American Scholar," directly challenged the ideal of scholarship developing in the colleges and theological schools. In the very decades that academicians were appropriating the German model of the theological encyclopedia, Emerson announced that the authentic vocation of the American scholar would never be claimed through timid and imitative subservience to the tutelage of Europe. Had he gone no further than urging a fresh and independent American literature, Emerson would simply have reiterated a conventional theme of academic oratory since the century's first decade.[47] But, in casting off the authority of Europe, he more fundamentally challenged all modes of American education that vested authority in "the mind of the Past" inscribed in literature, art, and institutions. The duties of the scholar "may all be comprised in self-trust," Emerson declared, and this fact defined the scholar's vocation, which was no less than the invention of America.

Recalling an ancient fable that the gods "divided Man into men, that he might be more helpful to himself," Emerson enunciated the doctrine that humanity was "present to all particular men only partially, or through one faculty; and that you must take the whole society to find the whole man." Society had, however, degenerated. There had been a Fall. What had begun as the diverse forms of a single, elemental human labor had scattered into specialized, separate functions with no significance beyond themselves. In this fragmented state, individuals were reduced to things, the sailor differing in no essential way from the rope on the ship. In the proper condition of society, the scholar was *"Man Thinking,"* but in society's degenerate state the scholar became "a mere thinker, or, still worse, the parrot of other men's thinking."

The task, then, was to regenerate scholarly work as a fully human social activity. This began, Emerson proposed, by recognizing that the most important influence on the mind of the scholar was direct encounter with nature that prompted curiosity about its fundamental order and meaning. "The ambitious soul sits down before each refractory fact; one after another," in Emerson's description, "reduces all strange constitutions, all new powers, to their class and their law, and goes on for ever to animate the last fibre of organization, the outskirts of nature, by insight." Immersion in concrete experiences disclosed integrated patterns of meaning. Intuition passed through particular experience to apprehend the wholeness of experience. As with nature so also with humanity, what appeared to be individual was in reality universal, and the scholar learned only by self-trust that "in going down into the secrets of his own mind, he has descended into the secrets of all minds. . . . The poet, in utter solitude remembering his spontaneous thoughts and recording them, is found to have recorded that, which men in crowded cities find true for them also." The scholar's critical ruminations on intuitive apprehensions discovered that the multiplicity of humans and the plenitude of facts were bound together by "the inexplicable continuity of this web of God." Nature revealed itself to be "the opposite of the soul," its beauty and its laws reflecting those of the mind and thereby serving as measures of the self's own reflective understanding. Thoroughly revising Calvin's observation that knowledge of God and knowledge of the self were "joined by many bonds," Emerson concluded that "the ancient precept, 'Know thyself,' and the modern precept, 'Study nature,' become at last one maxim."[48]

The immediately noticeable feature of Emerson's address is its comprehensive demolition of the scholar's unthinking reliance on "the mind of the Past." He focused his attack on habitual ways of reading the repository of that mind, books. An insatiable reader himself, Emerson did not assault the books but the reader, aiming to rehabilitate reading by radically redefining its purpose.[49] "The theory of books is noble. The scholar of the first age received into him the world around; brooded thereon; gave it the new arrangement of his own mind, and uttered it again. It came into him, life; it went out from him, truth."[50] But this scholarly act of "transmuting life into truth" was never perfectly accomplished, the conventional, the local, and the perishable never being entirely excluded. Hence, each age must write its own books, else a great mischief arises, in which "the sacredness which attaches to the act of creation,—the act of thought,—is transferred to the record." Atop this misapprehension was constructed a veritable manufactory of books, written by those "who start wrong, who set out from accepted dogmas, not from their own sight of principles." The actual meaning of the book, as a creative inquiry into nature's elemental form, was lost in the veneration of the text, and "instead of Man Thinking, we have the bookworm."[51]

The true significance of a book—including, it would seem, the Good Book—was its origin in a creative act, and its proper role was to "inspire" creativity in the reader, who "must be an inventor to read well." In the traditional understanding, humans read two divine "books," nature and Bible, on the assumption that Scripture guided the true reading of nature and the self. Readings of nature and human nature were thus corrected by regular comparison to the Bible. For Emerson, the Bible and all books were no longer authoritative guides to "reading" the world but, as it were, journals of the self's direct experience of the world and the insights deriving therefrom. He turned to the Bible not as an authoritative object of study but as an example for emulation, and thought of himself not as a commentator but as the potential author of a similarly evocative text.[52]

On those occasions when the scholar could go to nature and "read God directly," therefore, time was too precious to spend on the "transcripts" of readings by others. But *inventive reading*, reading that proceeded from faith that the mind common to the universe was individually present in the reader and all other individuals, could discern in the literature of the past the authentic utterances of what was "always true." Consequently, said Emerson, "when the intervals of darkness come, as come they must,—when the sun is hid, and the stars withdraw their shining,—we repair to the lamps which were kindled by their ray, to guide our steps to the East again, where the dawn is."[53] The sun, however, was not in the book but in the world, and the scholar drew vital energy from action in the world, which was "the preamble of thought, the transition through which it passes from the unconscious to the conscious." The world was the "shadow of the soul," and active encounter with the world rejuvenated the soul, providing the "raw material" of its invention. "When the artist has exhausted his materials, when the fancy no longer paints, when thoughts are no longer apprehended, and books are a weariness,— he has always the resource *to live*."[54]

The "self-trust" of the scholar rested on the conviction, the hope, that invention uncovered the infinite and vital ground of both nature and the self: "It is a mischievous notion that we are come late into nature; that the world was finished a long time ago. As the world was plastic and fluid in the hands of God, so it is ever to so much of his attributes as we bring to it."[55] The spirituality and inwardness that had so strongly marked the older ideal of catechetical formation, Emerson now reshaped into a process of self-culture that sought out the identities between the individual soul and the world's divine and molten core. His oration identified the American scholar not by reasoned definition of an existing social type but through a latent narrative of the seeker who has gone out from the inherited institutions of society "to perform the intellectual and imaginative labor of conceiving a new vocation for himself, and almost a new society in which this vocation might have meaning."[56] The scholar's inventive observation of the world thus summoned citizens to the possibilities resident and available in ordinary life, and the scholar's office was "to cheer, to raise, and to guide men by showing them facts amidst appearances." In the patient, even solitary, adding of observation to observation the scholar aspired amidst custom and common sense to have "seen something truly," and must hold to what he saw: "Let him not quit his belief that a popgun is a popgun, though the ancient and honorable of the earth affirm it to be the crack of doom."[57]

Intuition, Emerson thought, was itself simply the highest form of perception, and he used the word "seer" in a double sense whereby the imaginative observer was also the prophet.[58] In this assertion of the creative imagination as a source of quasi-religious authority, Emerson interpreted the scholar as an artist, skeptical of society's inherited truths and alienated from the norms of common sense.[59] Thinking—the reflective experience of concrete facts—recreated humanity as a social whole and grounded the life of democratic citizens in universal humanity. Should the scholar's instinct prevail as the truth about life for farmer, sailor, and merchant, it would be nothing other than "the conversion of the world." In an imitative society of complacency and avarice that had driven promising youths—including his own brothers—to disgust or despair, Emerson asked, what is to be done? If the scholar would "plant himself indomitably on his instincts, and there abide," the individual act would be the invention of society, the invention of America: "A nation of men will for the first time exist, because each believes himself inspired by the Divine Soul which also inspires all men."[60] Emerson thus indelibly stamped religious thought in America by his proclamation that the wholeness of life was to be apprehended, if at all, by the immediate, intuitive grasp of the "facts" of experience, concrete experiences providing the sole access to the eternal matrix of all experience. The educational ideal of transmitting a cultural heritage through textual scholarship was challenged by the image of the scholar as a social prophet emboldened by the American advent.

The Nature of Theological Language

Controversy over the public purpose of theology also brought second-generation theological scholars into conflict with one another about the nature of theological language. In one sense, their debate marked the challenge that theological perspectives influenced by German liberal theology of the nineteenth century posed for theological traditions largely derived from eighteenth-century British sources. Buttressed by the Scottish philosophy of common sense, the founding generation of seminary theologians had pursued a theology that would interrelate nature, society, and the human self within a harmonious system of divine law, "the moral government of God." Unambiguous words and invariant facts were intended to thwart skepticism and promote prescriptive moral standards, but in the act they tended also to nullify the symbolic and the historical. Resources from the theological scholarship of Schleiermacher and German Romanticism, mediated for many American intellectuals through Samuel Taylor Coleridge, opened an alternative.[61] But more importantly, the nature of theological language became a focus of debate because of uncertainty about how theology could be a voice for continuity in the individual denominational traditions, a voice for unity in the emerging national culture in which these traditions competed, and at the same time speak the language of nineteenth-century academic science. Could theology speak with a single voice in these diverse domains of American national culture? Or, was the breach irreparable between "the theology of the intellect and that of the feelings"?

In the years from 1849 to 1852 debate on these questions

crackled around Horace Bushnell's *God in Christ*, a collection of addresses delivered by the Hartford, Connecticut, pastor in 1848 at Yale, Harvard, and Andover on the nature of Christ, the doctrine of the atonement, and the relation of dogmatic theology to the religious life. Bushnell prefaced the collection with an extended essay on the symbolic nature of language, in which he presented the rationale for his revisionary approach to doctrine. The ensuing controversy engaged some of the leading theological scholars of the era, Edwards Amasa Park, Charles Hodge, Henry Boynton Smith, and John Williamson Nevin.[62]

For all of these thinkers, the nature of theological language had direct consequences for the certainty and authority of theology. All felt that theology was losing its intellectual influence and being thrust to the margins of the culture. Smith, for example, saw an intellectual conflict approaching in which Christian theology was assailed by doubts and "superseded by ethical, by social, and by metaphysical systems; we see it losing not only its traditionary, but also its intellectual hold, over many a sincere mind." In contrast to the optimistic assertion by Edwards Amasa Park that faith and science were interwoven and mutually confirming, Smith warned of an intellectual struggle over the comprehensive interpretation of experience, in which "each new science puts in its claim to modify some part of the sacred record."[63] He and his theological peers sought a point of certainty from which to begin the theological enterprise and variously identified the religious intuition, the authority of the biblical revelation, or a philosophically defensible theory of human nature as the basis of such certainty. But each of these options defined the nature of theology differently and implied a different scholarly task for the theologian. Each made a place for history near the center of theological scholarship, but each had a different view of the relation between history and revelation.

Bushnell, whose writings occasioned this particular controversy, proposed that the real nature of theology becomes evident from a general consideration of the character and capacities of language, as languages seem to have developed historically in societies. His views on language were set against the background of his general social theory, in which the church, the state, the school, and the family were not simply collections of individuals but "organic living bodies" that developed historically by virtue of inward powers that endowed them with distinctive character, character that was imparted to individual members.[64] Organic social life was the medium through which the individual came to expression, and language was the preeminent form of the social medium. John Williamson Nevin agreed fully with Bushnell on this point and underscored the necessity of the social creation of language for individual thinking.

> To think is to speak. Language is necessary, not simply for the communication of thought, but for its existence also and development. . . . The several languages of the world are the results, we may say, of so *many distinct efforts on the part of the soul, to evolve in an adequate way its own life, conditioned and determined by the circumstances in which it has been variously placed.* Each one accordingly is the standing type of the mental conformation, out of which it originally took its rise; and in this form, it rules and controls also the life of thought itself. Language once established becomes the necessary channel of thinking for the people to whom it belongs.[65]

Nevin's explanation is instructively typical of theological Romanticism at two key points. He both emphasizes that human thought never occurs in abstraction from concrete cultural forms, and at the same time he insists that it is the selfsame "soul," the universal determining feature of humanity, that moves along these diverse cultural channels toward full realization.

Bushnell began the introductory essay of *God in Christ* by asserting that language existed in two "departments," the first including all words referring to physical objects, sensations, and actions. In this department, the observed event mediated between observers and enabled the words with which they named it to take on specific meaning. The second department included words referring to thoughts or emotions, and its store of words had developed by using external "things" as symbols for the inner world of thought and emotion. Apart from "reference to matters of outward fact and history," *religious language* lay entirely within this latter department.[66]

It expressed the affective and intellectual core of a particular culture or of an individual self.

Bushnell then took a step beyond his preliminary proposition that languages were social creations. The analogical and symbolic relations between these two departments were social creations, indeed, but not arbitrarily so. Instead, the outer world was "a vast menstruum of thought or intelligence"; its objects were images or symbols of the soul's inner life and its spatial relations were a "grammar." Nature—a "vast dictionary and grammar of thought"—thus expressed "the universal Author" and did so in a manner that grounded the individual soul in the hidden and mysterious universal. The divine was encountered in this "logos of the forms of things," which revealed that "the outer world, which envelops our being, is itself language, the power of all language."[67]

When words were used as signs of thought, they were "only hints, or images, held up before the mind of another, to put *him* on generating or reproducing the same thought."[68] Meanings were always approximate, conditioned by historical perspective, and modified by personal experience. Hence, reflection on the nature of language demonstrated to Bushnell's satisfaction that the dogmatic propositions of a theological system did not have the univocal clarity that they were commonly supposed to have.

> They only give us the seeing of the authors, at the precise stand-point occupied by them, at that time, and they are true only as seen from that point—not even there, save in a proximate sense. Passing on, descending the current of time, we will say, for two centuries, we are brought to a different point, as when we change positions in a landscape, and then we are doomed to see things in a different light, in spite of ourselves. It is not that the truth changes, but that we change. . . . We are different men, living as parts in a different system of things and thinkings, denyings and affirmings; and, as our contents and our antagonisms are different, we cannot see the same truths in the same forms. It may even be necessary to change the forms, to hold us in the same truths.[69]

In response to Bushnell's proposal, some might object that through extended usage words obtained more determinate or univocal meanings. "There could not be," Bushnell responded, "a greater mistake." Even for theological writers living in the same era, a distinctive "chemistry of life" gave to the words of each a distinct signification. No two minds ever had the same impression of the word *sin*, for example. Instead, "the whole personal history of every man, his acts, temptations, wants, and repentances; his opinions of God, of law, and of personal freedom" entered into the connotations of the term and so "change the quality, and modify the relations of that which it signifies."[70]

Therefore, Bushnell found little evidence in Scripture or experience that supported the prospect of a "system of scientific theology," if by that phrase the theologian meant either a system that was unambiguous, determinate, univocal, and propositional in nature or a system that was descriptive of matters of outward fact and history. Rather than grasping for the misleading clarity implied by the term *theological science,* the theologian should instead recognize that religious language was symbolic, fluid, suggestive of multiple meanings and more evocative than descriptive in intent. In a word, it was poetic. Poets were the true metaphysicians.[71] Thus, manifold, even apparently contradictory perspectives on a symbol together gave a truer sense of the illusive, mysterious reality that the symbol entailed.[72] By way of illustration, he suggested that the more profound authors had an ability to present their subject from different perspectives, "bringing us round the field to show us how it looks from different points." In such a case, Bushnell presumed that the author "has some truth in hand which it becomes us to know," and proposed that "we are to pass round accordingly with him, take up all his symbols, catch a view of him here, and another there, use one thing to qualify and interpret another, and the other to shed light upon that, and, by a process of this kind, endeavor to comprehend his antagonisms, and settle into a complete view of his meaning."[73] By encountering a profound author, in other words, the individual recapitulated the historical education of humanity as a whole, which, "descending the currents of time," had been brought in successive ages to different perspectives on the truth.

Since God was "the universal Author" for whom the outer world that "envelops our being, is itself language," the search for the divine meanings hidden in the grammar of nature was likewise a symbolic perambulation that viewed experience from different perspectives in the hopeful endeavor "to comprehend his antagonisms, and settle into a complete view of his meaning." God the universal Author, in distinction from God the moral Governor, did not so much hand down decrees as stimulate a process of discovery, including self-discovery. Within the symbolic and analogical forms of life and language, dogmatic theology could not, in Bushnell's opinion, hope to support claims for its certain, univocal, and unchanging meaning. He therefore proposed that the balance of theological studies should incline toward the historical, the literary, and the practical. Theology should relinquish the supposedly "scientific" objective of "logical deductions and systematic solutions." Throughout, there should be a more sensitive attention to and greater sensibility for the symbolic and aesthetic in Scripture and religion: "If there is ever to be anything produced here that can reasonably be called a science, it will more resemble an experience than the dry judgments and barren generalizations hitherto called theology."[74]

The Hartford minister's challenge to theological science did not, of course, go unanswered. Princeton's Charles Hodge upheld the authority of the "positive doctrines" authoritatively revealed in an infallible Bible against Bushnell's "poetic sentimentalism" that in Hodge's opinion merged "all differences in doctrine, in aesthetic emotions."[75] The proper scientific status of theology, for Hodge, derived from its formulation of clear and consistent doctrine by means of "a careful collation of all the scriptural facts" bearing on the subject: "The doctrine does not profess to be an explanation of the facts, nor a reconciliation of them, but simply a statement of them, free from contradiction." The elemental biblical facts thus systematically arranged were themselves "to be received on the authority of God."[76]

"Scientific theology" received a quite different defense from John Williamson Nevin, who shared Bushnell's general views on the historical development of doctrine and the dependence of theological interpretation on historical context. But Nevin had appropriated Schleiermacher and the German historical theologians far more thoroughly than Bushnell and far more appreciatively than Hodge. He therefore defended academic theology not in terms of biblical doctrines transcendent of history but rather in terms of the theologian's capacity to investigate historically the organic unfolding of the essential form of the Christian life, institutionally embodied in the church. He found that Bushnell's tendency to set dogma in opposition to religious spirit went against Bushnell's own best instincts in arguing for the organic character of Christianity and the social construction of language. The spirit shaped organic institutions— schools and families, creeds and liturgies—just as comprehensively as it formed the individual person. "It is just because Christianity is a new life," Nevin observed, "that it must work like leaven into our whole existence," and generate in that existence knowledge as well as action, "theology or theoretic religion" as well as the religion of feeling and practice.[77]

Nevin insisted unwaveringly on the divine spirit as the immanent principle of development in human corporate life. Bushnell "read" the manifold forms of nature and found there the multiple meanings of "the universal Author"; Nevin read history and found the organic growth of creation toward its destiny. The key to this history of creation was the history of the church as the extension of the human life of Christ.

> If the fact of the incarnation be indeed the principle and
> source of a new supernatural order of life for humanity itself,
> the church, of course, is no abstraction. It must be a true, liv-
> ing, divine-human constitution in the world; strictly organic
> in its nature . . . the necessary, essential form of Christianity,
> in whose presence only it is possible to conceive intelligently
> of piety in its individual manifestations.[78]

In this development, "the supernatural has become itself natural . . . by falling into the regular process of the world's history, so as to form to the end of time indeed its true central stream."[79] Disciplined investigation of church history had the purpose of discerning this vital principle that gave unified life to the church through all outward historical changes and was, at one and the same time, the clue to universal destiny and the matrix of personal piety.

Bushnell regarded dogma as the source of controversy and division in church and society, and he therefore had proposed his linguistic "reduction or displacement of dogma" as a strategy that would clear the path for "an era of renovated faith, spreading from circle to circle through the whole church of God on earth."[80] Nevin shared the ecumenical hope for a renewed church as the center of what Bushnell had elsewhere called "a complete christian commonwealth." But Nevin explicated this hope in ways consonant with his organic theology of history, in order to make it compatible with his understanding of scientific theology. The great task in "the moral organization of society," as he saw it, was to solve the problem of church and state in such a way that "the power of christianity should be wrought intensively into the whole civilization of this country . . . fully to actuate and inform its interior collective life, filling its institutions as their very soul."[81] The historical study of Christianity therefore probed the fundamental moral structure of society, indeed—and here he moved close to Bushnell's vision—the moral structure of creation. According to Nevin's interpretation, when the creed affirmed the catholicity of the church, it was affirming

> That the last idea of this world as brought to its completion in man is made perfectly possible in the form of christianity, and in this form alone, and that this power therefore can never cease to work until it shall have actually taken possession of the world as a whole, and shall thus stand openly and clearly revealed as the true consummation of its nature and history in every other view. The universalness here affirmed must be taken to extend in the end, of course, over the limits of man's nature abstractly considered, to the physical constitution of the surrounding world . . . for the physical and moral are so bound together as a single whole in the organization of man's life, that the true and full redemption of this last would seem of itself to require a . . . renovation also of the earth in its natural form.[82]

In their agenda for theology, Bushnell and Nevin thus quite literally illustrated Sidney Mead's elaboration of Chesterton's aphorism that America is "a nation with the soul of a church."[83] Even more strongly put, Bushnell and Nevin postulated a nation whose soul *was* the church, the interior formative principle reshaping from within all social institutions and the individuals who inhabited them as part of the inexorable divine intent to renovate creation in its entirety.

In the decades leading up to the Civil War, the seminary theologians had shouldered the task of articulating the Christian foundations of a cultural consensus. But in the effort, they and their fellow church members skirted close to a crisis of religious authority by invoking Scripture, doctrine, and experience to sanction contrary courses of conduct, thus dramatizing the perennial dilemma that ethical principles, rather than reflecting "the moral government of God," arose from forces human, and therefore errant. They could scarcely have avoided agreement with Walter Lippmann's later dictum that "ethical codes cannot lay claim to unhesitating obedience when they are based upon the opinions of a majority, or on the notions of wise men, or on estimates of what is socially useful, or on a appeal to patriotism." In contrast to all such faltering human appeals, the antebellum theologians sought *theocentric ground for the American social ethic* in the "profound sense that a man's own purpose has become part of the purpose of the whole creation."[84] Responding to this search for religious certainty, Nevin proposed that sufficiently attentive inquiry into the varied experiences of historical life would discern a deep moral order and tendency, would find the norms of action by exploring what is and has been. He intended his scientific historical theology to be "the intellectual means of eliciting ethical imperatives from the study of reality," and in so doing he made the case for the social utility of theological science.[85]

If faith is to flourish, there must be a conception of how the universe is governed to support it. It is these supporting conceptions — the unconscious assumption that we are related to God as creatures to creator, as vassals to a king, as children to a father — that the acids of modernity have eaten away. The modern man's daily experience of modernity makes instinctively incredible to him these unconscious ideas which are at the core of the great traditional and popular religions. He does not wantonly reject belief, as so many churchmen assert. His predicament is much more serious. With the best will in the world, he finds himself not quite believing.

Walter Lippmann, *A Preface to Morals*, p. 56

THREE

THE CASE FOR THEOLOGY IN THE
UNIVERSITY, 1880–1930

The topics of theological debate from the Civil War era continued into the last quarter of the nineteenth century. The authority of the Bible and of Christian doctrine remained at issue in relation to theories of the historical development of doctrine, especially since doctrinal development was often associated with the still more controversial idea that the realities to which these doctrines pointed were also unfolding in history, that the divine itself was immanent in the processes of nature and human nature. By about 1880, these debates were consolidating theological parties—liberal and conservative—in the seminaries. Theologians in the conservative Princeton tradition were concluding that Darwinian evolutionary hypotheses were "antipodal to theism" and that theories of doctrinal development severed all connections between Christian creeds and the "immutable and immortal" truth infallibly revealed in the inspired text of the Bible.[1] Meanwhile, at Andover Seminary, the retirement of Edwards A. Park signaled a changing of the guard that brought to prominence the "Andover liberals," a group of younger theologians who self-consciously identified themselves with the legacy of Bushnell. They and their liberal contemporaries published books whose titles clearly announced their developmental perspective on theology: Newman Smyth, *Old Faiths in New Light* (1879), Theodore T. Munger, *The Freedom of Faith* (1883), Alexander V. G. Allen, *The Continuity of Christian Thought* (1884), or Egbert Smyth, *Progressive Orthodoxy* (1885). As "the new theology" became a recognizable movement, it prompted hostile or guarded reactions both in the scholarly journals and in the churches.[2] Throughout the decade and into the early 1890s, traditionalist forces were mobilized to block faculty appointments, scholars were interrogated regarding their views on biblical interpretation, and, as in the celebrated case against Charles A. Briggs of Union Theological Seminary, charges of heresy were occasionally brought before church judicatories.

But these continuing debates about the nature of theological language, about the historical development of doctrine and about the critical study of the Bible were now staged against a different institutional backdrop: the modern American research university, organized around graduate departments of instruction that identified their task as the extension of knowledge into new fields through original inquiry. The emergence of the American university may be said to have begun with the founding of research-oriented Johns Hopkins in 1876, and throughout the 1880s and 1890s the life of the new universities was buoyed by enthusiasm both for the enterprise itself and for the personal advancement of those who participated in it. In part, this energy derived from Americans returning from graduate study in Germany. Harvard philosopher Josiah Royce typified their outlook when he recalled his own days as a student in the German universities: "One went to Germany still a doubter as to the possibility of the theoretic life; one returned an idealist, devoted for the time to pure learning for learning's sake . . . burning for a chance to help to build the American university."[3] As Royce's recollections imply, hope fastened less on importing the German educational system than on shaping a distinctively *American* university. Daniel Coit Gilman, president of Johns Hopkins, would have encountered few dissenters from his argument that the American university should not merely emulate Europe but take its own form, "adapted to our institutions, civil and ecclesiastical, and to our times . . . the product of American thought adapted to American needs and ways."[4]

As historian Laurence R. Veysey has suggested, this ideal university that pursued learning on behalf of the American commonweal was interpreted by a rhetorical formula that combined practical social utility, specialized research, and the ideals of liberal culture.[5] The orientation toward social service derived urgency from the dramatic expansion of industrial cities at the turn of the century and derived focus from the participation of academics in progressive political action. The research agenda of the universities proceeded through the expansion of academic departments, with history, philosophy, sociology, psychology, and education having especially important consequences for the theologians. Amidst these social and academic changes, the ideal of liberal culture maintained education's historic responsibility to channel change by identifying and reinforcing continuities with the past. Though few advocated one of these purposes to the exclusion of the others, the balance and connections among them received differing appraisals with differing consequences for the public responsibilities of universities.

Theologians actively participated in this discussion of the university's public purpose, and in the 1880s and 1890s both theological liberals and theological conservatives argued that, for its future health, theology needed the university. But what sort of theology and what sort of university would this require, and what would be the consequences for church and ministry? Pointed replies to these questions came from two religiously attuned university presidents, Charles W. Eliot of Harvard and William Rainey Harper of Chicago, who wrote, in 1883 and 1899 respectively, on the proper character of theological study in the modern university. Their case for theology in the university provoked a lively debate, one that reshaped the nature of theology and the public role of theologians far more than they and their university colleagues initially anticipated.

Theology in the University

In May 1883, President Eliot expressed his opinion in the *Princeton Review* that dramatic changes in the social attitudes, political convictions, and scientific outlook of the educated public had wholly altered the environment in which the Protestant ministry carried out its work.[6] Socially, Eliot found not only that a smaller proportion of college graduates were entering the ministry than had been true a century earlier but that the other professions, with which ministry competed for the attention of students, had vastly increased their systematic training and public prestige over this same period. Intellectually, the altered cultural setting of ministry was most evident in the public's admiration for the "new method or spirit" of open and painstaking inquiry by which modern science pursued the truth. In Eliot's view, the scientific method of empirical investigation had set a new standard for intellectual honesty, which made dogmatism on the part of the ministry appear, by contrast, "deficient in intellectual candor." This new standard had shifted the ground on which knowledge, including theological knowledge, based its claims, and Eliot concluded that "even the ignorant have learned to despise the process of searching for proofs of a foregone conclusion."[7] Political ideas had changed as dramatically as scientific ones, Eliot declared, and this too exerted its influence on theology. Images of the deity as judgmental monarch were completely unsatisfactory to persons of philanthropic spirit, who believed in the power of democratic government "to improve the condition of the great masses of mankind." Protestant ministers, caught between modern democratic social ideals and their own outworn hierarchical metaphors, would not recover their cultural influence "until the accepted dogmas of the churches square with the political convictions of the people."[8] Clerical office and sacred doctrine no longer carried authority in their train. Instead, authority now derived from the personal attributes of the minister: vigorous intelligence, deep learning, and persuasive speech. General failure to consider the consequences of these changes for the work of the minister, Eliot concluded, had during the past forty years brought about "the decline of the ministry" in its intellectual influence and its standing among the professions.[9]

Eliot therefore proposed educational reforms that would better prepare ministers for their "proper place in modern society." Foremost, Eliot insisted that theological study must be carried on with the same freedom of inquiry for teacher and pupil that characterized

other fields of learning. "This academic freedom," Eliot further asserted, "is much more likely to be obtained in universities, and in
cities which are large enough to be centres of diversified intellectual
activity, than it is in isolated denominational seminaries." Second,
Eliot favored more rigorous academic standards for admission and
scholarships. The ministry had been greatly discredited in the eyes
of the laity, Eliot declared, by "the practice of imposing upon parishes, young men of small mental capacity and flaccid physical or
moral fibre." Finally, Eliot argued for the introduction of the elective
system to encourage concentrated pursuit of specialized research.
Since the information accumulated in the expanding academic fields
was now far too vast for *synoptic* mastery, elective *concentration*
brought about a more lasting educational achievement: the "acquisition of a right method in work and a just standard of attainment."[10]
Students possessed of individual initiative and self-reliance would be
attracted to, and thrive in, an elective system of theological study
that cultivated the ability to arrive at fresh conclusions based on sustained investigation.

Eliot's assessment quickly elicited sharply contrasting views
from Francis L. Patton, a professor at Western Theological Seminary
who subsequently served as president of Princeton University
(1888–1902) and Princeton Theological Seminary (1902–13). Patton
charged that Eliot's vision of the modern ministry so completely altered the traditional conception of the ministerial office "as practically to abolish it altogether."[11] He dismissed Eliot's assertion that
the social environment and status of the Protestant ministry and the
relations between clergy and laity had undergone fundamental
changes in the past century, suggesting instead that "it can only be
in a very limited sense that the scientific spirit has succeeded in alie-
nating popular sympathy from the clergy."[12] Eliot's proposals for
bringing the language of religion into conformity with the American
political vocabulary met Patton's resounding skepticism: "If the
American people have grown so republican that they cannot speak
of the kingdom of God . . . they have taken a long step in the direction of discarding Christianity altogether."[13] Patton, however,
doubted that such was the case and suggested that Eliot's views were
shared by only a tiny minority of the American public.

Patton countered Eliot's appeal for a ministry adapted to the modern era by insisting that, on the contrary, ministerial education above all required leaders trained to transmit faithfully the church's inherited teaching.

> It is ministerial education that is under discussion. And a ministry implies a church. The church, however, holds certain definite convictions regarding God, the future life, and a way of salvation through the blood of Jesus Christ. It is pledged to the propagation of this faith through all the world and its perpetuation through all time. To this end it educates and ordains a ministry. If the church had no definite convictions, it would cease to be; and if it ceased to have the definite convictions just referred to, it would have no need of a ministry and certainly no divine warrant for one.[14]

The study of Protestant theology, in Patton's view, was inalterably grounded in the fact that the minister was "a divinely appointed officer in a divinely founded institution, and that he is charged with the duty of declaring a specific and authoritative message in the name of God." If President Eliot's plan to adapt that authoritative message to contemporary intellectual sensibilities were actually adopted, Patton predicted, "the minister's office and occupation are gone."[15] Clearly, this exchange amounted to a clash of moralities. The appeal to dogmatic authority, which Eliot considered "deficient in intellectual candor," Patton regarded as admirable fidelity to the church's doctrinal traditions. Eliot, on the other hand, espoused the ethic of the modern university for which intellectual integrity began with the assumption that one cannot investigate a cognitive claim and at the same time insist that the claim is believable because the tradition has believed it.[16]

Sixteen years later, the principal themes of Eliot's analysis were taken up by President William Rainey Harper of the University of Chicago in a provocative essay entitled "Shall the Theological Curriculum Be Modified, and How?" Despite shifting the discussion from the ministerial vocation to the theological curriculum, Harper shared Eliot's view that theology had lost touch with the new social context: "While the environment of the seminary has utterly changed in this century, the seminary itself has remained practically at a standstill."[17] To set it moving, Harper enunciated two broad principles of curricular reform. First, the curriculum must incorporate the "assured results" of modern psychology and pedagogy, in order to train students in analytic methods that, taken into the ministry, would render them "more efficient as the years go by." Second, the curriculum must be "adjusted to the modern democratic situation" in order to bring students in touch with "the present state of society" and "the modern spirit of science."[18] Like Eliot, Harper believed that ministers derived social authority not from an inherited body of supernatural truths but from practical efficiency based on the trained and cultivated spirit of scientific investigation: "The seminary is not a place in which men are to . . . receive and adopt certain opinions. It is rather a place in which men shall be taught to think."[19]

Harper found the inherited theological curriculum too much influenced by "a narrow and exclusive spirit," a condition exacerbated by the rural isolation of the typical Protestant seminary. Like Eliot, he therefore advocated an urban, university environment that put both theology and theological students "in touch with modern life" and encouraged an interdenominational breadth of outlook through encounter with "other points of view." Instructional methods should emphasize elective courses and research seminars, thereby prompting students to investigate issues more deeply and to overcome the passive "superficiality" that characterized the catechetical inquiry of the traditional curriculum. In the same way that specialization was occurring in medicine, law, and education, theological students should also be given opportunities for specialization in different fields of ministry: preaching, pastoral work, Christian education, church administration, or medical missions. And, in addition to classroom instruction, they should acquire direct experience in the urban work of the church through a "clinical or laboratory method" of internships.[20]

Later that same year, the *American Journal of Theology* published a series of responses to Harper by five university and seminary presidents.[21] All found points of agreement with Harper, and several asserted that much of what he proposed was already occurring. Some thought President Harper's insistence on an urban location for theology overdrawn, but Charles C. Hall of Union Theological Seminary outdid both Harper and Eliot, finding the "monastic seclusion" of many theological schools a major problem and declaring that "if existing rural seminaries cannot be removed to towns, no new seminaries should be founded in country places."[22] This suspicion of the rural seminary had little or nothing to do with pragmatic principles of institutional management. Instead, it was a symbolic attack on the nineteenth-century separation of theology into denominational seminaries, a fateful decision, so it seemed to the liberals, that had prevented theology from sharing the modern advances of the American university. As theologians maneuvered to insure the intellectual centrality of church and ministry in a changing culture, contrasts between the intellectual bustle of a cosmopolitan university and the rather sleepy parochialism of the rural denominational seminary became ubiquitous stereotypes in turn-of-the-century literature of theological reform.

The administrators differed principally over whether the academic specialization and empirical investigation that characterized the modern research university ought to become the paradigm for Protestant ministerial education. Augustus H. Strong of Rochester Theological Seminary made the most emphatic statement in opposition to Harper: "The seminaries are not universities; they are professional schools. They were founded in order to make preachers, pastors, and missionaries, and not to make technical scholars and scientific specialists."[23] As Strong's rebuttal indicated, the recurrent question of whether or not academic theology contributed to the proper equipment of the church's ministry came to focus in this era on the authority that should be attributed to technical expertise achieved through specialized university research. What sort of education do ministers really need?[24] This was a question with high stakes, since the narrowing of theology to a specialized expertise not only heightened doubts about its pastoral utility but also reduced the clergy to theologians-at-second-hand, something akin to backyard astronomers, who looked to academic theologians for "original," constructive religious thought. But zeal for the progress of the research university obscured such ramifications, and very early in the twentieth century the Yale biblical scholar Benjamin W. Bacon argued vigorously for such authority, observing that advanced academic research in theology had rendered not only the laity but also the clergy dependent on the findings of the theological "expert and specialist": "To arrest this process of specialization is to condemn theology to a hopeless and contemptible inferiority to the other sciences. Specialization is indispensable, and this involves expert authority."[25] Both church and ministry would continue to decline in social influence unless they recognized that "the future of religion in this country" depended on the academic expertise of the theologians, the church's "strongest artillery."[26]

Three points in Eliot's and Harper's proposals epitomized the liberal intention to reform theology by situating it within the "diversified intellectual activity" of the university. First, the primary task of theology, its distinctive contribution *both* to the university *and* to the church, was the reformulation of Christian doctrine in terms of contemporary thought as that was represented in the emerging academic disciplines. This primary task implied, of course, that current theory in the disciplines was proceeding independently from explicit religious assumptions and that points of intellectual contact therefore had to be reestablished between the disciplines and a Christian theory of life. Second, theology must be liberated from authoritarian, intellectually isolating dogmatic interests in order to meet the ethical challenges of democratic society in the industrial city. In earlier centuries, Reformed theologians in America had insisted that the core of theology was "living to God," and that insistence was now refocused on the social ethics of urban society. Third, theological scholarship must proceed by the same methods of free and fully critical inquiry that defined academic work throughout the university. Academic freedom, so argued the liberals, must be understood not as the enemy but rather as the principal ally of religious commitment.

Fundamentalist scholars of religion sharply disagreed with these points but, by doing so, lost influence inside the universities and departed during the first decade of the twentieth century in order to found educational alternatives, from the Bible institutes of the 1920s to Fuller Seminary in 1947. Their evangelical successors would not return to the research universities in significant numbers until the 1960s.[27] This parting of the ways did not, however, simply align theological conservatives with the interests of the church and theological liberals with the interests of the university. Instead, debates between fundamentalists and modernists were so bitter precisely because both groups shared a commitment to the importance of scholarship for church and nation. However, each interpreted the nature and contemporary problems of the church and the nation quite differently and constructed a different role for theological scholarship with respect to those commitments. They agreed that Christian principles should provide the core of American civilization; agreed on the close relations of religion and education; agreed on the importance of Protestant world missions; agreed that Christianity was entering a crisis in all of these areas; but disagreed entirely about the strategies and the substance of the Christian response.

The theological liberals were not, of course, in full agreement among themselves about the shaping of modern Christian doctrine. But the various parties did share what historian William R. Hutchison has called a "modernist impulse," which included the conscious adaptation of religious ideas to modern culture, the idea that God was immanent in human cultural development, and the belief that society was struggling toward realization of the kingdom of God.[28] They also shared the conviction that the rise of the modern university was, simultaneously, both the most visible symptom of America's cultural transition and the key to theology's successful adjustment to the emerging new society. In 1897 Charles A. Briggs of Union Theological Seminary expressed their common opinion when he traced the historical progress of theological education through three institutional locations: the college, the graduate seminary, and the divinity school in alliance with the university. "We have only recently entered upon the third stage," Briggs observed, "and theological education in the future will advance in university lines."[29] The university-related divinity school—Harvard, Yale, Chicago, or Union Theological Seminary—became the liberal paradigm for contemporary theological scholarship, and during the first three decades of the twentieth century they regarded it as a pivotal institution for religion's leverage on American society.

A Theological Generation

As the proposals of Eliot and Harper attested, the liberals believed that the academic study of theology required dramatic reform precisely because the relationships among its defining communities—church, nation, and school—were undergoing a fundamental realignment. Encountering what many of them considered a "crisis" in the first two decades of the twentieth century, they appealed to the church to recognize "the fact" that America was "facing remarkable social changes in the immediate future. . . . The old order is indeed changing, yielding place to the new."[30] In 1907 Shailer Mathews of the University of Chicago Divinity School argued that in the institutional division of labor that characterized modern society, the church "has become only one of many directive forces." Consequently, it must "define its attitude toward the formative forces now at work" and "face the vital decision as to what part it shall have in producing the new world." In the American advance toward the future, the church was in danger of being left behind, a backwater in relation to the actual mission of Christianity in modern America. Motivating persons to embody the moral principles of Jesus in the concrete responsibilities of daily life was the "social office" of the church: "If it fulfills this office, it is as essential to social unity as is the school or the legislature. . . . If it neglects this office, it fails of performing its proper functions and will be outgrown—a danger which is not unexpected by some serious thinkers."[31]

The liberals numbered the modern university among the most important of the "directive forces" in society and did not find the directions it was taking altogether favorable to institutional religion or to religion's "social office" of contributing to "social unity." They therefore believed that the crisis was, in no small measure, an *intellectual* crisis for the church, one that required "reconstruction in theology."[32] The threat to the church's intellectual leadership was particularly apparent, the liberals believed, in the difficulty of retaining the religious allegiance of students and university-educated laity.

> The church of today is living in the midst of the most extraordinary intellectual transition that the world has ever seen. . . . When therefore, the church insists that in order to become one of its members one must assent to a series of doctrines embodying the cosmology, the psychology and the philosophy of the New Testament taken literally, it inevitably sets up a test which will compel a man under the influence of to-

day's scholarship to abandon not only a life of evil thinking
and evil action, but also the results of his education.[33]

This contradiction between university education and churchly teaching led not to irreligion among students but rather to religious interest that was finding expression outside the churches. Modern students, Newman Smyth opined, are more religious than they realize,
"but they are not frequenters of churches; and their doubts are their
creeds."[34] Harry Emerson Fosdick would later compose his autobiography, *The Living of These Days* (1956), as a representative life of the
turn-of-the-century student generation that had struggled with "the
endeavor to be both an intelligent modern and a serious Christian."[35]

By positing a contradiction between the inherited theology and
the thought patterns of a new era, Fosdick *did* speak for many theological liberals who thought of themselves as a distinct generation,
one challenged to restate the Christian faith in a form that was plausible in the modern world. Indeed, their sense of living in an age of
transition, of being a transitional "generation," provides an important clue to the intellectual orientation of liberal theologians in
America.[36] They believed that they stood far distant from the intellectual outlook of their immediate academic predecessors and that
their scholarly task involved not merely accumulating new information but reconsidering the fundamental assumptions that organized
that information. In *A Theology for the Social Gospel* (1918), Walter
Rauschenbusch summarized this generational distance by observing
that writers who had matured before the 1880s rarely comprehended
the sociological dimension of Christian doctrine. "We move in a different world of thought when we read their books," he concluded.
"The terms, the methods, the problems, and the guiding interests lie
far away."[37]

In part the assertion of generational distance simply reiterated
earlier ideas about the historical development of theology, but, more
importantly, it delivered an Emersonian mandate that each generation self-consciously articulate a theology appropriate to its own
time. Arthur Cushman McGiffert had stated in 1893 that the historian of Christianity "knows that every age which is not dead or stag-
nant has had, and that every age must have, its own theology, and

that the theology of no other age can fully meet its needs." Indeed, McGiffert underscored the negative side of this assertion by adding that to accept "absolutely unchanged, either in form or substance, and in its original sense, the creed of a past age, is to lose touch with the historic progress of the church and to fall behind fossilized and forgotten."[38] The revisionary task extended beyond doctrine to the entire structure of theological study, and William Rainey Harper's evaluation of the theological curriculum lamented that it preserved "many survivals from the oldest times" and that these survivals were "out of harmony with the whole situation as it exists today."[39]

This obsession with the harmony between theology and its contemporary context persisted among the liberals. William Adams Brown of Union Theological Seminary looked back in 1926, appraised a century of theological education, and concluded that the "old denominational intellectualist" approach to theology held little promise for the future. It erred both in restricting Christianity to the form of religion represented in a single denomination and in "the disposition to think of Christianity primarily as a series of beliefs, or at least of practices and experiences which follow upon the acceptance of such beliefs."[40] But a theology organized to propagate denominational teachings made no contribution to social unity. And a theology that supported those teachings on the basis of an immutable, supernatural authority made no contact with the presuppositions of scientifically educated persons, who had concluded that the fundamental processes of life were immanent to its operation: "The old philosophy with its clear-cut dualism between nature and the supernatural has been hopelessly discredited for multitudes of people. If they are to find God at all, it must be here and now. The mystery which is still the life-breath of religion must be found not outside the world but in the very structure of its mechanism."[41]

In his famous party manifesto of 1924, *The Faith of Modernism,* Shailer Mathews restated as a general feature of religions this supposed necessity of recasting inherited categories in order to make direct contact with contemporary life issues.

> Religions spring from human needs. Each has grown as its
> teachings and institutions have satisfied creative souls. Each

has become an enemy of progress when it has fastened upon
society the authority of the past. The ideals of the past have
then become the source of injustice for the present; the hopes
of the past, the conventions of the present; the spiritual
achievements of the past, the inhibitions of the present. . . .
The history of Christianity is one of successive applications
of a religious inheritance to new needs.[42]

The modernist theological project was a combat with the past, insofar as the past was identified with authoritative tradition that imposed a deadening constraint on the progress of the spirit. Consequently, what Mathews described as "applications of a religious
inheritance to new needs" became for liberal theologians an ethical
imperative. "The Church is halting between two voices that call it,"
announced Walter Rauschenbusch. "On the one side is the voice of
the living Christ amid living men to-day; on the other side is the
voice of past ages embodied in theology."[43]

As part of their sense of being a "generation," the liberal theologians thus assumed that ideas and institutions of an age are consistent with one another but that those of different ages are necessarily
in conflict, an assumption, it may be noted, that misconstrues the
empirical form of societies, which function with institutions and beliefs of various ages like the older and newer buildings that comprise
a city.[44] Their assumption about the necessary consistency of the
ideas and institutions of an age sharpened liberal antagonism toward
conservative theologians and, in particular, fundamentalists. Conservative theological movements, the liberals feared, would drag Protestant religious thought backward toward an unrecoverable past,
thereby making it unintelligible in the present. Indeed, in *The Faith
of Modernism*, Mathews characterized the human tendency to cling
to the past as the essence of sin. "The Modernist looks upon sin as
violation of the immanent divine will to good will and to progress
towards that which is more personal; a conscious yielding, because
of immediate pleasure to the backward pull of outgrown goods; a
violation of those personal forces both of God and human society
which make progress possible. Human nature is not corrupt, but ata-
vistic."[45] The insistence on adaptation carried with it, of course, the

implicit warning that theological conservatives who failed to adapt would, in McGiffert's evolutionary metaphor, become part of the fossil record. The "Darwinian" message to religion, and to religious thought in particular, was adapt or die. The modernists had no intention of allowing what they regarded as fundamentalist folly to carry the entire Protestant theological enterprise into extinction.

Few of the liberals, however, seem to have considered fundamentalism the main issue. The fundamentalist controversy, "despite the noise it made, was an ephemeral affair," recalled Harry Emerson Fosdick, and "the questions in dispute were not the great matters that confronted modern Christianity; they were trivial in comparison with the real issues of the day; and the whole uproar was not the noise of the main battle but the flare-up of a rear-guard action."[46] As Fosdick's interpretation implied, "the main battle" had less to do with conservative and liberal responses to the modern world than with the basic features of modernity itself. With respect to those basic features of modernity, the liberals generally agreed with Walter Lippmann's synopsis that "religion has become for most modern men one phase in a varied experience; it no longer regulates their civic duties, their economic activities, their family life, and their opinions." These phases of experience made their disparate claims on the modern person, and, as a consequence religion was "no longer the central loyalty from which all other obligations are derived." Amidst the jostling loyalties of modernity, religious loyalty often proved weaker than social or patriotic loyalties in the shaping of modern conduct. Divested of universal dominion, religion was now held supreme only within its own domain, and, indeed, "there is much uncertainty as to what that domain is."[47] Given this modern uncertainty about the unifying obligations of social life, the modernist theologians sought religious alternatives to an otherworldly fundamentalism and an altogether this-worldly humanism, and they were more troubled by the latter challenge than by the former.

The liberals sensed that this dispersal of the Christian social ethic marked the transition to a new age, and it gave their writing about modernity and modernism an ambivalence in which "the modern" was both promise and threat. In responding to the "diversified intellectual activity" of the university, they were more prone to

celebrate the trends toward unity than to extol the virtues of pluralism itself, more prone to emphasize the utility of modern academic
disciplines to Christian endeavor than to acknowledge their capacity
for construing the world in alternative ways. Throughout the liberal
theological project, the themes of historical continuity and historical
discontinuity coexisted in unresolved tension. In their books sympathetic openness to the modern world collided with anxiety about its
pluralism and its indifference toward religion.

"Historical generations are not born; they are made," Robert
Wohl has written; "they are a device by which people conceptualize
society and seek to transform it."[48] In a manner reminiscent of the
eighteenth-century revivalists' announcement of the "new light" or
Emerson's evocation of the American scholar, the modernists claimed
the voice of a generation in order to present their contemporaries
with a decisive, historic moment of transformation. The goal for this
generation of theological reformers was *a new, religiously based cultural synthesis*. Shailer Mathews enunciated the general liberal project with the pronouncement that "when culture is seen to be incom-
plete until it embraces religion, when a man will not be considered
educated who has no sympathies with right and God—when this
time comes, and not till then, will the genuine aim of culture be
realized."[49] In one sense, this pronouncement was not new at all but
simply the latest recurrence of the perennial reform impulse in
American Protestantism. But, in another sense, the call for "Christianizing the social order" announced a new perception of the social
and intellectual situation of Protestantism in America.[50] The liberals
assessed the modern industrial social order and concluded that the
church had been displaced from its traditional role of moral and
intellectual leadership, and they set for themselves the task of re-
interpreting the Christian tradition into the categories of modern
thought, in order to make that revised tradition the instrument of
the nation's moral and religious renewal. The success of this renewal
depended, particularly, on an alliance of theology with the university.
A university divinity faculty, they believed, had a primary religious
responsibility that it exercised not as custodian of a particular denominational tradition but as reformulator of "the philosophy of the
Christian religion" in the interests of the human good.

The Social Efficiency of Academic Theology

In their programmatic effort at adjustment or adaptation of theology to the patterns of modern thought, the liberals regularly invoked the rhetoric of *efficiency*. Some of the term's appeal derived, no doubt, from its energetic ring. "There is," said University of Chicago faculty member George E. Vincent, "a certain strut about the word, efficiency."[51] More substantively, however, *efficiency* connoted practical engagement with concrete issues, collaborative effort at solving problems, and successful response to tangible needs. It posited competitive success in the marketplace of ideas. It refurbished the evangelical theology of persuasion for the age of James, Dewey, and pragmatism. When, therefore, Shailer Mathews wrote on "Vocational Efficiency and the Theological Curriculum," he focused his attention on the "function" and "duties" of church and ministry in the contemporary situation. He began with the by now obligatory debunking of theological curricula developed for an earlier age: "What should we think of a law school which prepared men to practice in the courts of Queen Elizabeth, or of an engineering school that taught how to use pulleys but said nothing about electricity?" The first step in developing an adequate theological curriculum was determining the contemporary "duties of the church as an institution," in order to discover the minister's "function as leader." Typically, Mathews arrived at this determination by contrast with the past. "A century ago the duties of a church were simple," and Mathews summarized them as the maintenance of a particular theology and the persuasion of others that salvation lay in adopting these particular views. Consequently, the biblical languages and "denominational theology" encompassed ministerial training. The contemporary church, on the other hand, was marked by a strong consciousness of its social obligations and "is becoming an organization which is training its members to work for the welfare of the community in all its interests, physical as well as spiritual." Christianity was passing from a dogmatic "to a sociological conception of the content of religion," and Mathews therefore called for an overhaul of the theological curriculum in order to produce "leaders trained to lead the church in a changing social order." Ultimately, Mathews aimed for a new apostolate, "inspired to a social spirituality," that "organizes Christian forces into effectiveness."[52]

A significant variation of the liberal contrast between traditional religion and modernist "social spirituality" was developed in relation to the African American religious experience by Benjamin E. Mays, who had studied with Mathews at Chicago (Ph.D., 1935) and who went on to a distinguished career as president of Morehouse College from 1940 to 1967. In *The Negro's God as Reflected in His Literature* (1938), Mays argued that a debate of over a century and a half among African Americans had developed two contrasting ideas of God in response to their existential situation. One idea took the form of a "compensatory" otherworldly religion that enabled African Americans to endure oppression, and the other emphasized the justice of God and the importance of "struggle for social righteousness here on earth." In the present generation, popular religious literature had swung toward otherworldly patterns, while among African American writers and intellectuals Mays saw a move toward socialist theory and a tendency "to consider the idea of God as useless in any effort to reconstruct the world socially." This polarization presented black religious leaders with the challenge of recovering the alternative theological emphasis on divine justice that had once supported a "sense of social rehabilitation" and desire for freedom in order to address effectively "the point of social crisis" in the African American situation.[53]

This challenge to make Christian ideas efficient tools of social reform translated into an instrumental definition of the church as "the divinely appointed means by which the kingdom of God is to be realized" (or at least approach realization) in human society.[54] "The Christian demand for the Kingdom of God on earth," wrote Walter Rauschenbusch, "responds to the passionate desire for liberty which pervades and inspires the modern world," and *social* Christianity identified that desire for freedom with hope for the kingdom, thereby making "social solidarity" rather than "individual rights" the true foundation of freedom.[55] It was only the "theological inefficiency" of the older dogmatics, with its individualistic notion of redemption, that had forced "college men and women, workingmen, and theological students, to choose between an unsocial system of theology and an irreligious system of social salvation."[56] The times, Rauschenbusch announced, called for a social gospel that "evoked faith in the will and power of God to redeem the permanent institutions of human society from their inherited guilt of oppression and extortion," and he found the model for this faith in the prophetic God-consciousness of Jesus.[57] This prophetic consciousness, as Rauschenbusch presented it, reinterpreted the classic objective of theological study, Christian formation, by identifying the experiential substance of "personal conversion" as precisely the new sense of social solidarity.

> Other things being equal, a solidaristic religious experience is more distinctively Christian than an individualistic religious experience. To be afraid of hell or purgatory and desirous of a life without pain or trouble in heaven was not in itself Christian. It was self-interest on a higher level. . . . A Christian regeneration must have an outlook toward humanity and result in a higher moral consciousness. . . . The feeling which Jesus had when he said, "I am the hungry, the naked, the lonely," will be in the emotional consciousness of all holy men in the coming days. The sense of solidarity is one of the distinctive marks of the true followers of Jesus.[58]

But if what Mathews called the "sociological conception" of religion realized its *efficiency* only in effective ministerial function or persuasive exhortation to ethical social conduct or even a new ideal of Christian formation, it would not satisfy. Theology must also be an efficient contributor to the intellectual progress of universities. The liberals therefore *rethought the theological encyclopedia*—biblical studies, church history, practical theology, and systematic theology—in order to demonstrate that theology was an efficient tool of social reform precisely because it was fully compatible with university canons of scholarship. The linchpin for this liberal rationale for theology in the university was historical scholarship.

By emphasizing the deliberate adjustment or adaptation of theology to its social environment, the liberals asserted the historical contextuality of all theological reflection. "In the final analysis," said Shailer Mathews, theology was "the result of an attempt of the thinkers of an age to make religion intelligible to their fellows." Of necessity, therefore, theologians engaged in "the correlation of the facts of religion with the other things they know," and, because of this correlation, "the church is concerned with the results of modern scholarship, for scholarship is really determining the method of thought by which the church must formulate its own convictions."[59] This adaptive or correlative model of theology presupposed a functional interpretation of religion. Ideas and institutions arose to solve felt problems of individuals and societies; they endured so long as they remained effective tools for achieving human ends. In this approach modernist theologians found common ground with other university scholars who were inquiring into religious phenomena from the newer disciplinary perspectives of psychology and sociology. William James had stated the matter starkly in *The Varieties of Religious Experience*, with the summary observation that "the gods we stand by are the gods we need and can use, the gods whose demands on us are reinforcements of our demands on ourselves and on one another." It was the Darwinian principle of "the survival of the humanly fittest, applied to religious beliefs," and James concluded that "if we look at history candidly and without prejudice, we have to admit that no religion has ever in the long run established or proved itself in any other way."[60]

The functional interpretation of religion had a further ramification. The point was not simply that theological ideas changed over time in response to their social environment but the more thoroughgoing claim that Christianity was not primarily a set of beliefs but rather an evolving social organization: "The first duty of the student of Christianity is to seize the historical fact that it is the concrete religious life of a continuous, ongoing group rather than the various doctrines in which that life found expression."[61] Thus, doctrine was not the unchanging foundation of Christianity but rather a derivative from the fundamental social life of the church. Once again, modernist theologians agreed with James, who had argued that religious experience was "more fundamental" than theology. For his purposes, James had chosen a definition of religion that emphasized its personal dimension: "the feelings, acts, and experiences of individual men in their solitude, so far as they apprehend themselves to stand in relation to whatever they may consider the divine."[62] For the modernists, it was not solitude but society that provided the experiential base of theological reflection, and as the century proceeded they increasingly stressed the social dimension of religious experience and the social context in which the religious self came to expression. Shailer Mathews, for example, argued that theologies were "patterns derived from the total social life" of a community, rationalizing the most characteristic, if otherwise unspoken, premises of social organization and conduct. "That which was accepted as a matter of course in social experience," Mathews suggested, "was used to describe the relation of God to man." In one epoch this unifying pattern might be drawn from the organization of the state, in another from the economic relations of society, in yet another from scientific views about the relation between an organism and its environment. In all such cases, theology was a "technique of integration" that unified the dimensions of social life around a taken-for-granted pattern, and, in this sense, theology was "transcendentalized politics."[63] When the social structure changed, the "pattern-making process" began anew and the once reigning orthodoxy became "vestigial," unconnected with the new social conditions, "a sort of ghost of a previous social order," to be replaced by a new integrative pattern.[64]

By conceiving the history of Christianity as a social process of functional adaptation to a wider natural and social environment, the liberals refocused the inherited theological encyclopedia, beginning with *the fields of biblical studies and church history*. In their view, the theologian no longer went to the Bible and other Christian documents seeking "storehouses of doctrine." The "time-honored custom" of focusing religious scholarship on "an alleged revelation, which is assumed to operate independently of ordinary human experience" represented an approach that was completely "incompatible with the method of the scientific historian." Instead of focusing on religious documents, the modern historian of Christianity "centers attention upon the great on-going process of society's evolution, out of which documents may have from time to time emerged." The historic Christian literature was thus investigated as a means toward "the more ultimate task of recounting the social history of the Christian religion."[65] The Bible and other historical evidence enabled the scholar to study "the actual current of human experience, attitudes, convictions," in order to describe what that social experience was and to discern "the tendency of the historical process" exhibited in its institutional and intellectual development.[66]

This scholarly purpose of writing the social history of Christianity not only set aside the exposition of inspired doctrine but also moved away from the nineteenth-century organic model of history, in which an unfolding divine purpose left teleological traces accessible to the discerning scholar. Instead, modernist historical scholarship investigated the Christian movement as a free adaptation of religious life to changing and varied social contexts. This environmental approach to the social history of Christianity pursued the history of Christian thought by evaluating the function of theological ideas in particular societies, an approach that, characteristically, placed a premium on the harmony between the pattern of ideas and the structure of social institutions. According to Chicago's Shirley Jackson Case, the historical theologian could no longer hold "the traditional theory of a normative past, authenticated by special revelation" but must instead recognize that "history points the road and supplies a more or less adequate equipment for the journey, but it cannot formulate the complete itinerary nor can it fix the destination." The lesson to be learned from history was, therefore, that in every age the religious thinker could "justify his message" only by "the mandate of efficiency" in adjusting to the wider environment. Given this pragmatic reality, Case concluded, "the prophet" who intended to influence modern consciousness and conduct "must derive his sanctions not from the past but from the future."[67]

The combination of social history in the academy with social Christianity in the churches led to a reconsideration of *the field of practical theology.* Early in the century Gerald Birney Smith, a theological ethicist at the University of Chicago, lucidly reassessed this discipline in his programmatic essay *Practical Theology: A Neglected Field in Theological Education.* According to Smith, the recent reorientation of the churches toward social reform and of scholarly method toward historical research had led the purposes of the church and the purposes of the academy in opposite directions. This posed a conceptual problem for the unity of theology, a problem that Smith proposed to resolve through a fresh understanding of the field of practical theology.

According to Smith's analysis, traditional approaches to practical theology had emphasized "cultivation of ecclesiastical religious life" and conceived the minister as one "whose professional work is confined within the limits of the church." As a matter of fact, Smith concluded, the field as traditionally constituted "would be more accurately indicated by the use of some such term as 'ecclesiastics.'" But an ecclesiastical orientation for practical theology was inadequate to the current situation for two reasons. First, "with the decreasing importance of organized ecclesiasticism and the increasing importance of unconventional, adaptable Christian activity in our modern world," both church and ministry were redirecting their attention toward the task of social reconstruction and reform. The modern church's orientation toward contemporary society and its problems had already brought about pedagogical change through the advent of seminary courses in "Christian sociology," professorships of "applied Christianity," and the founding of social settlement houses to serve as training centers for theological students. For this reason, the field of practical theology must give more systematic attention to "the prophetic mission of the preacher," which "appeals to the citizens of the new world."[68] But, second, the dominance of the historical method in the scholarly study of religion had altered the task of the academic theologian from the systematic statement of immutable, revealed truth to the historical explanation of "religious beliefs by seeking to relate them to the vital problems and ideas which were current in the age in which the convictions took vigorous form."[69]

When these two points—the contemporary social focus of the church and the historical focus of the scholar—were considered together, a distinct irony emerged. "Not very long ago," Smith stated, the center of interest for the religious life had "coincided with the center of interest in biblical study, and the remembrance of this coincidence has by no means entirely vanished." Both piety and scholarship had approached the biblical text seeking truth that transcended history. But in the new situation, Smith judged, "the center of interest for the historical scholar has moved back twenty centuries, while the religious interests of men in general have moved forward into a new world."[70] Embodied in the chronological separation of first century from twentieth was a fundamental difference of attitude and purpose between the religious inquirer and the scholarly investigator. The academic theologian sought historical understanding through critical appraisal of evidence. The religious inquirer sought guidance for the impending spiritual and ethical judgments of social life. As Smith saw it, the "truth" pursued by historical scholarship and the "truth" that would guide contemporary social life "are so different in their psychological aspects that the teaching of the one does not necessarily involve the teaching of the other."[71]

Practical theology—newly understood—faced the task of combining both the historical and the ethical interests within "a complete theological education."[72] To accomplish this task, ministers and theologians must add to the historical perspective "a psychological view-point" on the Christian tradition, in order to insure that theology "embodies the psychological realities which make up religious experience." The minister and the theologian must come to understand the psychological processes by which doctrine, worship, and preaching actually motivated ethical decisions, inspired confidence, cemented communal ties, and adjusted lives to the social world; understanding these experiential dimensions of the Christian life required the academic perspective of social psychology as well as that of social history.[73] In this view, the discipline of practical theology pursued critical analysis of religious motivation and morale. Using the tools of theological modernism, the new practical theology investigated what Jonathan Edwards had called the "religious affections" in their connections to Christian doctrine and Christian ethics. As such, it both enhanced the minister's practical grasp of religion's social dynamics and made a distinctive contribution to theological scholarship.

> In order to give psychological evaluation to religious doctrines, a thorough study of the psychology of religious experience would be indispensable. If, as the science of religion today declares, all the historical manifestations of religion can be adequately explained only as we study the religious

life which expresses itself in these objective forms, practical theology would perform a valuable scientific function in constantly attempting a correlation of life and doctrine. This attempt would throw valuable light on the problem, now attracting widespread attention, as to what is the truly scientific method of studying theology.[74]

Finally, under the influence of social history and social psychology, *the field of systematic theology* came up for the same reconsideration received by biblical studies, church history, and practical theology. In 1910, the *American Journal of Theology* carried three essays on "The Task and Method of Systematic Theology" that presented the divergent views of Benjamin B. Warfield of Princeton Theological Seminary, William Adams Brown of Union Theological Seminary, and Gerald Birney Smith of Chicago. Warfield represented the conservative position and argued that "systematic theology" differed radically from "the science of religion." Systematic theology, in Warfield's view, properly began with the conviction that the Bible contained a special revelation of God, then took "the knowledge of God supplied to it by apologetical, exegetical, and historical theology" and systematically organized it "to make up the totality of our knowledge of God." By contrast, said Warfield, the science of religion in the tradition of Schleiermacher regarded Scripture as the record of human religious aspirations and shifted the object of theology from God to religion, defining dogmatics as a historical inquiry into the church's system of belief at a given point in time. But Warfield found a "leaven of agnosticism" in this effort to make the object of theology more accessible to humanistic inquiry, and he therefore derived theology from inerrant Scripture. Systematic theology was, "in essence, an attempt to reflect in the mirror of the human consciousness the God who reveals himself in his works and word."[75]

Since the liberals conceived the task of theological scholarship in relation to the canons of free, critical inquiry that characterized university scholarship, Warfield's prior allegiance to the authority of Scripture was not a position they were prepared to adopt. Religious authority "rooted in God's dictation and donation of truth" they found to be "no longer tenable." A theological position in which a "supernatural norm" had taken the place of "empirical testing is so out of harmony with the present method of science, that a system which avowedly seeks such a basis for its doctrines" transformed the investigator into "an advocate" whose "task is simply the practical one of expounding the beliefs of those who acknowledge certain presuppositions." In contrast, a modernist systematic theology "abandons appeal to a priori principles" and made its precepts "relative to human needs instead of being referred to any superhuman or prehuman source."[76] Theology ought to proceed by a method of empirical investigation, for which no presuppositions were, in principle, reserved from criticism.

Furthermore, Warfield's view of the specifically *systematic* aspect of systematic theology focused on the logical connections among Christian doctrines, on Christian theology as an internally consistent set of ideas. It represented the classic form of theological reflection within "the seminary ideal," a *catechetical inquiry* that appropriated a theological tradition and articulated its systematic structure with a view to its harmonious exposition. This definition of the systematic task the liberals considered fatally deficient. For them, the truly critical set of consistent connections were those that would interrelate in a coherent whole the ostensibly independent sectors of society: politics and law, medicine, the natural and the human sciences, economics, and religion. In their view, the explicitly *systematic* task of theology extended beyond internal doctrinal consistency to the "correlation" of Christian doctrine with theory in other intellectual domains. Just as modern religion pursued a new cultural synthesis so modern systematic theology was a *synthetic inquiry* that connected Christian ideas to the wider pattern of social thought. It was a fundamental and far-reaching reorientation of the theologian's work.

William Adams Brown pursued these general assumptions, as Warfield no doubt anticipated he would, by seeking to define the nature of Christian religious experience as the first step in delineating the task of theology. The nature of religious experience currently occupied scholarly attention, said Brown, because "the comparative method of study" was examining various religions and concluding that Christianity was "but one of a family of religions, all of them alike expressions of a religious instinct which is natural to man."[77] This comparative inquiry raised the question of the unique value of Christian experience that might justify its claim to supremacy or absoluteness. In part, Brown answered the question of value by introducing a quasi-empirical claim for Christianity's efficiency in meeting human religious needs.

> The proof that Christianity is really what its advocates have claimed it to be, namely, the final and perfect religion for man, is to be found in the effects which it produces and has ever produced in the lives of those who approach it in simplicity and faith. . . . The proof of its unique authority is not the fact that it has never changed, but that through all its many changes it has continued to meet the needs of the human heart as no other institution has done.[78]

But, since historical "values" may not endure, Brown argued that the theologian must push beyond the evidence of Christianity's practical benefits and deal with metaphysical questions, in order to demonstrate that the value of Christianity was not transient but "grounded in some permanent reality which forms part and parcel of the structure of the universe itself." Considered in this regard, theology was "simply a branch of philosophy"; it was "the philosophy of the Christian religion."[79]

Some years later this last point became the central theme of Brown's book *The Case for Theology in the University* (1938), which argued that theology could bring an ordering principle to the "intellectual disorder" and "chaos" in university education. Critics of the modern university were quite right in criticizing its lack of unifying intellectual principles, said Brown, and critics of theology were also quite right in denying that "dogmatic theology" could lend the requisite coherence. But in the form of "the philosophy of the Christian religion, or, in other words, the sum of the attempts to use the clue which Christian faith provides to bring unity and consistency into man's thoughts of the universe," Brown proposed that theology not only had a place in the university but could provide a cooperative and sympathetic "new universe of discourse" in which the university

could address the ultimate and most comprehensive issues of intellectual life. By the philosophy of the Christian religion he did not
mean a single, authoritative theology but rather "a common platform" of discussion that would ground and unify education as, by
analogy, he saw the Faith and Order Conferences of the 1930s establishing a common discussion among the differing churches of Western Christianity.[80]

Gerald Birney Smith's contribution to the debate over the task
and method of systematic theology began by criticizing German and
American scholars who had sought to build a norm for theology out
of Christian experience, by privileging the value judgments about
the world that were due to the influence of Jesus on human consciousness. Scholars "whose spirit is determined by the modern ideal
of research ask by what right a given type of religious experience can
be isolated from all other experience as the norm by which to test
doctrinal deliverances." In order to achieve a fully critical theology,
said Smith, the theologian will indeed study the history of religious
experience as part of the effort to understand the current situation.
But, efforts to salvage "the conception of an 'absolute' or 'final' theology" by appeal to a uniquely Christian experience was a regression
to "the authority method" in religious thought and "fundamentally
inconsistent with inductive procedure" in university scholarship.
The value of a particular theology in the past consisted in its practical
success at interpreting "the actual exigencies of human life." In the
same way, the validity of a contemporary theological position would
be determined by its functional effectiveness in interpreting "the
concrete conditions" of social existence and guiding an effective response to those "supreme tasks of modern life."[81]

Only by treating theological ideas as hypotheses to be tested
for their social efficiency could theology be regarded as genuinely
scientific. In this Smith differed from William Adams Brown, who
had assigned a "double task" to systematic theology of so stating the
Christian gospel "as at once to preserve its continuity with the past
and its living touch with the present."[82] In this formulation, Brown
gave equal weight to two norms for the adequacy of a theological
statement, whether it was appropriate to the Christian tradition and
whether it was comprehensible and plausible in the modern world.
For Smith, by contrast, the critical judgment was whether a religious

belief was practically effective and rationally defensible in the present, not "whether the solutions demanded by present problems do or do not correspond with the doctrine of some former age."[83] Contemporary theology might well draw interpretive insights from the experience embodied in past theological teachings, but it stood or fell on its investigation and interpretation of the modern religious situation: "It may be asked what guarantee there is that the outcome of such an empirical investigation as has been indicated will be a Christian theology. There is, of course, no such guarantee. . . . If there be any form of faith which is actually better adapted to bring to expression the vital realities with which religion deals, the theologian should be the first to discover it."[84]

If theology was to participate genuinely and fully in the life of the university, none of its constituent ideas—its hypotheses—could be exempt from critical examination, and the basis for that appraisal was the functional value of theological ideas for contemporary social life. As Smith clearly saw, this empirical effort to give reasoned, systematic articulation to social faith, however much it might employ resources from the Christian tradition, could not determine in advance that its solution would be a Christian solution.

As Smith understood it, "the field of theology is identical with that of the humanistic sciences," since theology, like economics, political science, sociology, and philosophy, dealt with the living problems of humanity. The differences among these sciences, said Smith, were not to be found in the object they studied "but rather in the specific purpose which is dominant in the mind of the investigator." Since the aim of the theologian's work was to propose the religious ideas that interpreted "the supreme significance of life," this interest of the theologian established a point of view on humans and their societies "not adequately represented by any other realm of scholarship," but it did so using methods and criteria that made it possible "to correlate" the theologian's "branch of learning with the other branches."[85]

The Sacred and the Social Process

It was encounter with the varied domains of the modern world, largely independent of religious premises, that constituted the religious challenge for the liberals. And, it was a *religious* challenge in the sense that it raised the question of—the doubt about—the unifying presence of God. When evaluating their various efforts to apply critical scholarship to the "needs" of the church or to correlate traditional Christian doctrines with the "needs" of modern humanity, it would be a mistake, therefore, to understand the watchword *efficiency* in merely practical terms. Behind the rhetoric of need, efficiency, and adaptation lay an explicitly religious dimension of the modernists' social and historical inquiry into the religious adjustment of each age to its environment. The "adjustment" they sought was an adjustment to the largest and most enduring features of what Shailer Mathews called "the actual current of human experience," the elemental processes of reality that made possible and supported the human enterprise.[86] "The environment which conditions our life," he said, contained, and still contains, "the personality-evolving elements of the universe" that brought humanity into existence. To these elements or forces, the Christian religion had given the name God, and "religion can be described as a phase of the life process which seeks by control or cooperation to get help from those elements of its cosmic environment upon which men feel themselves dependent by setting up social, that is, personal relations with them."[87] As Walter Rauschenbusch emphasized in all his writings, "a higher order" of social life would arise only because "spiritual forces build and weave it," and this force was God immanent in human labor: "By cooperating with God in his work they are realizing God." The modernists' rhetoric of adaptation and efficiency, in other words, sought to formulate the question of providence in a epoch of uncertain change. If they moved with a fair degree of vigor and confidence in society's "changing order," it was because they believed that the changes themselves were somehow of God. "All history," Rauschenbusch announced, "becomes the unfolding of the purpose of the immanent God who is working in the race toward the commonwealth of spiritual liberty and righteousness."[88]

The burden of authority that liberal theologians placed on the functional definition of religion, through the criterion of "efficient adjustment," could itself be questioned theologically and should have been questioned more than it was. One who did was the philosopher of religion George Burman Foster, who wondered by what criteria the theologian judged "adjustment" and who doubted that the enduring difficulties of human life were amenable to "efficient" resolution. In an essay entitled "The Contribution of Critical Scholarship to Ministerial Efficiency," he related those questions to the task of theology in the university.

Foster began by observing that the modern celebration of efficiency, with its emphasis on measurable results, failed to address the perennial questions of "the eternal meaning and mystery of existence." This was especially true because "our time is indeed an age of doubt, more widespread and more basic than the premature prognosticators of an age of faith seem to be aware of."[89] Indeed, there was a sense in which the American New World "began in doubt," doubting first the authority of the church, replacing it with the authority of Scripture, then coming to doubt that as well in the name of science or of "*bourgeois* customs recognized as 'good.'" This widening circle of doubt, Foster believed, had now extended to the limits of contemporary intellectual life and defied pragmatic resolution.

> What can our current "efficiency" do here—"efficiency"
> with its techniques and machinery and money and organiza-
> tion? At this point the tragedy of life passes beyond the help
> of such things. . . . The minister who cannot cope with this
> deepest need of the modern man may organize superficial and
> often impertinent reforms, but he cannot give the bread of
> life. He may minister to bodily wants—good enough in
> its way—but he leaves the soul in bewilderment and for-
> sakenness. In the end he loses confidence and abandons his
> fundamental task.[90]

Confrontation with "an age of doubt" caused Foster to ponder the apparent contradiction between theology as a critical scientific enterprise and as an enterprise "serviceable" to Christianity: "From the scientific point of view, theology seeks to be free from the control and needs of the church, to be determined solely by the truth-interest, by the impulse to know reality, and to regard no law but its own, and no authority save the compulsion of its own subject matter."[91] It might seem that this "scientific" method of systematic doubt would be of little religious use, since doubt was itself the religious problem that humans confronted in the modern world. But Foster thought otherwise. The impulse to know reality, what Foster called "the ethics of the intellect," was precisely what was needed by the church, if it was to avoid the flimsy reassurance of religious platitudes. This was particularly true since "ministers, like politicians, are especially tempted to debasement of the truth-interest—to sham learning, sham religion."[92] It was therefore theology as critical scientific inquiry that prepared the genuinely "efficient" minister. Theology as *catechetical inquiry* was no longer sufficient to meet "the needs and difficulties of our age of doubt and transition and growth." Instead, "the dissolution of orthodoxy" required that theology become a *synthetic inquiry* by which the student's theological formation "recapitulates and epitomizes" the wider cultural "experience of doubt" and in the process of reconstituting the relations of theology to the other academic disciplines simultaneously constituted a minister who was "personally prepared" to teach a religion that was "ever changing, ever in the making." Consequently, university education that tried students "in the fires of critical theological research" was the education with the best chance to "win the confidence of our bewildered and discouraged religious life." The governing purpose for academic freedom of inquiry was not simply the pursuit of truth abstractly considered but the formation of the truthful person, and, in Foster's opinion, this twist on the classic ideal of spiritual formation was the principal argument in the case for theology in the university.[93]

In the modern world institutions are more or less independent, each
serving its own proximate purpose, and our culture is really a
collection of separate interests each sovereign within its own
realm. . . . This separation of activities has its counterpart
in a separation of selves; the life of a modern man is not so
much the history of a single soul; it is rather a play of many
characters within a single body.

Walter Lippmann, *A Preface to Morals*, pp. 112–13

FOUR

INTELLECTUAL CENTER OF THE CHURCH'S
LIFE, 1930–1960

In 1934 the liberal vision for theological study received its codification. That year, a comprehensive four-volume survey, *The Education
of American Ministers*, appraised the faculties, students, and institutions engaged in theological education and offered an interpretation
of the relations of the theological school to the denomination, the
university, and the nation. Directed by Mark A. May, professor of
educational psychology at Yale University, the study had been conducted from 1929 to 1934, under the joint auspices of the Conference
of Theological Seminaries and the Institute for Social and Religious
Research. William Adams Brown of Union Theological Seminary
acted as theological adviser to the project and wrote the first volume,
which presented a synoptic interpretation of the statistics and surveys compiled in the succeeding volumes. Some twenty years later,
H. Richard Niebuhr collaborated with Daniel Day Williams and
James M. Gustafson in a similar diagnostic study organized by the
American Association of Theological Schools and financed by
the Carnegie Foundation, the results of which were published in

The Purpose of the Church and Its Ministry (1956), *The Ministry in Historical Perspectives* (1956), and *The Advancement of Theological Education* (1957). The continuities and contrasts between these two studies, roughly speaking the points of transition from Protestant liberalism to neo-orthodoxy, illustrate the primary dynamic of academic theology between approximately 1930 and 1960.

The Brown and Niebuhr reports were the most prominent in a series of interpretive surveys of theological education conducted between the 1920s and the 1950s that began with Robert L. Kelly, *Theological Education in America* (1924), and William A. Daniel, *The Education of Negro Ministers* (1925).[1] The immediate motivation of these studies was the desire to improve the quality of the Protestant ministry. As Kelly remarked, his own research had grown out of the belief that "methods used in educating Protestant ministers were inadequate," that "the quality of ministerial candidates had been on the decline for some time and that the churches faced a crisis because of the real or prospective dearth of leaders."[2] By mid-century, belief that raising educational standards could improve the quality of the ministry had led the mainstream churches to insist on genuinely graduate education in theology as the prerequisite for ordained ministry, an insistence that paralleled the general expansion of American higher education following World War II. A three-year graduate professional degree (today, the Master of Divinity) became the formal standard of ministerial education. The classic encyclopedia of biblical studies, church history, systematic theology, and practical theology persisted and, as reported by Brown and May, was augmented early in the century by work in ancillary social sciences, with education and psychology of religion "side by side with practical theology" and sociology "side by side with Christian ethics."[3]

The reports reflected—and reflected on—the ways in which racial division in churches and schools compounded the difficulty of raising the standards of ministerial education. By the time of the Brown-May report, the 224 theological schools in the United States and Canada included forty-one founded for the purpose of educating African American clergy. The presence of seminary graduates in the black churches remained small, however, and a 1931 survey of ministers in seven southern and five northern cities indicated that only 13 percent had graduate divinity degrees. In the same year, approximately 31 percent of African American seminarians had completed at least one year of college. Hence, the call to improve educational standards and resources in order to improve ministerial quality was especially pronounced for the education of African American ministers, and Benjamin E. Mays concluded that theology "trailed incredibly behind" other departments of black colleges in its academic standards and equipment. He lamented these statistics and asserted that, in fact, the African American minister needed better formal preparation than white clergy because opportunities for continuing education were so much more limited. In the South few libraries were open to blacks, the available libraries were inadequate, and "in many instances the kind of literature that is released to the Negro library is highly censored."[4] In the 1950s, the Niebuhr report found that, by failing to redress segregation and its religious consequences, "Protestantism as such is not coming to grips with its responsibilities for the church life and ministry of this dominantly Protestant segment of the society." Steps to improve the opportunities for black clergy education could not be separated from such broader needs as aggressive desegregation policies in the churches, stronger undergraduate education in religion, and strategies for recruiting African Americans for the profession of ministry.[5]

These surveys of theological education also presupposed that educational quality was directly linked to interdenominational cooperation in the preparation of Protestant pastors, leading them to identify the interdenominational, university-related divinity schools as the flagship institutions of the enterprise as a whole. In Brown and May's synopsis of the history of theological education, for instance, they linked the numerical increase of denominational seminaries in the mid-nineteenth century with "a progressive decline of educational standards" and treated the more recent past as an effort to respond to that problem.[6] In a similar vein, Kelly drew unfavorable contrasts in the 1920s between the denominational seminaries composed almost entirely of students from the sponsoring church and the interdenominational university divinity schools.[7] By the 1950s Niebuhr and his colleagues found that ecumenical relations throughout theological education had advanced, but unevenly. Their research did not indicate that the schools had become significantly more inter-denominational in the composition of their student bodies, and they lamented that faculties in the separate schools continued to be iso-lated from one another "behind denominational walls." The Niebuhr report therefore emphasized that "the life of the whole Church should become the context for all theological studies" and called for interdenominational exchanges of faculty as a way of combating the tendency of schools to become "ingrown."[8] The report did find, how-ever, that one source of denominational parochialism was breaking down: "the ecclesiastical circle" of faculty education, in which semi-nary faculty members received their educations entirely in schools affiliated with their own denomination, was being replaced by more pluralistic, interdenominational educations, often at the university-related divinity schools.[9] In general, all the surveys assumed that stu-dents began their ministerial educations possessed of a clear, some-times even rigid, denominational identity and that it was the purpose of theological education to expand the horizons of that identity by exposure to the thought and witness of ecumenical Christianity.

As suggested by their emphasis on standards of ministerial preparation within ecumenical Protestantism, these surveys of theo-logical education approached the "advancement" of theological study primarily in terms of the interests and responsibilities of the American churches. Hence, although Brown and Niebuhr were acutely conscious of the multiple institutional allegiances of theolog-ical schools, both theologians asserted that the fundamental, shaping community for theological education was the church and that only clarity about its relation to this community would enable the theo-logical school to order its responsibilities to other communities. Both, therefore, framed theological studies within a larger concep-tion of the church, its nature and its purpose. Despite sharing this initial assumption, however, Brown and Niebuhr differed signifi-cantly over the relationship between the church and other principal institutions of modern society. This difference is most clearly visible in the basic metaphor of the church through which each theologian communicated his central vision. Brown typically employed didactic and instrumental images that clustered around the metaphor of the church as *the teacher of the nations.* Niebuhr's recurrent metaphor portrayed the church as *the world's companion before God.* These different metaphors of the church entailed different proposals for "the aims of teaching and learning" in a divinity school and, in turn, different evaluations of theology's accountability to university and nation. The shift from one metaphor to the other may be interpreted as a theological response to the shifting status of mainstream Protestantism in American society during decades in which it relinquished its long cultural dominance and began to confront the heretofore little acknowledged religious diversity of the society.[10]

The Education of American Ministers

In selecting William Adams Brown to assess the state of ministerial education, his peers had chosen a scholar who epitomized the ecclesiastical portfolio that liberal theologians carried in their various denominations and on behalf of ecumenical Protestantism. Throughout his forty-four-year tenure on the Union faculty, Brown had vigorously engaged in the life of American Presbyterianism, in social gospel causes, in the interdenominational programs of the Religious Education Association, and in the beginnings of the world ecumenical movement. The range of Brown's influence was unusual, but the orientation was characteristic of his generation. Liberal theological educators had committed themselves to the proposition that federated action by the denominations could influence positively both church and society, and they intended that "efficiency" in matters religious should be fully equivalent to that in other sectors of society. It was, to borrow a phrase from H. Richard Niebuhr, the epoch of "the institutionalization of the kingdom."

Brown had been instrumental in the inaugural meetings in 1918 of the Conference of Theological Seminaries, predecessor to the present-day Association of Theological Schools, the interdenominational accrediting body for theological schools in the United States and Canada. The views he expressed in *The Education of American Ministers* thus culminated more than a decade of writing on the needs and purposes of theological education. Reflecting his own experience and that of the liberal theologians generally, Brown asserted that a changing social, economic, and intellectual environment threatened the displacement of the church from its traditional position as "an indispensable agency of public service," the organized fellowship charged with releasing and directing "energies which are to bear fruit not only in the development of Christian character in individuals but in the creation of a Christian society."[11] The church's failure to maintain its moral and intellectual leadership in society, said Brown, had been detrimental not only for the church but, more fundamentally, for society and its institutions. Thus, the characteristic theme of Brown's ecclesiology was one of reform and recovery: the ecumenical renewal of the church's "mission to organize society as a whole in accordance with the religious principle."[12]

Since the church had the public moral responsibility to make its "philosophy of life" central to the aspirations of the culture, Brown consistently depicted the church through images of its instrumental or mediating role. Its task was to adjust, adapt, or interpret the Christian gospel, in order that this message might act as a unifying spiritual force amid the diverse currents of modern social and intellectual life. This mandate required federated action by the churches and theological schools, action that found its justification beyond the churches themselves in the society they sought to serve. "In addressing ourselves to the tasks that we face in our own country and in our own church," Brown stated at the centennial of Lancaster Theological Seminary, "we are not merely doing our immediate duty; we are fitting ourselves to co-operate with our fellow-Christians of other churches and of other lands in that co-operative study through which alone the church of Christ can be put in the position to fulfil its ecumenical function as the teacher of the nations."[13]

Just as the preeminent function of the church was its teaching function as interpreter of the gospel to the world, so the minister, according to Brown, was "above all else a teacher" of individual and social moral philosophy.[14] The seminary, in turn, found its proper calling as "the teacher of teachers." Theological classrooms instilled "the ideals which must inspire the leaders of the next generation, as they go out to interpret Christianity to the men and women who must live their lives under the new conditions now confronting us."[15] Thus, when Brown asserted that the unifying purpose of theological education was "the training of students for the ministry," he envisioned a series of instrumental relationships running through seminary, ministry, and church toward the social order, whose reorganization "in accordance with the religious principle" was the church's definitive mission.

Brown warned that this social mission was invariably impeded by excessive denominationalism, that "narrow view of life" which, by identifying Christianity "with the form of religion represented in one's own communion," limited the purpose of the denomination to propagating a certain set of beliefs and, consequently, turned the church inward on its own life and factional disputes. Denominationalism failed to recognize that just as persons "differ in their theories of the State and of the school who may yet share the common life of citizens and engage together in the quest for knowledge, so there is a bond of union between Christians which persists in spite of their differing philosophies."[16] Preparation for the "specialized ministry" of different denominations and different fields of endeavor must not obscure the "core" held in common: the body of common knowledge that united the separate studies of the curriculum and the unity of the church that encompassed the various denominations. By "seeking unity through variety," theological inquiry ought to instill "sympathetic understanding with our fellow Christians for the purpose of effective cooperation" on behalf of society as a whole. Since "unity in variety" was precisely the problem that confronted democracy itself, Brown believed that the ecumenical churches could provide a model for the conduct of public life as a whole, and that demonstrating "how this can be done will be the supreme office of the seminary of tomorrow."[17]

This same "problem of unity in difference" was the topic of Brown's address to the Conference of Theological Seminaries in June 1920. Reminding them of their cooperation with one another during the world war, Brown asked the member schools of the conference whether common interests commended continued meeting. As he saw it, the task was to insure "that religion has its rightful place in this country of ours and makes its contribution to the ideals and purposes that are to shape our national future." Things held in common—from faith in God and Christ to belief in the moral order of the universe and the ultimate triumph of right—must be made integral elements in "the education of the rising generation."[18] Brown appealed to the theologians, "the teachers of the teachers of religion," to map a national strategy that would "mold the Christian sentiment of the future" and educate students in the principle of "unity in difference" that undergirded the modern ecumenical movement and that had such importance for world political life.[19] In the aftermath of war and "the stupendous task of world reconstruction," American Protestants were called to achieve a new understanding of "the function of the Church in our democratic society," an understanding that defined *church* as the federated denominations engaged by word and deed in the moral and spiritual education of humanity. Despite its faults, the interdenominational church remained, said Brown, "the one social institution touching men of all races and nations and callings which exists to spread faith in a good god and to unite men in a world-wide brotherhood."[20]

Perhaps the most succinct characterization of the ecclesiastical stance adopted by Brown and his peers is *liberated denominationalism.* They aimed not to reject their denominational traditions but to open them toward modern American society and toward one another. By aligning themselves with movements of social reform and with university scholarship, they not only intended to shape the national culture but also to carry out an opening of the denominational mind. Seminary presidents, deans, and faculty accepted leadership in the Federal Council of Churches, the Committee on War and the Religious Outlook, and in the Interchurch World Movement following World War I.[21] Indeed, the Brown-May report led directly to the formation of an interdenominational accrediting body, the American Association of Theological Schools. The liberals were equally active within their respective denominations promoting reformist perspectives on denominational identity. Among the Baptists Walter Rauschenbusch was instrumental in forming the Brotherhood of the Kingdom, an organization of pastors and educators committed to "infusing the power of religion into social efforts."[22] Similarly, Edward Scribner Ames and other Disciples of Christ professors at the University of Chicago established the Campbell Institute, an association of ministers with graduate degrees who promoted theological discussion and contributed to "the literature of the Disciples of Christ" in ways that soon made this group a wide-ranging forum for liberal theology within the denomination.[23]

These and comparable movements in other denominations self-consciously attempted explicit correlation between inherited denominational culture and contemporary life. *For the denomination*, the most important consequence of this correlation was a more or less deliberate intent to transform denominational identity through interaction with larger cultural movements. Such transformations, to the extent that they were persuasively achieved, argued for the continuing pertinence of the denomination's tradition within the larger context of American religious life. From the liberal perspective, denominational culture was most effectively transmitted by consciously transforming it. *For the student*, such transmission by transformation mediated between denominational culture, especially the inherited denominational theology, and those intellectual questions and social commitments that had originally led the student toward the ministry. Harry Emerson Fosdick wrote for his student generation when he recalled in 1956:

> What present-day critics of liberalism often fail to see is its absolute necessity to multitudes of us who would not have been Christians at all unless we could then have escaped the bondage of the then reigning orthodoxy. Of course the revolt was not the whole answer! Of course it left out dimensions of Christian faith which would need to be rediscovered! Despite that, however, it offered a generation of earnest youth the only chance they had to be honest while being Christian.[24]

The liberals' goal for individual students was parallel to their goal for the denominations: to reorient them away from the preservation of traditional ideas toward active, transforming intellectual engagement with public life and the currents of modern thought. Philosopher of religion George Burman Foster aptly summarized the expansive liberal pedagogy:

> It may be said that usually the candidate for the ministry— young though he may sometimes be—enters the divinity

school as a finished religious and theological product, but that
in consequence of his studies there he departs, unfinished,
growing, aware that his personality, with its religion and its
theology, are alike in the making. A divinity school that
achieves such a result has fulfilled its function in the life of
the human spirit.[25]

By their *liberated denominationalism* the liberal theologians
helped "invent" the twentieth-century form of mainstream Protestantism. Although terms such as "mainstream" or "mainline" did
not figure in their rhetoric, this more recent terminology nicely captures their sense of the churches' institutional responsibility for a
"central" spiritual tradition within the American commonwealth
and their tacit assumption that others—notably fundamentalist
Protestants and Roman Catholics—had either rejected or stood outside of this central tradition. They regarded their own denominations
as tolerant institutions, committed to federated action in the public
sphere and willing to transform a religious heritage in order to
achieve a broader religious and social consensus. They conceived of
theology less as doctrinal studies grounded in specific confessional
traditions than as an ecumenical inquiry into common human experience and the transpersonal forces that challenged and nurtured that
common experience. They were institution builders who believed in
the power of institutions to better the human lot. Their confidence
arose not so much from a sense of personal righteousness as from
the conviction that the values to which they aspired were congruent
with the heart of things. This commitment to a consensus around
which a plural Protestant tradition could sustain its religious hopes
and cooperatively institutionalize its moral influence within the nation went far to define the modern self-conception of the mainstream.

In many respects, 1934 was the last possible moment that a
report so thoroughly grounded in the assumptions of liberal Protestantism could have plausibly interpreted the intellectual life of
American divinity schools. During the very years that Brown and
May were accumulating their data, the American theological climate
was shifting. In particular, Brown's classically liberal formulation of

the church's social role as "teacher of the nations" was receiving increasingly severe criticism from a significant group of younger theologians. In the year following publication of the Brown report, H. Richard Niebuhr, recently appointed professor of Christian ethics at Yale Divinity School, joined Wilhelm Pauck of Chicago Theological Seminary and Francis Miller of the World Student Christian Federation in publishing a book with an unequivocal title, *The Church against the World.* All three found American Christianity so entangled with the values and assumptions of national culture and capitalist economics that it was unable either to assert its own independent identity or to exercise a genuinely formative influence on the society in which it participated. Their rhetoric of "entanglement," "domestication," "captivity," and "accommodation" manifested their resolve to challenge liberal Protestantism's operative model of the church's relation to the nation. At least in Niebuhr's case, however, the elaboration of an alternative model was a task that took time to accomplish, and the immediate response was therefore limited to an emphatic protest. "Our position," they wrote, "is in the midst of that increasing group in the church which has heard the command to halt, to remind itself of its mission, and to await further orders."[26]

The Theology of Crisis

Niebuhr and his collaborators depicted the 1930s as a time of social dislocation and catastrophe, a time of transition estranged from the assumptions that had guided the nineteenth-century epoch, stretching from the French Revolution to World War I. In Niebuhr's characterization, the dominant spirit of the nineteenth century had been shaped by the industrial revolution, imperialistic nationalism, the rise of the middle class and the political emancipation of the individual, the increase of scientific knowledge and its technological application. Material progress had combined with the emphasis on personal freedom to induce an "anthropocentric" attitude toward life, "characterized not only by its evaluation of man as the central fact in reality but also by its ambition to subject all things to human control and by its assumption that such control is possible."[27] The intellectual fruit of this development was modern humanism, with its elimination from social life of all but human objects and purposes. The nineteenth-century assumption that "intelligence" applied to human problems could bring about progress was characteristically attended by optimism, and the collapse of this symptomatic optimism under the weight of world war and economic depression had now called attention to the failure of the underlying assumption.[28]

In the opinion of Wilhelm Pauck, this cultural crisis was at root a crisis of existential meaning, exemplified by the superficiality of mass culture, on the one hand, and, on the other hand, by the disillusionment of intellectuals with the commonplace convictions that heretofore had undergirded the civilization.

> It is likely that at all times in human history many men and women have spent their lives unaware of *the deeper meanings of existence.* But surely there have been few historical periods in which men were so disillusioned about the meaningfulness of life as they are in our own era. . . . *Depth seems to be the one dimension strangely absent from the life of the present generation.* A spirit of uncertainty has shaken, it seems, all positive convictions. . . . When we ask ourselves how this situation has come about we answer, usually, that we are experiencing a crisis of civilization, that we are living in the end of an era, that we are members of a period of cultural transition.[29]

But, if this crisis was a crisis of culture, it was also and equally a crisis for the church. "In the crisis of the world," Niebuhr wrote, "the church becomes aware of its own crisis; not that merely of a weak and responsible institution but of one which is threatened with destruction."[30] A "domesticated" Christianity—by which Niebuhr meant liberal Protestantism in particular—had absorbed the most characteristic values of the culture, had too often been reduced to the "spirit of devotion" that motivated actions justified on other than religious grounds, and had accommodated itself to the culture's confidence in the efficacy of technical reason by transmuting its religious mission into "programs and ideas of social planning" that would insure its value to democratic society.[31] Liberal Protestantism, in sum, had sought "to prove its usefulness to civilization, in terms of civilization's own demands."[32] But, in so doing, it had lost any distinctively Christian interpretation of the culture and now found employment only as "*the teacher of the prevailing code of morals* and the pantheon of the social gods."[33]

The problem of modern American Christianity was not, in other words, that it was locked in a clearly defined struggle against a powerfully coherent secular ideology. Instead, so it seemed to Niebuhr and his colleagues, the dispersed, specialized activities of the professions and the independent domains of modern intellectual, industrial, political, and religious life had pursued their separate courses, all the while loosely suspended in a cultural mood of pragmatic optimism, religiously glossed by association with the doctrine of providence. This national culture, wrote Francis Miller, was laced with tacit religious assumptions, setting great store by humanitarian ideals, championing the sanctity of individual "personality," displaying "a vivid sense of world mission." The "national religion" that was developing, Miller concluded, was a flimsy construction that appealed to "national culture as the ultimate frame of reference" for existential meaning and ethical decision.[34] Twenty years later Will Herberg's sociological analysis *Protestant, Catholic, Jew* (1955) would similarly name the defining paradox of American religion as "this secularism of a religious people, this religiousness in a secularist framework."[35] In 1935 the authors of *The Church against the World* found the superficiality of this "American way of life" unlikely to endure the challenges of modernity. Depth was "the one dimension strangely absent."

In this sense, liberal Protestantism suffered not merely from an error of social strategy but from a specifically religious failure. A cultural crisis had come to pass, said these critics of liberalism, because the church had become so enmeshed in the prevailing ethos that it could not render critical judgments, whether of self-criticism or cultural criticism. The neo-orthodox rhetoric of "depth" claimed a profundity to social experience that could neither be manipulated nor even fully comprehended by technical reason. The liberal church had so ignored this depth dimension as to render itself not merely trivial, but dangerous, by unwitting sanction of the uncriticized exercise of power in political and economic life. Both church and culture were victims of bad faith, a bland confidence in the sufficiency of humanity and human institutions that "has not eliminated faith but substituted a worldly for a divine faith," directing fidelity not toward God but toward nation, wealth, and industry in the "anthropocentric" faiths of nationalism, capitalism, and industrialism.[36] Now, with the collapse of confidence in "the social gods," the church that had accommodated itself to them would share their fate. "The question which we raise in this situation," said Niebuhr, "may best be stated in the gospel phrase, 'What must we do to be saved?'"[37] If, during the nineteenth century, the church had engaged in a social "program of salvation," the present moment of futility and demoralization had quite properly forced the church to remember "that it is not a savior but the company of those who have found a savior."[38] By raising the question of salvation, the church was not advocating irresponsible retreat from social obligation. Rather, said Niebuhr, the question arose because the church recognized its incapacity to give effective aid to those with whom it was entrapped.

Niebuhr took this "moment of crisis" to be a time not of despair but of opportunity for the church to recover its bearings and mission, to divest itself of entangling alliances and to recover its independence, "to turn away from its temporal toward its eternal relations and so to become fit again for its work in time." The liberal theologians had sought to correlate theology with modern thought because social and intellectual change seemed to threaten the church with irrelevance. Niebuhr came to the contrasting conclusion that the actual threat against the church was being made "not by a changing world but by an unchanging God."

> The "cracks in time" which now appear are fissures too deep for human contriving, and reveal a justice too profound to be the product of chance. The God who appears in this judgment of the world is neither the amiable parent of the soft faith we recently avowed nor the miracle worker of superstitious supernaturalism; he is rather the eternal God, Creator, Judge, and Redeemer, whom prophets and apostles heard, and saw at work, casting down and raising up. He uses all things temporal as his instruments, but resigns his sovereignty to none.[39]

In depicting the "cracks in time" as disclosures of deity, Niebuhr was following the theological analysis of culture proposed by Paul Tillich, who in 1933 began a long and extraordinarily influential American career by leaving his native Germany for a faculty position at Union Theological Seminary. Niebuhr was particularly drawn to Tillich's notion of *Kairos*, the moment when "time is invaded by eternity," when history reached a crisis that opened the way for something new and thereby confronted humans with the responsibilities and possibilities of their situation. For, although every age was related to the eternal, *consciousness* of this relation arose only in times when theological symbols had "lost their symbolic character as pointers" to the ultimate and when institutions presumed to be self-sufficient were shaken by social upheaval. In such times "when the relation of all existence to the ultimate source of meaning and existence becomes apparent in judgment, then," Niebuhr declared, "the consciousness of Kairos and of the responsibility of man come to their climax."[40]

> We now stand in the Kairos, in the moment when the judgment of the eternal upon time and all things temporal and the responsibility of the temporal to the eternal become evident in the events of the period. We are not facing merely a transition from one stage of culture to another, from one religion to another. . . . We are rather in a situation in which the whole question of the meaningfulness of existence is brought before us in such a fashion that we can not escape it, a period in which every social institution and religious symbol is challenged as to its right to existence. The eternal invades time and places every temporal form in question. There is in this not only judgment but also challenge to create such forms, such a culture and religion as will express the meaningfulness of all reality as a meaningfulness derived from the relation to the ultimate.[41]

As these extended citations indicate, Niebuhr was attracted to Tillich and commended him to American audiences for three general reasons. First, he shared Tillich's view that the nineteenth century had defined religion as the progressive historical pursuit of (human) ideals and had insufficiently recognized the sacred as fact, limit, and problem of life. The liberal theologians had understood the divine as the immanent power that was the condition for personal and social life, but they had tended to characterize it as sustaining and progressively developing that life. They encountered the sacred, to recur to Shailer Mathews's phrase, in "the personality-evolving elements of the universe," and they emphasized the continuity, even harmony, between the human enterprise and its cosmic setting. As a consequence, Niebuhr concluded, the myth of progress had obscured the precarious contingency of all human ideas and institutions, and "the word *God* has been made the symbol, not of the last reality with which man contends, but of his own aspirations."[42] For Niebuhr, as for Tillich, the deity encountered in the *Kairos* was "the unconditional" that opened new possibilities for the self not by confirming but by confounding human hopes. The disposition of the cosmos toward the human enterprise was enigmatic, ambiguous in its meanings, and therefore not amenable to human religious "adjustment."

This interpretation of divine sovereignty regularly recurred in Niebuhr's writing. In his historical study of American Protestantism, *The Kingdom of God in America* (1937), he found that faith in the divine kingdom had given a note of temporal urgency to the religious revolutions of the sixteenth and seventeenth centuries. The important element in the early Protestant expectation of the end and the new beginning was not the millenarian rhetoric in which it was couched "but rather the conviction that life is a critical affair, that nothing in it is abiding, that nothing temporal is able to bear the weight of human faith, and that salvation is possible only through giving up allegiance to the passing world and setting one's hope upon the eternal." The sense of crisis fostered "a revolutionary temper" among those who anticipated the in-breaking rule of God, because it confronted them with "the necessity of facing the ultimate realities of life." During the eighteenth century, said Niebuhr, the preaching of Jonathan Edwards had graphically communicated this same sense of the precariousness of existence. In the Awakening sermons of Edwards, "the coming kingdom appeared not as a goal toward which men were traveling but as the end which was hastening toward them; and now it was no longer simply the great happiness which men might miss but also the great threat which they could not escape."[43] Even when, in *The Purpose of the Church and Its Ministry,* Niebuhr described the overarching purpose of the church as "the increase of the love of God and neighbor," the progressive movement of love that a reader might infer from the word *increase* was overturned by the sovereign determiner of destiny: "The problem of man is how to love the One on whom he is completely, absolutely dependent; who is the Mystery behind the mystery of human existence in the fatefulness of its self-hood, of being this man among these men, in this time and all time, in the thus and so-ness of the strange actual world. It is the problem of reconciliation to the One from whom death proceeds as well as life."[44]

Niebuhr's second reason for commending Tillich's theological analysis of culture was that Tillich's notion of *Kairos* suggested a model of historical existence in which the necessity for ethical decision arose from the enigmatic fatefulness of life at least as often as from human planning. Both the unanticipated contingencies of life and the unanticipated consequences of ideals actively pursued brought individuals and societies to unforeseen intersections of choice. The "necessity of facing the ultimate realities of life" made decisions unavoidable, but responsibility for those decisions had to be accepted without the support of false certainties derived either from supernatural decrees or from a cultural mood of optimism. Since human plans were historically contingent and human decisions inescapable, nothing could be taken for granted either as the assured basis for conduct or as the self-evident message to be taught to "the nations." The ethical significance of the cultural and religious crisis was a situation "in which every social institution and religious symbol is challenged as to its right to existence."

Third, Tillich's way of formulating the crisis of existential meaning not only raised an ethical challenge but also the intellectual challenge to create theological symbols that would "express the meaningfulness of all reality as a meaningfulness derived from the relation to the ultimate." Could theological language imaginatively suggest the moment when "time is invaded by eternity?" Could the language of transcendence be retrieved as the basis for responsible citizenship in a democratic society? At the root of questions about the "right to existence" of theological symbols was Niebuhr's conviction that no other influence had more deeply affected contemporary thought than "the understanding that the spatio-temporal point of view of an observer enters into his knowledge of reality, so that no universal knowledge of things as they are in themselves is possible, so that all knowledge is conditioned by the standpoint of the knower."[45] Theology could not fruitfully proceed without completely rethinking the relations of the relative and the absolute in history, and such rethinking, in Niebuhr's estimation, must work out the theological implications of the modern judgment that all religions were historically contingent and that Christianity had no privileged point of view on time, eternity, and truth.

Throughout his work but especially in *The Meaning of Revelation* (1941), Niebuhr therefore took up the difficult rhetorical task of composing theological models that recognized fully the historical contingency of theological symbols. "The patterns and models we employ to understand the historical world may have had a heavenly origin," he wrote, "but as we know and use them they are, like ourselves, creatures of history and time."[46] Nonetheless, Niebuhr aimed to evoke through those symbols a transcendent referent for the meaning and conduct of personal and social life. The time-bound character of any human concept did not imply for him a retreat into subjectivity that relinquished this transcendent reference.

> It is not evident that the man who is forced to confess his
> view of things is conditioned by the standpoint he occupies
> must doubt the reality of what he sees. It is not apparent that
> one who knows that his concepts are not universal must also
> doubt that they are concepts of the universal, or that one who
> understands how all his experience is historically mediated
> must believe that nothing is mediated through history.[47]

With this chastened confidence in the communicative power of theological language, Niebuhr set about to craft theological models or patterns that exhibited not only the historical contextuality of the model but also directed attention to critical features in "the actual pattern of reality."[48]

For biblical scribes and rabbis, prophets and poets, the welter of their past experiences had revealed a comprehensive pattern of intelligibility, Niebuhr suggested, and "with that pattern in mind they made their choices in an ever critical present."[49] This was the case because historically contingent, particular events might be experienced as revelatory, in the sense that they suggested general ways of ordering or interpreting life as a whole.

> By revelation in our history, then, we mean that special occasion which provides us with an image by means of which all the occasions of personal and common life become intelligible. What concerns us at this point is not the fact that the revelatory moment shines by its own light and is intelligible in itself but rather that it illuminates other events and enables us to understand them. . . . Through it a *pattern of dramatic unity* becomes apparent with the aid of which the heart can understand what has happened, is happening and will happen to selves in their community.[50]

In no small measure the power of such "great common patterns" derived from the fact that, by a complex interaction, the same pattern or model thematized the ideas humans held about themselves, their societies, and the world. Through a pattern's suggestive analogies, human "efforts at self-control (ethics), at social construction (politics), and their attitudes toward their ultimate environment (religion) are in consequence influenced by similar ideas."[51] He wrote *The Kingdom of God in America* in order to pursue the question of "whether there is in the history of American Christianity a pattern which may perform a similar function for us."[52]

Looking back over the course of American history, Niebuhr found such a *"fundamental* pattern" operative in the covenant theology articulated by the Reformed theologians of colonial America. Whether in colonial psychology, political theory, or metaphysics, the covenant idea fastened on the experience of loyalty to a community and generalized features of this experience as the structure of social and religious relationships. The covenant envisioned "the world as a peculiar kind of society in which all parts are bound to each other by *promises*," and it defined the human in terms of the capacity to commit the self "as a promise-maker, promise-keeper, *a covenanter in universal community."* In this covenant tradition, the kingdom of God to which a John Cotton, a Roger Williams, or a Jonathan Edwards had been "loyal was not simply American culture or political and economic interest exalted and idealized; it was rather a kingdom which was prior to America and to which this nation, in its politics and economics, was required to conform." Such notions of participation in a universal community were present, Niebuhr observed, at the founding of American democracy, and "one may raise the question whether our common life could have been established, could have been maintained and whether it can endure without the presence of the conviction that we live in a world that has the moral structure of a covenant and without the presence in it of men who have achieved responsible citizenship by exercising the kind of freedom that appears in their taking upon themselves the obligations of unlimited loyalty, under God, to principles of truth-telling, of justice, of loyalty to one another, of indissoluble union."[53] The churches had to take their not inconsiderable share of responsibility for the present cultural crisis, because in their moral entanglement with the society they had lost their transcendent principle of critical judgment. The covenant theology was a historical reminder that attentiveness to and articulation of this transcendent reference were the churches' fundamental cultural responsibilities.

Companion to the World

Against this background of the theology of crisis and its consequences for ethics and theological language, Niebuhr sought to resolve the church's "entanglement" with culture and to delineate the church's appropriate role in national life. The churches of liberal Protestantism did not, to his mind, have sufficient critical distance from the American polity to discern and appraise its tacit norms and values. He sought to clarify the constitutive loyalties of American Christianity through an image of the church that defined its *importance for* the culture in terms of its *independence from* the culture and that grounded this independence in a fully historical standpoint that was nonetheless oriented toward a transcendent reality. As a consistent element of this model of the church, he sought an understanding of the theological school that would "nurture men and women whose business in life it will be to help men to see their immediate perplexities, joys and sufferings in the light of an ultimate meaning, to live as citizens of the inclusive society of being, and to relate their present choices to the first and last decisions made about them in the totality of human history by Sovereign Power."[54]

Niebuhr experimented for almost a decade before he achieved a "pattern" that in some measure satisfied these objectives, and the development toward this pattern is evident in his changing presentation of the church from *The Social Sources of Denominationalism* (1929) to *The Kingdom of God in America* (1937).[55] In the earlier book, Niebuhr had directed a withering attack against the social captivity of the churches, arguing that it was naive to believe that doctrinal differences were the basis for the denominational divisions in American Christianity. Where William Adams Brown had appealed for a new study of denominational symbolics so that students might learn the convictions and ideals of other churches,[56] Niebuhr had been prompted to write *The Social Sources of Denominationalism* by his sense of the misleading futility of understanding denominational differences in this way.[57] Not doctrine but class and race sustained the social life of the churches.

> The denominations, churches, sects, are sociological groups whose principle of differentiation is to be sought in their conformity to the order of social classes and castes. It would not be true to affirm that the denominations are not religious groups with religious purposes, but it is true that they represent the accommodation of religion to the caste system. They are the emblems, therefore, of the victory of the world over the church, of the secularization of Christianity, of the church's sanction of that divisiveness which the church's gospel condemns. Denominationalism thus represents the moral failure of Christianity.[58]

In an analysis reminiscent of Shailer Mathews's view that theology was a projection of social organization ("transcendentalized politics"), Niebuhr portrayed the relation of Christian theology to society largely as a matter of sociological placement in which doctrines "change with the mutations of social structure, not vice versa."[59] So, for example, "disinherited" groups, by virtue of their alienation from the dominant culture, might gain a moral insight into the meaning of the gospel that could provide a basis for the renewal of the church.[60] But this privileged point of view was gradually lost as the "sect" advanced in social standing, evolving into a "denomination" that participated more fully in the surrounding culture.

Having mapped the social and historical coordinates of the churches' "accommodation . . . to the caste system," Niebuhr nonetheless concluded his analysis by suggesting that the church must embody *a new cultural synthesis,* one which would reorder culture around Christian loyalties. The church, he said, "can save neither its self-esteem nor its existence nor yet the finer values its thinkers, prophets, artists and its toiling masses have wrought out, unless it is made captive to some compelling and integrating ideal which will restore to it a sense of the whole and will equip it with an ethics commensurate with the scope of its interests and of its world-embracing organization."[61] Employing rhetoric similar to that of William Adams Brown, Niebuhr expressed hope that "such an ideal as that of the Gospels" would inspire the "latent energy and devotion" of humanity to seek an "organic integration of mankind into a functional whole."[62] The religious task was a "synthesis of culture" that was built on "a common world-view and a common ethics." Civilizations that have achieved such a synthesis have received it from their religion, he concluded, and without a cultural synthesis no civilization has flourished or made an enduring contribution to the human enterprise.[63]

But Niebuhr was soon dissatisfied with this faith in the inspirational power of religious ideals; the attack on the optimistic aspirations of "the nineteenth century" that subsequently appeared in his writings of the 1930s was explicitly directed at liberal Protestantism but surely contained a measure of self-criticism as well. Not only did a Christian synthesis of culture place unwarranted dependence on human good will or devotion to the Christian ideal in order to motivate efforts toward cultural renewal, but the formal difference between cultural synthesis, which he applauded, and accommodation, which he attacked, was in reality quite unclear. "Synthesis" and "entanglement" tended to be moralistic terms of approval or disapproval rather than a way out of the dilemma of historical and cultural relativity.

In his contribution to *The Church against the World*, Niebuhr experimented with another analytic model: a cycle or oscillation in the church's life that passed through historical phases of conflict, alliance, and identification in relation to the surrounding culture. The phases of this cycle were not unlike the transition from sect to denomination described in *The Social Sources of Denominationalism*: "A converted church in a corrupt civilization withdraws to its upper rooms, into monasteries and conventicles; it issues forth from these in the aggressive evangelism of apostles, monks and friars, circuit riders and missionaries; it relaxes its rigorism as it discerns signs of repentance and faith; it enters into inevitable alliance with converted emperors and governors, philosophers and artists, merchants and entrepreneurs, and begins to live at peace in the culture they produce under the stimulus of their faith; when faith loses its force, as generation follows generation, discipline is relaxed, repentance grows formal, corruption enters with idolatry, and the church, tied to the culture which it sponsored, suffers corruption with it."[64] But at the moment the church's distinctive identity dissolved in the culture, Niebuhr did not, as in *Social Sources of Denominationalism*, hold out the hope of a new cultural synthesis. Instead, he announced that only the dynamic turn of *a new cycle* in the church's relation to culture could retrieve its proper religious mission: "Only a new withdrawal followed by a new aggression can then save the church and restore to it the salt with which to savor society."[65]

Although the dynamism of this model became characteristic of all his later models of the church, subsequent restatements suggest that he found its formulation here unsatisfactory. In this cyclical movement, what was the principle that gave direction? In this dynamism, what was the dynamic? Undoubtedly the church moved in and through history, but in the midst of movement how did it make a judgment about whether or not it was "on course," without recourse to ahistorical supernaturalism that Niebuhr regarded as unacceptably naive? What he wrote in 1935 about the "revolt" within the church could also be said of his own position: It had not yet fully analyzed its situation and hence remained uncertain of its end and strategy; it was "a protest rather than a theory and a plan of action." It was this theory "based upon a clear analysis of the situation" that he now required, if the church hoped to avoid sacrificing its ethical nerve to sentimentality or the futility of premature action. Whatever its form, the "theory of the Christian revolution" must be based in theology rather than borrowing its central premises from psychology or sociology, and it must elaborate a strategy that "always has a dual character," engaging in the affairs of the world while yet knowing that "its main task always remains that of understanding, proclaiming and preparing for the divine revolution in human life." Faced with the difficulty of sustaining this duality without lapsing into "the monism of other-worldliness or of this-worldliness," Niebuhr believed that "the theory of the Christian revolution is beginning to unfold itself again as the theory of a divine determinism, of the inevitable divine judgment, and of the salvation of men by the suffering of the innocent."[66]

The Kingdom of God in America presented a new pattern that combined the dynamic view of the church moving through history with the idea of divine sovereignty to form a dialectical tension between the rule of God and cultural existence in the world. "This dialectic," Niebuhr wrote, "is expressed in worship and in work, in the direction toward God and the direction toward the world which is loved in God, in the pilgrimage toward the eternal kingdom, and in the desire to make his will real on earth."[67] Neither movement solely toward eternity nor movement solely toward the world adequately expressed the "theocentric" orientation of Christian faith toward God and world, since the eternal God was one who worked redemptively in the world and since the world did not derive meaning from itself but only from God. But by suspending the vitality of the church, the faith by which it lived in the world, from the divine sovereignty, Niebuhr's dialectical analysis generated a difficulty for faith's institutional embodiment that he described as *the dilemma of constructive Protestantism*. This, he believed, had been the religious dilemma of the seventeenth-century Protestant colonists of North America, and it was not simply the perennial problem faced by protest movements whenever they proceed from criticism to the actual responsibility of applying their principles to institutional leadership. Instead, Protestantism's dilemma arose from its conviction that social construction depended on the divine initiative, not on the implementation of human plans. Apprehension of the near approach of the rule of God might well be said to provoke a sense of crisis that "fosters a revolutionary temper," but could it also become the basis for "construction of a new order of life?" As Paul Tillich had written, protest in the name of divine sovereignty had generated the "inner dilemma of Protestantism" by which "it must protest against every religious or cultural realization which seeks to be intrinsically valid" even though at the same time "it needs such realization if it is to be able to make its protest in any meaningful way."[68] Since "it was evident that men lived in a crisis and that they could not stand still but were hastening either to destruction or to life," this sense of the immediacy of divine power in their midst had evoked a decision from the Protestant colonists to "press into the kingdom," employing their fragmentary vision of it in order to establish congregations, schools, and governments. Insofar as the nation later continued this venture to build a society on the self-critical principle of divine sovereignty, America, thought Niebuhr, was "an experiment in constructive Protestantism."[69]

Since "constructive Protestantism" believed the authentic church was "not an organization but the organic movement of those who have been 'called out,'" the movement's "crystallization" in institutions, although inevitable, denied "what Christianity is" in the very act of conserving it. For this reason, what Niebuhr referred to as "the theory of the Christian revolution" was also and always a theory of "permanent revolution" in which human construction was contingent on the "Sovereign Power" of history. Institutions performed the necessary function of consolidating the gains of revolutionary epochs and transmitting to the next generation what would otherwise be lost when the moment of dynamism expired. Still, "since the goal is the infinite and eternal God, only movement or life directed toward the ever transcendent can express its meaning." The relation between the nature of the church as movement and as institution could not, therefore, be explained in the liberal terms of progressive institutional embodiment of permanent religious ideals within a changing cultural environment. Rather, the encounter with the unconditional amidst the conditions of history forced perennial reappraisal of all institutions and the ideals they purported to serve, alike human and therefore transient.[70] To communicate the challenge of basing a constructive venture on a contingent vision, Niebuhr displayed a fondness for navigational metaphors, in which the theologian gained some sense, by triangulation, of his relative location within the historical scene. Such a sailor, "who seeks his bearings by consulting the charts his fathers used when they set out on the voyage he is continuing, by noting all the corrections they have made upon them and by looking for the stars which gave them orientation may claim at least that he is trying to be true to the meaning of the voyage."[71]

As amplified in *The Purpose of the Church and Its Ministry*, this dialectical analysis defined the church not in terms of its essence or nature but underscored instead the orientation of the church within history "by defining certain poles between which it moves." Several of these polarities were internal to the church, its local and its universal, its Protestant and its Catholic aspects, for example. These various internal polarities—the list was not exhaustive—were encompassed by two external ones, the relation to God and the relation to the world. *Polarity* thus connoted not only the presence of opposing properties or powers within the church but also an orienting attraction toward a particular object or in a particular direction. Among the polarities, the orientation toward God influenced all others, and consequently the world was not the object of orienting attraction for the church in the same way that God was: "World, rather, is companion of the Church, a community something like itself with which it lives before God. The world is sometimes enemy, sometimes partner of Church, often antagonist, always one to be befriended; now it is the co-knower, now the one that does not know what Church knows, now the knower of what the Church does not know."[72]

This triadic metaphor of church and world as companions locked in life before the sovereign God marked a significant departure from earlier American metaphors of the church. The organic metaphor of church and world, exemplified in the Protestant Romanticism of John Williamson Nevin, had identified the church as the soul of civilization, its influence suffusing and ultimately directing the whole of history. "The supernatural has itself become natural" in the progressive evolution of the church, according to Nevin, "by falling into the regular processes of the world's history, so as to form to the end of time indeed its true central stream."[73] Niebuhr's model also differed from William Adams Brown's instrumental metaphor of the church. Brown's metaphorical relation of a teaching church to a learning world was replaced by the relation of "co-learners" in a long, human inquiry lived out "before God." As a consequence, the relation of the church to nation and school did not presuppose models of social consensus built on either "the essence of Christianity" or "the philosophy of the Christian religion" but assumed instead a permanent diversity of "standpoints" or "points of view" in American culture. Church and world might have extended conversation about the existential and ethical problems of common life together, but the theologian could in no way assume, as had Brown, that it was the church's "mission to organize society as a whole in accordance with the religious principle."[74] Instead, Niebuhr's triadic relation of church, world, and God implied that to educate persons "for the ministry of the Church is to train them for ministry to the world and to introduce them to the conversation of Church and world, a conversation in which both humility and self-assurance have their proper place."[75]

Intellectual Center of the Church's Life

When in the 1950s Niebuhr appraised the aims of theological education, he made this theory of the church the axis of his analysis. Confusion and uncertainty existed in theological schools, he observed, largely because of lack of clarity about the nature of the church and about the church's relation to the wider culture. Without a definition of church, he thought it impossible adequately to conceive education for ministry in the church. He thought it equally impossible to organize a curriculum in Bible, church history, theology, and practical theology without "clarity about the place of these studies and acts in the life of the Church." And, "unless the relations of the Church to religion in general, to the particular religions and to secular culture have been intelligibly defined," he thought it impossible "to achieve more than superficial correlation of studies in the history and philosophy of religion, in psychology and sociology, with the older disciplines" of the fourfold theological encyclopedia.[76]

He rejected as superficial the notion that the religious community within which the theological school carried out its work and whose aims and values it represented consisted simply of the denomination that had founded and funded it. Instead, he concluded that despite "their denominational affiliation and their service of denominational purposes the theological schools usually give evidence of sharing in a community of discourse and interest that transcends denominational boundaries."[77] Neither was the nation the primary communal context of theological study. The purpose of Christian theology was not simply to contribute to shaping national identity. On this point Niebuhr shared Will Herberg's opinion that, in American popular culture, self-identification as "a Protestant, a Catholic, or a Jew is understood as the specific way, and increasingly perhaps the only way, of being an American and locating oneself in American society." But to understand these particular religious traditions as "alternative ways of being an American" had come to mean, said Herberg, that "the religion which actually prevails among Americans today has lost much of its authentic Christian (or Jewish) content." Such a relation between religiosity and national identity, both men thought, undercut any properly religious "sense of transcendence."[78] Although denominational affiliations and American national life were both "conditioning elements" in the work of theological schools, Niebuhr therefore asserted that "the primary context in which the ministry and theology do their work is neither denomination nor nation but the Church in its wholeness." He found this ecumenical context of study apparent in courses in Bible, church history, and theology: "With few exceptions teachers and students do not engage in a denominationally restricted discussion but participate in a Protestant and a Christian conversation or debate about the ultimate problems of faith and life."[79] Hence, Niebuhr described the modern minister as a *pastoral director*, in order to stress the minister's responsibility to represent the church's long tradition, "its conceptional frames of reference, its moral orientation in the world of good and evil." He intended this emphasis on tradition to counterbalance the American practice of voluntary church affiliation, which pressed the minister to become simply "the representative of a fleeting majority of living and local church members."[80]

Even if, however, "the Church in its wholeness" had replaced the denomination as the primary *context* of theological study, in Niebuhr's view, the church catholic no more than the denomination should be confused with the primary *object* of theological study. "The confusion between part and whole is not to be avoided by denying the reality of the parts," he insisted, "but only by the acceptance of diversity and limitation and the corollary recognition that all the parts are equally related in the whole to the ultimate object of the Church."[81] Hence, for mainstream Protestantism at mid-century a greater danger than confusion of the denomination with the whole church was confusion of the church, considered as an ecumenical whole, with the ultimate object of theological education.[82] Instead, the ultimate object that oriented the theologian's work was the final sovereignty of God over a created order in which the church's comprehensive purpose was the exercise and the extension of the love of God and neighbor. From Niebuhr's perspective, ecumenical Protestantism no less than the individual denominations stood under judgment, since exaltation of the church led to the mistaken—indeed, idolatrous—effort "not to reconcile men with God or to redirect their love and ours toward God and the neighbor but rather to convert them to Christianity."[83] Such an exaltation of the church, whenever it prevailed, undercut the theological school's striving genuinely to *be theological*, since education that accepted service to *the church* as its ultimate purpose "necessarily becomes indoctrination in Christian principles rather than inquiry based on faith in God; or it is turned into training in methods for increasing the Church rather than for guiding men to love of God and neighbor."[84]

The implications of this model of "constructive Protestantism" were evident in Niebuhr's choice of the phrase "intellectual center of the church's life" to designate a theological school. "*Intellectual* center" was a bold choice in the 1950s. The intellectual has not been a uniformly popular figure in America, and among the most prominent of the intellectual's detractors have been the advocates of religion. Protestant and Catholic scholars alike had been hard pressed to nurture an intellectual tradition in the face of the churches' demand for practical devotion. In many respects, the situation had not changed appreciably since the mid-nineteenth century, when Andover Seminary's Bela Bates Edwards ruefully remarked that "it is an impression, somewhat general, that an intellectual clergyman is deficient in piety, and that an eminently pious minister is deficient in intellect."[85] During the years of "McCarthyism" and the cold war, intellectuals felt themselves beset on all flanks, and in his 1954 presidential address to the American Historical Association, Wisconsin's Merle Curti commented on the tenor of the times that "most observers who have written on the theme agree that popular suspicion of the critical role of intellectuals has increased, that it has become more intense, and that demagogues are exploiting it as never before in our history."[86] To speak of the religious scholar as an intellectual therefore raised a number of questions and possible contradictions. Still, it seemed to Niebuhr the best term to describe the way ahead, and his reasoning is partially illuminated by Richard Hofstadter's later usage in *Anti-Intellectualism in American Life* (1963). There, in a contrast reminiscent of Niebuhr's critique of liberalism's "anthropocentric" faith in pragmatic intelligence, Hofstadter sharply distinguished the idea of intellect from the idea of intelligence: "Whereas intelligence seeks to grasp, manipulate, re-order, adjust, intellect examines, ponders, wonders, theorizes, criticizes, imagines. Intelligence will seize the immediate meaning in a situation and evaluate it. Intellect evaluates evaluations, and looks for the meanings of situations as a whole."[87] From this distinction, it followed that intellect was stimulated less by the instrumental utility of ideas than by the "playfulness" of thought that implied "a special sense of the ultimate value in existence of the act of comprehension." Hence, to be the member of a profession was not necessarily to be an intellectual. The professional was "a mental worker, a technician," who may *happen* to be an intellectual by virtue of bringing to the profession "a distinctive feeling about ideas" not actually required by the job.[88] At stake in such distinctions was the difference between the divinity school of William Rainey Harper and Shailer Mathews oriented toward "ministerial efficiency" and the divinity school of Niebuhr which provided the occasion for "the intellectual love of God." In short, Niebuhr's "intellectual center" connoted critical distance between theology and the practical needs of church and nation, an independence that was the basis for its genuinely distinctive service to the purposes that the church served.

This critical distance, as Hofstadter also noted, had been part and parcel of the modern notion of "intellectuals" as a social class. First in Europe and then in America, the intellectual had been identified with political and moral protest, and this meaning was quite evident in the first American use of the term that Hofstadter found, by William James in 1899.

> We 'intellectuals' in America must all work to keep our precious birthright of individualism, and freedom from these institutions [church, army, aristocracy, royalty]. *Every* great institution is perforce a means of corruption—whatever good it may also do. Only in the free personal relation is full ideality to be found.[89]

But, although the intellectual's protest against "social faith" comports well with Niebuhr's own aphoristic definition of theology as "the theory of the Christian revolution," his decision to name the theological school an *intellectual* center did not entail the anti-institutional individualism of the Jamesian intellectual. The theological school as intellectual *center* signaled Niebuhr's appreciation for a point Jacques Barzun would make in *The House of Intellect* (1959), that intellect was a collaborative cultural achievement, "the communal form of live intelligence" composed of disciplined habits of reasoning, acquired bodies of knowledge, and established channels of communication.[90] Without such institutional embodiment, the wondering, imagining, and intuitive intellect of Hofstadter's characterization had no social context of expression and influence. Still, Niebuhr explicitly distinguished actual seminaries from "the idea of a theological school," insofar as the latter represented direct intellectual engagement in the church's purpose of extending the love of God and of neighbor. A theological school arose *"wherever and whenever there has been intense intellectual activity in the Church,"* he wrote, "while institutions possessing the external appearance of such schools but devoid of reflective life have quickly revealed themselves as training establishments for the habituation of apprentices in the skills of a clerical trade rather than as theological schools." This intellectual activity of the church, which *"centers on occasion* in a theological school" manifested the "dilemma of constructive Protestantism" in its educational form and was a variation on the distinction between doctrinal knowledge and "the sense of the heart" that had been at issue among American theological scholars since the age of Edwards.[91]

The intellectual activity that in the first instance characterized such an "intellectual center" was the "response of nascent love toward God and neighbor which seeks to know the beloved, not with the question of whether it is worthy of love, but with wonder; not for the sake of power over the beloved but as overpowered." This understanding of theology stood in the tradition of Jonathan Edwards not only in the general sense that it was "theocentric" but more particularly in the primacy it gave to the piety of aesthetic adoration in establishing the ethical orientation of Christian theology. In this sense, theology was not for Niebuhr simply ancillary to other actions of the church but was itself a primary action: "Such a movement of the mind toward God and the neighbor-before-God is characteristic of the Church in all its parts but it is the first duty and central purpose of the theological school."[92] As this also suggests, Niebuhr built the complex object of theological study directly on his triadic model of the church: "What is known and knowable in theology is God in relation to self and to neighbor, and self and neighbor in relation to God."[93] Intellectual "triangulation" charted the church's relative location in its movement through time and space, gradually establishing "the communal point of view and perspective of the Church" which put it "into a relation to its Object and makes possible an understanding of it that is impossible from every other point of view."[94]

There were other perspectives directed toward the divine reality, Niebuhr affirmed, but they were oriented differently from the orientation characteristic of Christian faith. So, by analogy, a nation could be known by the patriot and by the international observer, yet in different ways and with different ethical ramifications. The theologian was necessarily conversant with these alternate perspectives, and the historical and interpretive studies that sustained the Christian point of view as a living tradition were not simply a restatement of what historically the church had "said." Inevitably the scholar reinterpreted an element of the Christian tradition or perhaps its meaning as a whole and did so in a context thoroughly permeated by contemporary "secular" thought.

> At no time in the past has the gospel been understood and communicated without the aid of "secular" conceptions about the world, man, his psychology, his society. The theological student needs to understand modern politics, psychology, philosophy and sociology not simply for the purposes of finding a language into which he can translate convictions and ideas once stated in the terms of another language but in order that he may reappropriate what earlier men meant when they used their words and concepts to speak of God and salvation.[95]

The reasoning of faith required a dialogue between the churchly and the secular points of view—the two companions before God—in order to present a comprehensible statement of the Christian point of view itself (comprehensible even to the Christian).

Niebuhr envisioned a permanent plurality of faith perspectives in society—both those that might be characterized as religious and those that might be characterized as secular—and he imagined that church and world would remain co-learners in this pluralistic circumstance. This conception of the church affected his understanding of the proper task of theology in the university. Unlike William Adams Brown, for whom "the philosophy of the Christian religion" provided a unifying framework for the diverse conversation of the modern university, Niebuhr repudiated for theology any role as "queen of the sciences." Theology must "develop its own methods in view of the situation in which it works and of the object with which it deals" and do so, he believed, "without becoming the vassal of methodologies developed by rational inquiries directed toward other objects and existing in connection with other nonrational activities of men besides faith."[96] However, the theologian cultivated this distinctive perspective not to isolate theology from the conversation of the university but precisely to make a distinctive contribution to that conversation. In a university, the role of theology was critical rather than directive, joining other disciplines in what the theologian, at least, took to be a common inquiry into the way "every individual, group, and institution is directly related to the Transcendent—whether positively in trust and loyalty or negatively in distrust and disloyalty. . . . As fellow servant of truth in this sense theology takes its place in the university alongside other inquiries, never separated from them, never dependent upon them, never isolating itself with them from the totality of the common life which is the universe." At most, Niebuhr stated, the university had a hidden theological ingredient in its commitment "to try to understand what is true for all men everywhere in the universal community and to communicate the truths it understands without bearing false witness against any neighbors, whatever their loyalties or privileges." Although the predispositions of modern society made it easy to overlook this ultimate accountability, a university attentive to this commitment would recognize that it was "as directly responsible to the Transcendent in the performance of its duties of study and teaching" as states were in the administration of law or churches were in acts of preaching and worship.[97]

Walter Lippmann observed that "in the modern world institutions are more or less independent, each serving its own proximate purpose, and our culture is really a collection of separate interests each sovereign within its own realm." As participants in these multiple institutions, the modern person experiences the self as "the center of a complex of loyalties," commanding only a segment of the self, such that modern "conflicts between institutions are in considerable measure conflicts of interest within the same individuals." The institutional separation of independent social activities, therefore, had "its counterpart in a separation of selves; the life of a modern man is not so much the history of a single soul; it is rather a play of many characters within a single body."[98] Niebuhr's dialectical portrayal of the church responded to this modern condition of societies and selves by a theological inquiry into the nature of human allegiances. Human communities did not come into being and endure, in Niebuhr's opinion, apart from confidence in institutions and fidelity to the causes or ideals those institutions represented. Equally, the human individual received and elaborated a sense of self within this fabric of trust and loyalty. Human life was not lived without faith, in this double sense of the term. The issue, then, was the adequacy of the objects in which humans placed their confidence and to which they devoted their loyal service, an adequacy measured by the capacity to nurture particular loyalties through a final, unifying loyalty. But in the multiplicity of purposes and allegiances, was there a worthy final goal to which others were subordinate, or a "final unifying consideration that modifies all the special strivings?" Amid the multiple loyalties to religious communities, to nations, to schools, it was the church's responsibility faithfully to embody the proposition that the citizens who populate these institutions—religious and secular—"are first of all citizens of another, prior, and universal Commonwealth."[99] Apart from such a comprehensive sense of obligation and of confidence, neither society nor the self could hope for integrity.

> To be a self is to have a god; to have a god is to have a history, that is, events connected in a meaningful pattern; to have one god is to have one history. God and the history of selves in community belong together in inseparable union.[100]

*The disesteem into which moralists have fallen is due at bottom to
their failure to see that in an age like this one the function of the
moralist is not to exhort men to be good but to elucidate what the
good is. . . . The true function of the moralist in an age when usage
is unsettled is what Aristotle who lived in such an age described
it to be: to promote good conduct by discovering and explaining
the mark at which things aim.*

Walter Lippmann, *A Preface to Morals,* pp. 318–19

FIVE

THE BACKGROUND OF POSSIBILITIES

In 1961 Daniel Day Williams, Niebuhr's collaborator in *The Advancement of Theological Education,* published a long essay entitled
"Tradition and Experience in American Theology." In this piece,
which interpreted the key developments of theology in America
from Jonathan Edwards to the middle of the twentieth century, Williams argued, rightly I think, that there is no "American theology,"
if one means by that a distinctively American mix of religious beliefs. But Williams went on to say that religious diversity, the voluntary character of church life in America, and the democratic assumptions of the society had produced a distinctive problem for Christian
theology and a distinctive theological method for addressing that
problem. The problem arose because the American disestablishment
of religion gave no formal preference to any tradition and permitted
an open hearing for all. In this pluralistic setting, no simple appeal
to the belief and practice of a particular tradition could, of itself, offer
a publicly persuasive reading of the American religious circumstance
as a whole. At the same time, the theological impulse toward a com-

prehensive interpretation of reality and the social impulse toward public cohesion left religious thinkers discontent with sheer plurality of opinion.

This unresolved tension between the pluralistic particularity of religious traditions and the theological drive toward comprehensive interpretation gradually imparted a distinctive character to theology in America that "does not consist in agreement about particular doctrines, but in *a way of thinking* about the relation of doctrine to the religious life and to the life of the church."[1] Not an American theology but an American method for doing theology had arisen from the need to offer comprehensive theological interpretation to a religious and social life indelibly marked by religious diversity. According to Williams, the thematic coherence of this "way of thinking" came to expression in an appeal to *experience* as a basis for cooperation and understanding among religious groups. Historically, he said, American theologians had advanced the interpretation that a "common experience" underlying differing doctrinal symbols offered the possibility for religious community that respected, but transcended, difference.

In the context of religious diversity, this *common experience* became a systematic theological principle, a functional criterion for the adequacy of doctrine that implied a pragmatic method of theological analysis and critique. Doctrines that failed to illuminate the exigencies of personal existence, that failed to make pertinent contact with wider social experience, or that failed to promote ethical behavior would, it was assumed, likewise fail to retain their hold on the public imagination. Indeed, the acknowledged common experience of the society might reforge inherited beliefs in ways that led to "the creation of new symbols which are endowed with the power of supporting social unity." Pluralistic America, said Williams, required a theological method that transcended confessionalism in order to "search for the thread of common experience which runs through a variety of doctrinal expressions."[2] Religious diversity was suffused with unifying experiential themes, and it was the vocation of ecumenical Protestant theologians to identify and articulate these unifying themes in order to speak influentially in the constitutive conversations of civic life.

Williams saw, of course, that the theological connotations of *experience* had shifted over the centuries of American history. In the thought of Edwards and Bushnell, experience had referred to the vital principle of personal religion for which nature, Scripture, and the interaction between them disclosed an intelligibility that was "an earnest of the divine faithfulness and an expression of the divine beauty." To social gospel theologians such as Walter Rauschenbusch, experience tested the practical social worth of particular beliefs, on the assumption that the decisive "proving ground for religious and ethical convictions" was actual ethical behavior by those who held these convictions. The empirical theology of "the Chicago School," from Shailer Mathews to Henry Nelson Wieman, identified experience with the stream of collective experience, "the social process," whose course and flow could be delineated through theological categories.[3] In each case personal experience was shaped by, expressed through, and incorporated in ever wider social communities that were themselves ultimately encompassed by the created order. As such, the history of American reflection on the theological meaning of *common experience* pressed "toward a theology of the human community."[4]

Theological attentiveness to the empirical, according to Williams, thus became a means in the context of religious pluralism for giving attention to the divine presence.

> Perhaps the most important root of theological empiricism was the belief, derived from the Christian faith and present in the American consciousness from the Puritans and Edwards to the present, that a sufficiently faithful and realistic attention to the direction of historical events will disclose the hand and judgment of God. American theological empiricism in all its forms has an inward relation to the doctrine of Providence, whether this be expressed in Calvinist determinism, in ideas of progress, or in the criticism of progressive optimism.[5]

Williams proposed that a theological interpretation of American experience, by identifying the continuity in its diversity, narrated the presence of God in American history. Later in the decade comparable readings of American experience were given by the religious historian Sidney E. Mead and the sociologist of religion Robert N. Bellah, who identified a *religion of the republic* or *civil religion* that interpreted public life in terms of a transcendent reference. A "definitive element" in the American sense of nationality, Mead wrote in 1967, has been "the conception of a universal principle which is thought to transcend and include" the national and religious particularities of the people who populated America. What Mead called "a theonomous cosmopolitanism" in the American tradition meant that, at its best, the religion of the republic was not a mere celebration of the American "way of life" but, as Bellah argued, "a genuine apprehension of universal and transcendent religious reality as seen in or, one could almost say, as revealed through the experience of the American people."[6]

Experience in American Theology

Williams's interpretive category *common experience* soon became problematic, however, because it rested on two fragile assumptions, first, that Americans shared a common cultural history and, second, that this common experience could bear a coherent theological interpretation. But by mid-decade, leading theologians were questioning whether or not theological language actually made intelligible connections with common experience, that is, whether theological categories plausibly interpreted the *ordinary experience* of everyday life. At the same time, the civil rights movement was raising pointed questions about whether the national experience was indeed a common experience or was not instead a conflicting assemblage of *particular experiences* shaped by race and class. The intellectual and social consequences of these two challenges made it increasingly clear that the common experience assumed in Williams's analysis was in fact the particular experience of theologians from "the Protestant establishment,"[7] with their characteristic strategies for relating theology to a threefold public of church, nation, and university. The reshaping of American religious life that began in the sixties dispersed the cultural energies of mainstream Protestantism and dramatically reopened controversy about the civic, academic, and churchly bearings of theological scholarship. *Experience* was shifting from the interpre-

tive presupposition for an American theological project to the principal contested issue of American theological debate. Hence, appraising
the purposes of theological schools and scholars in the contemporary
American context involves reconsidering Williams's analytic categories: common experience, tradition, and the creation of symbols that
point "toward a theology of the human community."

The first dimension of the issue manifested itself during the
mid-sixties, in debate about the lack of connection between theological language and the common experience of concrete, everyday life:
the day-to-day experience of citizens, students, or professors, and
members of religious communities. Langdon Gilkey's synthetic
appraisal, *Naming the Whirlwind: The Renewal of God-Language*
(1969), described the sense of unreality and meaninglessness that
had attached to talk about God because such language made no apparent contact with life in "the secular world." The "*new* character"
of the theological situation, Gilkey believed, was that this sense of
the unreality of Christian theological language now manifested itself
not only abroad in the culture but even in the church, which was
searching for the experiential foundations of its words, its worship,
and its works.

> The world was within the Church, belief was saturated by sec-
> ular doubt, and no one, either in pew or in pulpit, was sure a
> divine Word had been heard at all or a divine presence mani-
> fested. In such a situation, the theology that was unable to re-
> late itself to ordinary experience was bound to falter—and it
> did. . . . The present unreality and so seeming impossibility
> of theological language about God stems fundamentally, we
> believe, from this split between our existence in the secular
> world which all Christians share, on the one hand, and a theo-
> logical language, on the other, that has had no essential touch
> with that world.[8]

The "split" between theological language and the common secular
world was similarly evaluated in *The Analogy of Experience* (1973)
by philosopher John E. Smith, who argued that Christian theology
had lost and must recover its character as a philosophy of lived experience. Like Gilkey, Smith found that the contemporary tempera-

ment was concerned "for experience, for the actual suffering and undergoing that makes up our encounter with the world and each other" and consequently was baffled, even repelled, by Christian ideas that failed to provide an illuminating "diagnosis of the human predicament."[9]

In response to this cultural impatience with "meaningless" God-talk, Gilkey's strategy was to analyze the tacit presuppositions of "the secular spirit" itself, a cultural mood which he summarized as the "radically this-worldly" view that humanity is "set within a contingent, relative, and temporal context in which no ultimate order, coherence, or meaning—either in terms of an eternal rational structure or a sovereign divine will—appears, and so in which man is forced (or enabled) to create by his own powers whatever meaning his life on earth may achieve."[10] Gilkey chose not to repudiate this secular spirit but rather to argue that it failed to provide symbolic forms capable of adequately interpreting its own lived experience. Within secular life he then identified those situations in which a "dimension of ultimacy appears in ordinary experience," a dimension that can be appropriately thematized through theological symbols. "Inevitably in any culture, secular or religious," Gilkey concluded, "religious discourse or myths appear in relation to the mysteries of our origins, our limits, our ambiguity and evil, and our hopes for the future."[11] Particular theological traditions developed symbolic forms that interpreted in distinctive ways these general situations of human limit and possibility. Experience, as Smith explained, had a shared character and a public form because individual experiences presupposed "the belief that experience is continuous" and individuals could in fact compare their respective reports of what they have encountered. In this cumulative social labor, experience was not merely immediate, subjective, and individual; but "experience takes on an objective form as custom, tradition and habitual life which serve as the basis of all human community." In Smith's estimation fruitful engagement with the contemporary cultural mood required retrieving and reworking an experiential tradition in American theology that stretched back to Jonathan Edwards and that sought "to connect the meaning of theological ideas with human experience and to show their bearing on the life of each individual."[12]

The cultural eclipse of theological language, which thinkers such as Gilkey and Smith appraised and attempted to overcome, subsequently received various diagnoses. Certainly, the vigor and visibility of evangelical Protestantism throughout the seventies could be taken to demonstrate that the interpretive power of traditional theological language was undiminished in that sector of American religion. But theologians in mainstream seminaries and university-related divinity schools have most often concluded that the general difficulty Gilkey identified has, if anything, intensified. "Does ultimacy appear to us in the twentieth century at all?" Gilkey had asked. "Is there any way in which the unconditioned, the transcendent, and the holy manifest themselves to secular men?" He took this to be the basic question for "a prolegomenon to theology."[13] Dissatisfaction with the theological responses to this question, on the part of the theologians themselves, has raised a recurrent lament that theology is "marginal" to the intellectual and practical concerns of modern social institutions. No community, it seemed, actively promoted theological scholarship or regarded theology as important to its ongoing health. Theologians were not accorded the hearing among intellectuals and politicians that Paul Tillich and the Niebuhr brothers were recalled to have received at mid-century. And this "marginalization" was said to characterize not only the relation of theology to nation and university but its relation to the churches as well.[14] Not only could theology be regarded as a parochial or sectarian intrusion into politics or higher education, but it also stood at several removes from the concrete religious tasks of persuasion and compassion that occupied the daily labors of congregations and ministers. Summarizing the consequences of theology's "marginality" for ministerial education, Edward Farley of Vanderbilt Divinity School wrote in 1983 that "the present ethos of the Protestant churches is such that a theologically oriented approach to the preparation of ministers is not only irrelevant but counterproductive."[15] Theological inquiry had, from Farley's perspective, lost its audience in the churches; it was no longer one of the capacities recognized as needful for carrying out the duties of ministerial leadership.

I have argued that, in the opening phase of American theological inquiry, *the seminary ideal* had portrayed a coherent spiritual discipline in which the complementarity of piety, civic leadership, and learning in the life of the scholar was analogous to the ideal social harmony among church, nation, and school. From the outset of the American experiment, these idealized harmonies were subjected to centrifugal social forces that made the religious coherence of America and the religious coherence of the self the dominant theological problems. The three publics of theology and the increasingly diverse assumptions and life disciplines each implied became ever more difficult for theologians to coordinate. Theologians, in brief, had difficulty establishing the theory, symbols, course of action, and audience implied in their own lived experience. The crisis of the meaningfulness or intelligibility of God-language represented a crisis of the search for a "common human experience," that is, a shared form of life for which religious language made sense. In this search, academic theology was becoming increasingly abstract not merely because it was becoming more technical but, more important, because its community of intelligibility was becoming increasingly diffuse. The eclipse of God-language was, in other words, a crisis in the communal frame of reference for theological reflection. Theology had lost both its publics and its Public.

Daniel Day Williams had written his essay, of course, at the beginning of one of the most turbulent decades of modern American history, a critical decade in the movements for the civil rights of African Americans and women, a decade of controversy over the conduct of war in Southeast Asia, a decade of political assassination. In the course of social conflict and trauma, the decisive differences in the experiences of Americans seemed to arise from race, class, or gender, and these far overshadowed the diversity of denominational theological traditions that had been the primary subject of Williams's reflections on the religious diversity of America. The election of a Roman Catholic president, the religious changes set in motion by the Second Vatican Council, widespread cultural interest in Islam and Asian religions, and the growth of Protestant conservative and evangelical churches not only drew new attention to the diversity of the nation but evoked different categories for understanding that diversity. By the seventies, a cultural "center," once claimed by mainstream Protestantism, became increasingly difficult to discern amid the compelling assertion of alternatives. Americans had begun redrawing the mental map of their pluralism.

This cultural cartography has been especially pronounced in American higher education, including the theological schools. Women and minorities, on faculties and among students, have challenged the priorities of theological study and called for a greater diversity of representation and for a curriculum that more adequately engaged this diversity. In so doing, they have presented a second challenge to the assumed threefold public of theological studies, by offering *a new version of the classically American appeal to experience* for the material of theological reflection and the criteria of theological judgment. Unlike Daniel Day Williams, however, they have not associated experience with the underlying commonalities of American life. Instead, *experience* underscores the particular, the individual, the distinctive, that marks the boundaries of ethnicity, gender, class, and race. Williams had appealed to *common experience* in order to establish a principle of cultural unity that counteracted American religious pluralism. More recent American theologians have appealed to *particular experience* in order to resist an imposed unity. A group of women scholars engaged in a collaborative analysis of theological education, the "Mud Flower Collective," has crisply stated this affirmatively pluralistic outlook on the contextual relativity of intellectual inquiry: "We take with utmost seriousness our racial and ethnic differences as fundamental to our work. We will attempt to lift up rather than gloss over our various perspectives and priorities. Among us, as should be the case throughout theological education, cultural pluralism is critical to examining the value of what is taught and what is learned."[16] The insistence that thought is socially embedded requires that thinkers become critically reflective about their experiential starting points, and the "Collective" goes on to assert that "to do theology ourselves we must begin with our experience of ourselves in relation."[17]

As historian David A. Hollinger has recently remarked, contemporary American thinkers have become "situation-conscious intellectuals," whose perspectives on the culture are strongly marked by a sense that perceptions, beliefs, and ideals are temporally contingent and socially shaped. *Experience*, in short, is culturally constructed. Broadly speaking, the trend of recent intellectual history has been toward the critical analysis of ideas in terms of the social location of the thinker and the social group in which the thinker participates, a trend away from speech about the universal or the common and toward what Hollinger describes as the particularity of "ethnos-centered discourse."[18] When compared to the discourse of scholars shaped by Reformed Christianity and its extension in twentieth-century "mainstream Protestantism," this gives every appearance of a sharp departure. Even granting the important conceptual space that Richard Niebuhr cleared for plural perspectives in American culture, the general orientation of the Reformed/ mainstream academic tradition had consistently inclined toward encompassing differences in broader ecumenical or civic commonalities.

Emphasis on the particularity of experience by these "situation-conscious intellectuals" has not, however, simply turned "ethnos-centered discourse" inward onto the cultivation of group life and identity. On the contrary, their work has been ethically engaged with the "situation," underscoring the scholar's responsibility for social criticism. Critique of inherited practice attends and reinforces the new attention to pluralism, by drawing out the implicit moral structure of historical narratives, insisting on the scholar's moral accountability within history, and evaluating not only the "interests" that shape scholarly retrieval of the past but also the expectations that orient action toward a future. The religious experience of gender, class, or racial groups is taken to point beyond itself to structural inequities in the society as a whole, thus pointing as well to normative principles or idealized social relations that cast judgment on present circumstance. Even the most "situation-conscious" among the theologians are discontent with unqualified allegiance to what Jonathan Edwards had earlier called "a private circle or system of beings, which are but a small part of the whole." They have instead proposed that "the situation" discloses transcending principles of justice and that the particular community represents the plight and the aspirations of encompassing human communities.[19]

These were notes sounded early and eloquently by Martin Luther King, who for reasons of principle and of strategy believed that "constructive alliances" not "isolation" represented the road for African Americans to "achieve our humanity's full stature." In his book *Where Do We Go from Here?* (1968) King challenged African Americans with the conviction that "abused and scorned though we may be, our destiny is tied up with the destiny of America." The struggle of African Americans for civil justice was funded, in King's view, by the conviction that "America must be a nation in which its multiracial people are partners in power," and he therefore saw in the solidarity of black Americans not only the hope for their own renewal but the hope for the renewal of national life on the basis of the common good, "enlarging the whole society, and giving it a new sense of values as we seek to solve our particular problem."[20]

> In the days ahead we must not consider it unpatriotic to raise certain basic questions about our national character. . . . All these questions remind us that there is need for a radical restructuring of the architecture of American society. . . . Let us, therefore, not think of our movement as one that seeks to integrate the Negro into all the existing values of American society. Let us be those creative dissenters who will call our beloved nation to a higher destiny, to a new plateau of compassion, to a more noble expression of humaneness.[21]

The recent work of Cornel West similarly proposes that the most intractable divisions in American society, those constructed around race, are at one and the same time tragic realities and fateful misapprehensions of the situation. Both liberal and conservative social critics, writes West, "fail to see that the presence and predicaments of black people are neither additions to nor defections from American life, but rather *constitutive elements of that life.*" To create the social space for genuine difference requires public debate oriented by commitment to the common good. "To establish a new framework, we need to begin with a frank acknowledgment of the basic humanness and Americanness of each of us," West declares, "and we must acknowledge that as a people—*E Pluribus Unum*—we are on a slippery slope toward economic strife, social turmoil, and cultural chaos."[22] On this model, different trajectories of tradition and experience, even if they do not arise from the common experience presupposed in

Williams's earlier analysis, may converge in identifying an arena of common problems. The diversity of communal heritages and experiences, the variegated forms that identity may take, it is argued, need not derive from a common experience in order to represent and promote the common good.

The assumption that academic theology addresses or interprets a *common experience* that lends religious coherence to American life has thus fractured along two lines: the relation of theological interpretation to *ordinary experience* and the relation of theological interpretation to *particular experience*. Along one fracture, theologians have encountered the nagging sense of distance between academic theology and the concrete experience of communities—even and especially religious communities. The issues here might be generally characterized as *the difficulty of convoking a public* for theological study. Along the other fracture, theologians have struggled to enunciate the ways in which difference and particularity might contribute to "a theology of the human community." In this case, the issues might be generally characterized as *the difficulty of establishing coherent relationships among diverse publics*. As I will indicate in the next section of this chapter, difficulties in the relation of academic theology to its publics have their parallels in difficulties with the scope and coherence of the theological curriculum, the relationships among the elements of what was once called the theological encyclopedia. For this reason, proposals for the reform of theological education have recapitulated the contest over *experience* in recent American theology, and rhetoric of identity and diversity, of pluralism and unity, floods the discourse.[23] The current reappraisal of theological study is so thoroughgoing precisely because it is pursuing heavily related basic issues, simultaneously and interactively, both as questions about its coherence as a discipline and as questions about its relationships to a traditional threefold public in nation, academy, and church. In pursuing this double agenda of public accountability and disciplinary coherence, the debate, of course, partially replicates the "seasons of reform" in theological education that have been illustrated in the preceding chapters. In no small measure, therefore, the changes that contemporary scholars prescribe for theological study today will depend on their evaluation of the success of earlier efforts to resolve these issues and their evaluation of the extent and power of the *distinctive* features in the current situation.

Theology and Its Publics

Without pretending that any single scheme can offer a full descriptive appraisal of the diverse contemporary proposals for reforming theological studies, I do think that history helps. In part, it helps because it affords a clearer sense of what is distinctive in our current religious situation and what is a feature or tendency of longer duration. Theological reformers have difficulty remembering this very obvious point. From revivalism, to transcendentalism, to liberal modernism, to the neo-orthodox assault on the modernist impulse, the theologians encountered in the preceding chapters have displayed a remarkable tendency to establish their theological positions by repudiating the immediately preceding "generation." The premium that the academic community places on the production of "original" research has, of course, exacerbated this tendency. To the extent that current interpretations of the theologian's work incline toward this same tradition of anti-traditional intellectual lurching, it is time, I believe, to pause and take a more measured account of our predecessors, their failings and their achievements as they are seen from our own limited standpoint. Only so will we also take the measure of our own context. Not every wheel requires reinvention. But some do.

As an experiment in historical reading of the relationships between contemporary theological scholars and their publics, I will therefore interpret recent proposals for the reform of theological education in terms of two traditional understandings of theology. In using these traditional definitions to describe recent reform proposals, I will also recast the definitions in order to suggest how they might fruitfully address the contemporary aims and purposes of academic theology. The first, encountered especially in chapter 1, regarded theological study as a *catechetical inquiry.* Its principal aim was the transformative appropriation of Christian teaching, such that this teaching functioned as a wisdom about the conduct of life. It took the form of questions and answers that probed the meaning and consequences of basic Christian affirmations. So, for example,

Martin Luther opened his *Large Catechism* with the first of the Ten Commandments—"You shall have no other gods"—and was immediately prompted to ask, "What does this mean, and how is it to be understood? What is it to have a god? What is God?"[24] Luther then responded to these questions in such a way as to guide the educative meditations of the reader. The second definition, encountered especially in chapter 3, regarded theological study as a *synthetic inquiry*. Its governing purpose was the articulation of plausible relations between Christian teaching and other interpretations of the modern world—philosophical, scientific, psychological, historical—such that theology proposed a coherence for conduct in the manifold domains of modern life. It assumed that, while Christian traditions might prompt distinctive questions that shaped a distinctive perspective, these were questions and perspectives not on an exclusive religious domain but on the common life of all. And, it set about to argue how this was the case. Both models, it will be recalled, included both a characteristic public stance and a distinctive professional formation of the theologian. And, both entailed a curricular organization of theological study designed to achieve these societal and personal purposes. The current contests over *experience* in academic theology have disrupted and partially reconfigured both models.

Catechetical inquiry formed the theological student in a tradition. As such, it assumed a community of relative stability, a community that had confidently identified the important questions a proper "catechism" should ask, even when it did not agree on the answers. A "given" set of questions about the purposes and conduct of life provided a framework within which particular moral choices or religious practices could be intelligently debated, and this catechetically ordered debate gradually molded a church's culture. In the current disruption of academic theology's relation to its historic publics, numerous scholars have called for retrieval of the catechetical dimension to theological inquiry, which would mold personal religious identity and ecclesial culture.

In the long history of such appeals for academic theology's catechetical contribution to the church,[25] the perennial question in religiously plural America has, of course, been "which church?" But in previous eras it was popularly assumed that this was roughly identical to the question "which denomination?" And the longstanding contribution of seminaries to denominational formation had reinforced that assumption. Since the 1970s, however, theologians and social analysts have become increasingly persuaded of the denomination's decline, both as a mediating institution between congregations and wider publics and as a mediator of personal religious identity. Not only does denominational religion face a situation of ever more scarce financial resources for its social and religious enterprises, but, especially among the mainstream denominations, denominational affiliation seems to play a declining role in the religious identity or spirituality of individual church members. Gender, ethnicity, race, educational attainment, or class are widely regarded as more determinative of religious identity than denominational membership.[26] Hence, recent reflection on the nature and purposes of theological education has struggled with the relation to its ecclesial public and sought to understand, in the phrase of Joseph C. Hough and John B. Cobb, the connection between "Christian identity and theological education."

Many commentators have agreed with Hough and Cobb that the basis for reform of theological education must be a "strong conviction about who we are as a Christian people," but they have disagreed over the concrete locus of this sense of Christian peoplehood. In their own proposal, for example, Hough and Cobb emphasize *the church as a global institution*, whose local manifestations ought to be informed by awareness of its world historical context. They and others have called for the "globalization" of theological education and would replace the question "which church?" with the question "what is the place of the church in the history of life on this planet?"[27] Such proposals perpetuate the classic emphasis of mainstream Protestant theological educators on education which will open students to ecumenical horizons. But, the parallel to earlier mainstream ideals is only partial. This is the case because, in its earlier form, the mainstream ideal for "Christian identity" had assumed that students possessed a relatively clear denominational religious identity, which seminary education could *expand* by cultivating appreciation for the complex mix of traditions that made up Christianity as a whole. In the present religious environment, however, the problem is less often expanding a denominationally shaped Christian identity than it is consolidating such a Christian identity for students who come to their theological studies with little in the way of informed allegiance to the particular traditions of the churches. To respond to the rather nebulous sense of Christian identity among many seminarians, the late James Hopewell, a historian of religions at Emory University, proposed an alternative answer to the question "which church?" by suggesting that *the local congregation* should become the paradigm for theological education. Rather than dealing at high levels of generalization about church, world, and people, said Hopewell, theological inquiry should be concretely "directed to finding out how church and world are in fact instantiated in a particular place, what forms the historical and ecumenical context of a local church, what makes the church local, and what constitutes its human situation and informs its response as a church."[28] Carried to its conclusions, such a proposal might reintroduce some features of the apprenticeship that once characterized reading divinity and that constructed parallels between the subjects of theological study and the concrete intellectual practices of ministry. Other educators have wondered, however, whether a congregational paradigm for formation provides students the necessary critical principles to appraise and, when necessary, challenge the moral and religious assumptions of local Christian practice.[29] In sum, uncertainties about the relationships among local, denominational, and general manifestations of Christian tradition have left theological educators perplexed about the ways in which commitments to each of these various manifestations can work to correct the others in the process of catechetical formation.

Such uncertainty about the catechetical power of academic theology has manifested itself in criticism of the theological curriculum, often popularly expressed as discontent over the bifurcation of theological "theory" and religious "practice." Of course, the conviction that Christian ideas should directly influence the conduct of life has long been paramount among American Protestant theologians, who from diverse perspectives have shared the view that theology was a theory of lived experience, that it was, in Jonathan Edwards's phrase, "the doctrine of living to God by Christ." But, as Langdon Gilkey's analysis made clear, questions about whether this any longer remained the case generated a sense of crisis among theologians of the sixties. In order to reestablish the function of theology in common experience, proposals for curricular reform in the 1960s and 1970s regularly employed the educational metaphor of building a "bridge" between "theory" and "practice." But, by the beginning of the eighties, scholars concerned with the reform of theological education were concluding that the theory-to-practice model was less a resolution of the relation of theology to common experience than a symptom of the problem. In 1979, for example, Robert W. Lynn, vice-president for religion at the Lilly Endowment, sharply criticized the curricular reforms of the sixties, finding that for all their "melodramatic talk" about a crisis in theological education that required radical new models, these proposals actually reduced to the "now shopworn idea" that education must move from theory to practice through "a two-phase curriculum, one stage devoted to 'academic' work and the second to 'practice-centered' or 'professional' studies." Was it the case, he asked, that these parallel distinctions between academic and professional, between theory and practice, were "fated to be the boundaries that will always encase the seminary curriculum?"[30]

In response to Lynn's question, theological ethicist Joseph C. Hough reflected on the educational politics implied by the theory-practice dichotomy. Hough attributed "the lack of coherence in theological education today" primarily to the conflicting claims of the academic disciplines in the university, on the one hand, and, on the other hand, the requirements of church constituencies, especially clergy who emphasized the need for functional skills of professional ministry. Hough, in other words, elaborated the political implications of the seminary's origins as a "hybrid creation," operating between the spheres of the church and of higher education, by suggesting how curricular debate had implied that "theory" entailed an allegiance to the academy and "practice" an allegiance to church and clergy. "The continuing tension between the claims of conflicting and powerful professional groups on faculty members and theological schools as a whole," Hough argued, "constitutes the political boundary for the present discussion of reform in theological education." In reply to Robert Lynn's query of whether the theory-practice dichotomy was fated to be the conceptual boundary of the theological curriculum, Hough replied that it was so fated "unless we can find concrete ways to modify the impact of the political realities on which that distinction rests and from which it continues to exercise its powerful influence."[31]

Nor was the felt separation of theory from practice the only point of "fragmentation" in the theological curriculum. The alignment of theological disciplines with other academic disciplines dissipated the controlling or governing questions that ordered catechetical reflection. As Gilkey had warned, this dispersal tempted the theologian to become "an amateur in cultural analysis," borrowing methods and issues from other fields, and produced a problem of method concerning "the sources, content, and criteria of theology as a form of thought."[32] Edward Farley, responding to such considerations in several essays and in his influential book of 1983, *Theologia: The Fragmentation and Unity of Theological Education*, developed a historical argument for the unity of theology. Classically understood, he said, theology was "a cognitive disposition and orientation of the soul, a knowledge of God and what God reveals." At the same time, this Christian sagacity was "a wisdom which can be promoted, deepened, and extended by human study and argument," and since this was the case the term theology had also meant a disciplined course of study.[33] Farley traced the "dispersal" of this unitary study into the fourfold theological encyclopedia of Bible, church history, dogmatics, and practical theology during the eighteenth and nineteenth centuries. In the twentieth century, Farley asserted, these four historic fields had become independent scientific disciplines more closely allied with various humanistic fields in the university than with one another. Meanwhile, ministry had come to be circumscribed functionally in a set of ecclesiastical duties and skills, and a double problem thus arose. First, how should one explain the unity of the four separate disciplines that collectively comprise theological studies? Second, how did these four academic disciplines actually contribute to ministerial formation? Farley concluded that the educational dichotomy between academic theory and ministerial practice reflected and reinforced these problems rather than solved them. Retrieving a unified purpose for theological study therefore required a renewed understanding of the nature of theological inquiry itself as a cognitive disposition, or wisdom, directed toward God.[34] In this way, reconsideration of the theological curriculum has combined with the more general concern for the formation of "Christian identity" in order to emphasize the nature of theology as a set of interpretive capacities or a process of practical reasoning rather than as a system of beliefs or a collection of "subject-matters" to be mastered. Theologians were reintroducing into theological study the classic educational concern for formation.

Hence, the contemporary rethinking of theology as a catechetical inquiry includes rethinking its character as a *critical inquiry*, that is, an inquiry which aims to achieve reflective awareness about the standards of judgment appropriate to some prior, ongoing human activity. In the case of theology, that ongoing human activity is the activity of Christian communities, and the educational intent is to form a capacity for critical judgment with respect to the life of these communities.[35] In the 1980s, the desire to cultivate this critical capacity refocused curricular attention on what Gerald Birney Smith had once named the "neglected field": practical theology.[36] Smith had found it necessary to rethink practical theology at the beginning of the century, because he believed it was inadequate to restrict the term to a set of clerical functions that maintained the ongoing activities of churches. Changing understandings of ministry and of theological scholarship, he thought, required a reconsideration of the underlying purpose of these practices in order to reshape them for the present age. Similarly, contemporary reconsideration of practical theology has concerned itself less with training for concrete ministerial functions, preaching, for example, than with rethinking theology itself as an enterprise of practical reflection, constantly reevaluating the use of time and energy by the church in light of an interpretation of the church's history and its role in the wider society. The work of the ministry for which theological students are trained, in this view, is a work of reflective practice, cognizant of the minister's responsibility to the church's corporate memory which funds or informs practice.[37] This effort includes a renewed emphasis on the hermeneutical relationship with the past, in which the inquirer is pressed to be self-conscious about his or her own historical context and the contextual predispositions that influence the scholar's perspective on the temporal life of individuals and institutions. The emphasis on reflective practice in the new practical theology has often taken a critically transformative stance both toward the Christian tradition and toward the surrounding society. From this transformative posture, Don Browning writes, the "overall dynamic is the reconstruction of experience." When common sense understanding of ordinary life is disrupted, "when inherited interpretations and practices seem to be breaking down, practical reason tries to reconstruct both its picture of the world and its more concrete practices."[38]

In an era when the environing community of theological study does not have relative stability, as Browning's comment suggests, catechetical inquiry cannot simply mean the formation of students by critical reflection on inherited practice. When communal cultures are in disarray, there is especial urgency to the observation of Harvard theologian Ronald Thiemann that "theological inquiry has the particular aim of seeking a critical reconstruction of the community within which it operates."[39] This notion of the "critical reconstruction of the community" retrieves another dimension of catechetical inquiry and its questions. Indeed, I think it is a dimension that needs to be accentuated, and an important clue to its character comes from the most penetrating of the Protestant interpreters of ecclesial culture, John Williamson Nevin. In his 1847 study of the great doctrinal standard of the German Reformed Church, the Heidelberg Catechism, Nevin observed that the catechism was the product of the religious life of the Reformed Church at the time, and it was the product in a particular sense. The catechism, he said, so embodied the church in speech that it was "recognized and responded to by the Church at large as its own word."[40] That is, the "genius" of the Heidelberg Catechism was its capacity to convoke a public, to call a public into self-conscious life by articulating its unspoken or hitherto unrecognized common life. Thought of from this perspective, catechetical inquiry poses the questions that disparate groups and individuals have failed to discern as common or shared questions, but that, having once been expressed, convoke a wider public and name its common cause. In convoking this public it raises the possibility of spiritual formation for those who acknowledge their life within this newly named community.

This convocative capability of theological inquiry is, perhaps, the common thread that runs through the various contemporary appeals for a "public theology." Theologians have long claimed a role of interpreting national life. But, as we have seen, the "ground rules" for this public role are the subject of a longstanding debate and have, perhaps, never been less clear than today. The contemporary affirmation of cultural diversity, for instance, has sweepingly challenged the Christian theologian's role as the bearer of a national religious consensus. And, when "pluralism" is combined with the chronic American split between public and private, any role for theology beyond the community of religious affiliation becomes even more problematic than usual. The theologians have thus concurred with those social analysts who find that a process of privatization of religion, already evident in the eighteenth century, has culminated in the twentieth by restricting the role of religion to the composure of private life and the influence of theology to internal communication within religious communities. As the legal scholar Stephen L. Carter has recently observed in *The Culture of Disbelief,* "We often ask our citizens to split their public and private selves, telling them in effect that it is fine to be religious in private, but there is something askew when those private beliefs become the basis for public action."[41] Hence, a religious thinker who ventures to take a position on economic, political, or cultural issues facing the American commonwealth is likely to be regarded simply as the representative of one "interest group" among many involved in a general competition for social power or influence. There is, moreover, an especial skepticism directed toward "interest groups" who have the temerity to claim that their "interest" is the common good. "Religion," concluded sociologist Robert Bellah in 1982, "no longer had a public role, because religion was no longer seen as the bearer of a public truth."[42]

Theologians have sought to overcome this enforced privatization, in part, by proposing new coalitions as the communal basis for religious interpretations of national life. Historian of Christianity Martin E. Marty, for example, has stated the "need for an awakened public church," a communion of churches "mainline, evangelical, Catholic," that was "especially sensitive to the res publica, the public order that surrounds and includes people of faith." He and others have challenged such a publicly oriented church to enunciate a "*public theology*" that would "interpret the life of a people in the light of a transcendent reference."[43] The call for *public theology*, in other words, seeks to promote the theologians' historic role in civic debate by simultaneously honoring distinctive religious communities and by appealing for a more inclusive community of theological interpreters, less subject to the charge (and the fact) of pleading a special interest. At the same time, the call for public theology also reasserts the traditional vision of theology as the bearer of social transformation. Recent expositors of public theology, attempting to articulate the critical theological principles for reform, have both directed attention to a common life that underlies social and cultural divisions and criticized the moral, political, and social assumptions tacit within the intellectual and institutional forms of that common life. By reclaiming this two-point agenda, writes Linell Cady, public theologians will "contribute to the upbuilding and the critical transformation of our common life."[44]

As the example of public theology reminds us, the historic public of academic theology in the Protestant tradition has never simply been the church. Instead, since the colonial period, the formation of the theologian has been not toward a single public but rather toward a threefold public, comprised of church, nation, and academy. As chapters 2, 3, and 4 have argued, it was the dispersal of this threefold public into relatively independent domains of responsibility that prompted the mode of theology that I have called *synthetic inquiry*, theological scholarship explicitly organized to establish plausible, systematic connections between religious thought and the major domains of modern life as these were embodied in national economic and political life or in the disciplines of American higher education. Theology as synthetic inquiry thus arose contextually from theology as catechetical inquiry in order to meet the challenge of convoking manifold publics as a single, coherent public whose common questions could be the basis for formation of the theological student. Doubts about the possibility of such an enterprise have disrupted the connnections of theology to its publics and especially the connection between church and university.[45]

In the years since Williams's essay, these disrupted connections have arisen primarily from three substantial shifts in the relation between theological education and its university public. First, the emergence and rapid expansion of departments of religious studies in colleges and universities provided a fresh academic embodiment of scholarship in religion, one that pursued, as its "foremost" responsibility, studies that were "intrinsically multi-cultural, directed to more than one religious tradition." Especially since the 1970s, these departments have sought to organize their work not only, obviously, to avoid "sectarian bias" but also to distinguish their curricular form, method, and purpose from the fourfold theological encyclopedia aimed at ministerial education.[46] Second, also during the seventies, theological seminaries relaxed the historic tension between academic and churchly loyalties and turned increased institutional emphasis toward their denominational connections and responsibility to provide educational services to church and ministry.[47] Third, a 1976 report by George Lindbeck of Yale Divinity School concerning the ecclesiastically independent university-related divinity schools identified a further symptom of the diverging publics of theological scholarship. Through their engagement in "the academically and intellectually responsible transmission and development of particular religious heritages," Lindbeck asserted, university divinity schools had long constituted "the main institutional bridge between the university and organized religion in our society," but now, Lindbeck feared, "they seem to be losing their function of mediating between the university on the one hand and religious bodies on the other."[48] Meanwhile, academic nomenclature, which with increasing frequency distinguished between "religious studies" and "theological studies," was mirroring distinct institutional embodiments attended by dispute—sometimes sharp dispute—about contrasting educational purposes and commitments.[49] The dual accountability of theology to academy and to church was, perhaps, moving toward a separation, with "religious studies" oriented toward the university and "theological studies" oriented toward the churches. Commonly, the issue turned on a point familiar in American higher education since the close of the nineteenth century, namely, the notion that theology appeals to special criteria for its truth claims and that theologians have prior commitments to the truth of their theological assertions, thus placing their scholarship beyond appraisal by the general criteria for truth that characterize, at least in principle, the scholarship of universities.[50] Frequently these debates over the relation of commitment to critical inquiry focused on the relation between a theologian's freedom to pursue questions of truth in his or her discipline and a theologian's religious commitment to and participation in a church. But the modern condition is constituted precisely by responsibility amidst the contending multiplicity of commitments, and William F. May has argued, rightly in my judgment, that "the university should organize itself around the principle that the truth must be pursued without compromise, and not around the principle that membership in the academic community intrinsically demands the shattering of ties to all other communities that make claims to insight and truth."[51]

During the past twenty years, as the preceding examples perhaps suggest, the most intractable difficulties have not involved the relations of academic theology to any one of its publics but rather the development of styles of theological reflection that effectively addressed and connected different publics. The dual responsibility of theological education to the church and to the modern university, in particular, has prompted innumerable, sometimes polemical, essays. And in some cases, such as the seminaries of the Southern Baptist Convention, disagreement about the constraints that doctrinal orthodoxy places on academic research has generated considerable institutional friction. Despite apparently widespread interest in the academic study of religion not only in departments of religious studies but in such fields as English, history, and classics, some interpreters have concluded that universities today are so secularized as to be inhospitable to explicitly Christian perspectives on scholarly work. The historian of American religion George M. Marsden, for example, has described the century from the 1870s to the 1970s as one in which the nation "moved from an era when organized Christianity and explicitly Christian ideals had a major role in the leading institutions of higher education to an era when they have almost none." In the most recent past universities have been marked by the pursuit of technical disciplines disinterested in larger questions about the intellectual unity of the university and by "an aggressive pluralistic secularism." "In the name of equality and the rights of women and minorities," pluralistic secularism, according to Marsden, "questions all beliefs as mere social constructions, challenges what is left of the old consensus ideology, attacks the Western-oriented canon, and repudiates many conventional ethical assumptions." In light of his analysis, Marsden makes two prescriptive proposals. First, religiously committed scholars should advocate a broader tolerance in the academy that "would involve allowing all sorts of Christian and other religiously based intellectual traditions back into the discussion" from which they have been largely excluded in the past generation. Second, says Marsden, Christians may need to "recognize that they are part of an unpopular sect" and begin building "distinctly Christian universities" that will provide alternatives to the predominantly secular universities of contemporary America.[52]

Such sweeping polarizations could perhaps be tested by a survey of university faculty attitudes toward religious commitment, but it is perhaps more to the point to recall why academic theologians engaged themselves in the life of universities in the first place. Since they wished to understand the interdependence of all life, they had no desire to isolate Christian theology and ethics from critical points of view in order to maintain the unique, historic identity of Christianity. Instead, they believed that insofar as Christianity was interested in "the truth about life" its proponents needed to be able to test its claims to truth against other interpretations, perhaps especially the ones that were most critical.[53] Still more, they recognized that persons generally do not fully know what they believe until they are called upon to articulate it, and, hence, they thought that Christian faith needed the university precisely in order to clarify for itself, through expression, what its own orientation in fact was.[54] Presumably, they also hoped that they would be included in university discussion not because it had been unfair for some academics to exclude them but because they had something interesting to say. Articulating the connections of theology to the life of universities and of the nation has not, in short, been an "extra assignment" that academic theologians have undertaken but rather a task they took to be constitutive of theology as a catechetical and a synthetic inquiry.

The Background of Possibilities

In the preceding sections of this chapter I have taken Daniel Day Williams's clue, that *experience* has been a key category throughout the history of theological scholarship in the American Protestant tradition, in order to map the contemporary intellectual issues facing theological education. In the context of religious pluralism, said Williams, theologians desired to offer a persuasive interpretation of the American religious circumstance as a whole but could not do so by simple appeal to the belief and practice of any particular tradition. They therefore turned to experience as a potential source of commonality amidst their differences. *As a source for theological reflection,* the boundaries between particular experience and common experience have proven permeable and perennially contested. Some, like Emerson, sought to heighten the authority of the personal by claiming for intuition an apprehension of common experience in its wholeness. Others sought to order personal experience by emphasizing the authority of collective experience expressed in traditional belief. Certainly, experience did not prove to be any sort of escape hatch from diversity. At the same time that experience became a source for theological reflection, it also became *a criterion for theological judgments,* on the pragmatic argument that theological ideas "mattered" because they had a bearing on the common conduct of life. This experiential pragmatism, as we have seen, launched a long effort by academic theologians to demonstrate the social utility of "theological science." As a criterion of theological reflection, experience proved a severe master for the theological scholars, constantly challenging them to demonstrate the meaning of systematic theological reflection for everyday life in church and civil society.

Thus, the category *experience* connotes many things. It can refer to what everybody knows or what is intensely private and inaccessible to the public gaze. It may underscore the immediacy of the present by calling attention to a "defining moment" in the life of a group, or it may instead call to mind the seasoned professional, whose "experience" qualifies her for the job. The impact of its employment in theological inquiry has been manifold, and it has been slippery as it changed its shape. It is omnipresent. Nevertheless, its employments are both important and important to understand, in order to retrieve and reconceive the purposes of academic theology and the cultural vocation of theological scholarship.

In order to consolidate the most important meanings of the concept *experience* in American theological scholarship, I will set forth three interpretive principles not directly from the theologians themselves but rather from the American thinker whose analysis of experience best captures its cultural significance, William James. I will then conclude by proposing how attention to experience as source and criterion for theology has historically shaped the vocation of the theological scholar as a *public intellectual* by orienting inquiry "toward a theology of the human community."

In *The Varieties of Religious Experience,* James observed that "the lustre of the present hour is always borrowed from the background of possibilities it goes with."[55]

> Let our common experiences be enveloped in an eternal moral order; let our suffering have an immortal significance; let Heaven smile upon the earth, and deities pay their visits; let faith and hope be the atmosphere which man breathes in;— and his days pass by with zest; they stir with prospects, they thrill with remoter values. Place round them on the contrary the curdling cold and gloom and absence of all meaning which for pure naturalism . . . of our time is all that is visible ultimately, and the thrill stops short, or turns rather to an anxious trembling.[56]

From this suggestive image, my initial Jamesian observation on experience is that the comprehensive interpretive stage on which human action is set largely determines the particular actions in which a human will venture to engage. The *background* James portrayed includes consciously held values or beliefs, cultural moods fostering optimism or gloom, and widely available but unspoken assumptions that "envelop" their inhabitants so completely as to be beyond discussion. Such notions—about the capacity of humans to change, about the overarching direction of change, about the exercise of power, about the limits to power, or about personal and corporate identity—are what Shailer Mathews and H. Richard Niebuhr, in their different ways, spoke of as the "patterns" of coherence that delineate a civilization. Without such a background of possibilities, the foreground of human agency lacks the comprehensive interpretive pattern that situates thought and conduct, that orients it toward the "prospects" of some hoped-for future. "The lustre of the present hour is always borrowed from the background of possibilities it goes with."

James's metaphor has several similarities to the quotation from Walter Lippmann's *Preface to Morals* with which this book began. Both men thought that the "events" of life have a "dignity" or stir with "prospects" because they are situated within a comprehensive pattern of meaning. In Lippmann's phrase, it is the sense of being "an actor in a great and dramatic destiny" that prompts and sustains ethical engagement with the world by persons and groups. Loss of this "theory of the meaning and value of events," by contrast, leaves the actor innervated by the sense of being the victim of massive, but mutely incoherent, social and natural forces. For the theological scholars surveyed in the preceding narrative, this "background of possibilities" as the theater of moral action has been the governing preoccupation of their academic inquiry. Hence, as Daniel Day Williams suggested, the empirical orientation toward experience as source and criterion for theological judgments displays strong continuities with the emphasis on providence characteristic of the Reformed theological heritage in which the beginnings of American theological scholarship were so deeply rooted. Attentiveness to lived experience and the clues it gave as to its larger—its comprehensive—context gave continuity to the quite different views of the scholarly enterprise advanced in one era by Nevin or Emerson and in another by Mathews or Niebuhr.

At no point in American history, of course, was this "background of possibilities" seen in a single way, and the plurality of perspectives has itself been a continuing concern of the theologians, most notably in the past twenty years. This pluralism of possibilities James also recognized, and it yields a second Jamesian interpretation of experience. "The obvious outcome of our total experience," he wrote, "is that the world can be handled according to many systems of ideas, and is so handled by men, and will each time give some characteristic kind of profit, for which he cares, to the handler, while at the same time some other kind of profit has to be omitted or postponed."[57] Hence, in the final book of his career, *A Pluralistic Universe* (1909), James reversed the flow of influence between "the background of possibilities" and "the present hour." Now it was particular personal and collective experiences and interests that shaped the world in order to give "some characteristic kind of profit" to the interpreter. Our particular experiences, James declared, were the root, by analogical extension, of the comprehensive background.

> The only material we have at our disposal for making a picture of the whole world is supplied by the various portions of that world of which we have already had experience. We can invent no new forms of conception, applicable to the whole exclusively, and not suggested originally by the parts. All philosophers, accordingly, have conceived of the whole world after the analogy of some particular feature of it which has particularly captivated their attention.[58]

In so stating the situation, James assumed a world in which alternative backgrounds were present and available, in a kind of malleable reciprocity with particular experiences. "Why," he asked, "may not the world be so complex as to consist of many interpenetrating spheres of reality, which we can thus approach in alternation by using different conceptions and assuming different attitudes."[59] At certain times or for certain groups the background may seem to possess a large measure of coherence. As such, some will accept it as the starting point of scholarly reflection, while others will strenuously resist in the name of an alternative rendering. Indeed, a good part of the development of academic theology has unfolded as argument, between revivalists and "old Calvinists," between modernists and fundamentalists, over which background presuppositions should remain stable and which required change. In such intellectual combats, the most pervasive background presuppositions are, of course, well-hidden, and it takes an unusually acute "hermeneutic of suspicion" to discover the convictions tacitly *shared* by the opposing sides. It is the very rare American scholar who actually delivers an answer to the Emersonian question "Why should not we also enjoy an original relation to the universe?" But despite these caveats, James's central point remains, that the world described is always *our* world, shaped by the interests with which we approach it and fashioned "after the analogy of some particular feature of it which has particularly captivated our attention."

For this reason, both the background of possibilities and our common experiences, James believed, were fluid. Neither consisted of clearly bounded entities: "the Christian tradition" or "biblical faith" or "the African American experience" or "the church." On the contrary, "the concrete pulses of experience appear pent in by no such definite limits as our conceptual substitutes for them are confined by. They run into one another continuously and seem to interpenetrate."[60] Neither the Christian tradition nor secular experience presents itself as an inherent unity. Indeed, the theologian's most demandingly creative work may be precisely the process of sorting the melange of culturally available ideas into interpretive categories such as *Christian* and *secular*. This Jamesian consideration is especially important in relation to the current emphasis on the contextuality of theology among that large group of us who fall within David Hollinger's category of "situation-conscious intellectuals." When "context" and "situation" become paramount for interpretation, our descriptive premises about the context go far toward determining our judgments about it. The prescription follows from the diagnosis. Delimiting the situation, identifying its distinctive features, and placing it within larger contexts are descriptive judgments of conceptualization that profoundly influence the normative and ethical judgments of the theological interpreter.[61]

Consequently, self-consciousness about the interests and prejudgments that inform the theologian's own perspective have never been more critical. This, it would seem, is one reason that contemporary theological education has been concerned about issues of student formation. Critical knowledge of the intellectual traditions of Christianity are indispensable to the theologian's self-critical approach to scholarship. Perhaps most important, knowledge of this manifold heritage, like historical knowledge generally, can free the student from bondage to the present by suggesting alternatives from earlier, quite different approaches to theological inquiry. Indeed, the task of interpreting contemporary situations with resources from the tradition underscores the incredible extent of Christian theological diversity and the very different readings of situations that will result from interpreting them through one theological category rather than another.

Third, James believed that experience is fluid in yet another way. It is only partially assimilated to or determined by the categories of social thought, only partially "social experience." Features of experience constantly confound human efforts to comprehend or domesticate it. Hence, James suggested that "the strung-along and flowing sort of reality which we finite beings swim in" was "non-rational" in the sense that "life, experience, concreteness, immediacy, use what word you will, exceeds our logic, overflows and surrounds it."[62] Long before James so named them, the non-rational features of experience were classic locations for theological rhetoric that took account of both the ordering background patterns of tradition-shaped experience and the unassimilated otherness of existence as limit, disruption, and fatefulness. This "exceeding" aspect of reality has, in varied forms, been a stock feature of the divine presence as depicted by American theologians, especially those influenced by the Reformed tradition from Edwards to Niebuhr and Gilkey. Recurrently, in particular cultural moments of crisis, the utterly free power of a transcending God has symbolically represented the radical limit to human institutions, human ingenuity, or human projects of fulfillment.

In these three ways, James found the background of possibilities morally charged with human aspiration. By emphasizing the interplay between "our common experiences" and "the background of possibilities," he called attention to the background of possibilities precisely as *possibilities*, not necessities or foregone conclusions. So varied, so apparently unrelated, so often contradictory a set of open possibilities entails some appraisal of what is realistically possible or plausible. It includes elements that are imaginatively available to challenge and extend the range of what we consider possible by posing a new possibility. In this respect, the work of the theologian is the envisionment of a "believable" hope; in Walter Lippmann's phrase, "ideals are an imaginative understanding of that which is desirable in that which is possible."[63] Theological scholarship is an act of the moral imagination actively engaged in appraising and refashioning "the background of possibilities" that invests the particular events of human life with some more enduring meaning. The religious impulse, as John Dewey understood, includes the imaginative capacity for the construal of the wholeness of all that is.

> There actually occurs extremely little observation of brute facts merely for the sake of the facts. . . . Facts are usually observed with reference to some practical end, and that end is presented only imaginatively. . . . The idea of a whole, whether of the whole personal being or of the world, is an imaginative, not a literal, idea. The limited world of our observation and reflection becomes the Universe only through imaginative extension.[64]

Dewey further believed that the self came to some sense of unity not simply in terms of itself but by being directed beyond itself, and so "its own unification depends upon the idea of the integration of the shifting scenes of the world into that imaginative totality we call the Universe."[65]

This imaginative enterprise of integrating the universe (the self) made theological scholarship, as Niebuhr had proposed, itself an expression of the religious sensibility. Exploration and appraisal of the background of possibilities is a historical, systematic, and ethical inquiry that involves the theologian in comparison, analysis, and imaginative synthesis. General considerations in this process involve testing the shared reference points, symbols, and tacit assumptions that order and prompt action in the world. On its analytic side, then, American theological inquiry has sought to render explicit the tacit presuppositions which, as the background of possibilities, give meaning and context to specific beliefs and practices. Its responsibility has been the critical ethical appraisal both of that background and of the actions that the background sanctioned. But on its visionary side, the theological impulse presumes that the concrete world of meaningful action derives coherence and confidence from the imaginative conception of the good at which a civilization aims: "If civilization is to be coherent and confident it must be known in that civilization what its ideals are. There must exist in the form of clearly available ideas an understanding of what the fulfillment of the promise of that civilization might mean, an imaginative conception of the good at which it might, and, if it is to flourish, at which it must aim."[66]

American theologians have concentrated their work on proposals about the shape and the reshaping of this background, and there has been considerable continuity to the process itself even if the "answers" given at particular junctures of the conversation or by different partners in the conversation have been quite diverse. But, in what I think were their best moments, they were less interested in the triumph of a particular vision than in persuading their fellow citizens that without such rigorously debated envisionments the ethical conduct of personal and civic life would atrophy.

This attentiveness to the responsibilities of scholarship for social criticism, to the interlacing of theory and practice in lived experience, and to the normative social ramifications of particular experience points with considerable urgency to a public agenda for professional intellectuals within universities and theological schools. Not surprisingly, throughout the humanities and the social sciences, the vocational shorthand is that the times call for "public intellectuals."[67] But, the term *public intellectual* cannot usefully define the cultural vocation of a theologian in the lineage I have described unless one also recalls the questions that such theologians have distinctively raised about their publics and their Public.

The distinctive questions posed by the theologian as a public intellectual are clarified if we recall John Dewey's dictum that *publics* arise whenever "human acts have consequences upon others." The perception of this fact provokes efforts "to control action so as to secure some consequences and to avoid others." An action moves from the private to the public domain whenever the extent and scope of the consequences of acts are so extensive as to require control, whether by inhibition or promotion. In this view, "the public consists of all those who are affected by the indirect consequences of transactions to such an extent that it is deemed necessary to have those consequences systematically cared for." The industrial era has so enormously expanded and complicated these indirect consequences that there are now "too many publics and too much of public concern." I concur with Dewey's opinion that amid these overlapping and competing parties the resultant manifold public "cannot identify and distinguish itself." For this reason, the principal problem of democratic society is "primarily and essentially an intellectual problem," namely, the fact that, as the ties that link human action become ever more complex, the symbols that will "convert" society into community are no longer able to make overt the links which bind it together. "The Public will remain in eclipse," therefore, until it elaborates "the signs and symbols without which shared experience is impossible."[68]

Historically, academic theologians in the Protestant tradition have understood their role to be just this activity of convoking "the Public," or making it visible, through the proposal of symbols that make "shared experience" possible. Publics are of different extent and organized for quite different purposes, and the American religious circumstance is such that the theologian is rarely immediately accountable to a single public. The previous chapters have proposed that uncertainties about the purpose of theological study have arisen historically from the shifting relations among theology's three publics—church, academy, and nation—and the difficulty of the theologian has been systematic interpretation of these public obligations. Decisions about public priorities have precipitated reforms that redefined the vocation of the theologian. In attention to *the public,* the theologian as *intellectual* may take up a variety of stances. As we have seen, theologians in one aspect are "Emersonian intellectuals," impatient with institutions, alienated from inherited patterns of belief, loyal to ideals that hover in the vicinity of society and lure thought beyond itself. In another aspect, after the manner of John Williamson Nevin, they inhabit what Jacques Barzun called "the House of Intellect" and regard tradition not as the "dead hand of the past" but as a genetic code that vitalizes and forms present experience. Although in both aspects the intellectual is regarded as an agent of change in the society, these two connotations of the designation intellectual imply different understandings of the relation between the ideal and the actual, tradition and innovation, the processes of change. But in neither case is the theologian as *public intellectual* simply one who makes pronouncements on concrete issues "of public moment." In these seasons of reform, theologians conceived the

possibility of an ultimate public that challenged these more proximate publics with its comprehensive purposes: the city of God, the
kingdom of God, the universal commonwealth, the divine republic.
As Edward W. Said has recently argued with regard to intellectuals
in general, they employ "universal principles" in order to establish
a position of critical independence from the institutions which would
otherwise co-opt them and thus undercut their cultural challenge.[69]
To return to a phrase I earlier borrowed from Thoreau, theological
inquiry proceeds from the hypothesis that critical appraisal of
"where we are" entails reflection on "the infinite extent of our relations." The historic task of theological inquiry in America has been
to propose and appraise the ultimate context of self and culture, "the
infinite extent of our relations." Changing and highly particular social experiences (". . . where we are . . ."), in turn, have exerted pressures that have reshaped the interpretive frame. In short, the idea of
God has functioned to propose the ultimate public in which all more
proximate publics cohere, in which contending loyalties are adjudicated, and which generalizes the human scope of what any particular
person, race, nation has suffered or undergone.[70]

Such a vocation, of course, has its clear and present dangers.
Any intellectual who sets out to grasp the world as a whole and to
offer a "universal solution to its problems" is, as Vaclav Havel has
recently asserted, always susceptible to becoming the ideologue of a
regime. But all vocations of any importance have their serious dangers, which does not mean they should not or cannot be attempted.
Havel therefore goes on to say that when some intellectuals seek
to understand the concrete affairs of life in more global terms,
they recognize the "mysterious nature" of that global context and
humbly defer to it. For the long tradition of Protestant theologians I
have reviewed in this book, it is the aspiration to engender a debate
about the global context of our lives—but with humility—that has
been at stake in their convictions about the final sovereignty of God
in all human affairs. In principle, they agree with Havel that the
"sense of responsibility for this world has not made such intellectuals identify with an ideology; it has made them identify with humanity, its dignity, and its prospects."[71] Daniel Day Williams correctly
identified the intent of their work when he said that they sought a
"theology of the human community."

In using the term "public intellectual" to describe the vocation of the theologian, I wish to underscore the extent to which American theological inquiry has so persistently oriented itself toward the public good and the fact that it has so regularly aligned itself with other university disciplines in their regard for the public good. I believe this to be the proper vocation for theologians in America, and I will call on the sociologist Edward Shils to explain why. There are, Shils explains, intellectuals by office and intellectuals by disposition. The former group populates government, business, and the professions in order to carry out tasks that require intellectual labor. But intellectuals by disposition are those in every society "with an unusual sensitivity to the sacred, an uncommon reflectiveness about the nature of their universe, and the rules which govern their society." Shils argues that in this respect there is a close relation between intellectual activity in all its forms and the religious.

> Differently disciplined, both the religious and the scientific
> dispositions at their most creative, have in common the striv-
> ing for contact with the most decisive and significant symbols
> and the realities underlying those symbols. It is therefore no
> stretching of the term to say that science and philosophy,
> even when they are not religious in a conventional sense, are
> as concerned with the sacred as religion itself.[72]

If this is the case, the scholarly study of religion has the opportunity and the responsibility—perhaps opportunity and responsibility to distinctive degree—to reflect on the meaning of "the most decisive and significant symbols" that order public life, to raise the question of "the infinite extent of our relations," a question that sometimes challenges customary paths and sometimes retraces those paths to glimpse what their makers truly saw. In this reading of the theologian's vocation, retreat to the internal concerns of the university and the jargon of its scholarly disciplines would be a retreat from the very point of scholarship and religion alike. To withdraw from the work of the public intellectual would separate theological scholarship not only from its historical social purpose but also, perhaps, from the sacred itself.

NOTES

Introduction

1. Dorothy Ross, *The Origins of American Social Science* (Cambridge: Cambridge University Press, 1991); Arthur J. Vidich and Stanford M. Lyman, *American Sociology: Worldly Rejections of Religion and Their Directions* (New Haven: Yale University Press, 1985); Peter Novick, *That Noble Dream: The "Objectivity Question" and the American Historical Profession* (Cambridge: Cambridge University Press, 1988); Gerald Graff, *Professing Literature: An Institutional History* (Chicago: University of Chicago Press, 1987); Paul Starr, *The Social Transformation of American Medicine* (New York: Basic Books, 1982); Robert Stevens, *Law School: Legal Education in America from the 1850s to the 1980s* (Chapel Hill: University of North Carolina Press, 1983).

2. W. Clark Gilpin, "Basic Issues in Theological Education: A Selected Bibliography, 1980–88," *Theological Education* 25 (Spring, 1989): 115–21; more recent studies include Ray L. Hart, "Religious and Theological Studies in American Higher Education: A Pilot Study," *Journal of the American Academy of Religion* 59 (1991): 715–827; David H. Kelsey, *To Understand God Truly: What's Theological about a Theological School* (Louisville: Westminster/John Knox, 1992); David H. Kelsey, *Between Athens and Berlin: The Theological Education Debate* (Grand Rapids: Eerdmans, 1993).

3. Russell Jacoby, *The Last Intellectuals: American Culture in the Age of Academe* (New York: Noonday, 1987), ix, 5–6, 17, 147.

4. The most useful historical bibliography is by Heather F. Day, *Protestant Theological Education in America: A Bibliography* (Metuchen, N.J.: American Theological Library Association, 1985).

5. The phrase "the idea of a theological school" comes from H. Richard Niebuhr, *The Purpose of the Church and Its Ministry: Reflections on the Aims of Theological Education* (New York: Harper, 1956), 95–134.

6. With respect to this effort to sustain national religious homogeneity within a wider political context of diversity, William H. McNeill has remarked that "the political diversity of Europe thwarted the heart's desire of nearly all the intellectually sensitive men of the time by making impossible the construction of a single authoritative, definitive, and (as almost everyone also desired) enforcible codification of Truth. Yet, ironically, the failure to construct a world-view commanding general assent was the great achievement of the age." See McNeill's *Rise of the West: A History of the Human Community* (Chicago: University of Chicago Press, 1963), 642.

7. Readers of American religious history will recognize this paragraph as an all-too-brief and all-too-simple summary of the seminal work by Sidney E. Mead, *The Lively Experiment: The Shaping of Christianity in America* (New York: Harper, 1963).

8. Paul K. Conkin, *The Uneasy Center: Reformed Christianity in Antebellum America* (Chapel Hill: University of North Carolina Press, 1995), pp. ix–xiv.

9. David Tracy has discussed theology's threefold public in several of his writings, but in the present connection see especially "Theology, Public Discourse, and the American Tradition," in *Religion and Twentieth-Century American Intellectual Life*, ed. Michael J. Lacey (Cambridge: Cambridge University Press, 1989), 193–203.

10. I owe to my teacher and colleague Jerald C. Brauer the notion that being "out of step" is sometimes an institutional virtue; see "A History of the Divinity School: Creatively Out of Step," *Criterion* 29 (Autumn, 1990): 12–17.

11. Niebuhr, *Purpose of the Church*, 1.

12. Ibid., 9.

13. In my thoughts about the import of religion and the voluntary sector for public life, I have been greatly instructed by several recent books from the pen of Robert Wuthnow, especially *The Struggle for America's Soul: Evangelicals, Liberals, and Secularism* (Grand Rapids: Eerdmans, 1989) and *Christianity in the 21st Century: Reflections on the Challenges Ahead* (New York: Oxford University Press, 1993).

14. R. H. Tawney, *Religion and the Rise of Capitalism: A Historical Study* (New York: Harcourt, Brace, 1926), 8.

15. Walter Lippmann, *A Preface to Morals* (New York: Macmillan, 1929), 3.

16. Ibid., 9–10.

17. Henry David Thoreau, *The Works of Thoreau*, ed. Henry S. Canby (Boston: Houghton Mifflin, 1937), 356–60.

Chapter One

1. H. C. Porter, ed., *Puritanism in Tudor England* (London: Macmillan, 1970), 182–83.

2. Sidney E. Mead, "The Rise of the Evangelical Conception of the Ministry in America (1607–1850), in *The Ministry in Historical Perspectives*, ed. H. Richard Niebuhr and Daniel Day Williams (New York: Harper, 1956), 237.

3. George H. Williams, *Wilderness and Paradise in Christian Thought* (New York: Harper, 1962), 143–57, 187, 190.

4. Increase Mather, *Ichabod* (Boston, 1702), 75. In this and subsequent quotations from sources of the seventeenth and eighteenth centuries, the spelling, capitalization, and punctuation have been modernized.

5. [Jonathan Mitchell], "A Modell for the Maintaining of Students and Fellows of Choise Abilities at the Colledge in Cambridge," *Colonial Society of Massachusetts Publications* 31 (1935): 301–22. Mitchell cited Rev. 10:9–10.

6. Mead, "Evangelical Conception of the Ministry," 207–8.

7. Daniel Calhoun, *The Intelligence of a People* (Princeton: Princeton University Press, 1973), 42–43.

8. Joan R. Gunderson, "The Search for Good Men: Recruiting Ministers in Colonial Virginia," *Historical Magazine of the Protestant Episcopal Church* 48 (1979): 455–59.

9. For surveys of this method of theological instruction, see Mary Latimer Gambrell, *Ministerial Training in Eighteenth-Century New England* (New York: Columbia University Press, 1937); William Orpheus Shewmaker, "The Training of the Protestant Ministry in the United States of America, before the Establishment of Theological Seminaries," *Papers of the American Society of Church History*, 2d ser. 6 (1921): 71–202; J. William T. Youngs, Jr., *God's Messengers: Religious Leadership in Colonial New England, 1700–1750* (Baltimore: Johns Hopkins University Press, 1976), 17–24.

10. Harry S. Stout, *The New England Soul: Preaching and Religious Culture in Colonial New England* (New York: Oxford University Press, 1986), 57; Roland H. Bainton, *Yale and the Ministry: A History of Education for the Christian Ministry at Yale from the Founding in 1701* (New York: Harper, 1957), xi.

11. Phyllis Vine, "The Social Function of Eighteenth-Century Higher Education," *History of Education Quarterly* 16 (1976): 417–19.

12. Edmund S. Morgan, *The Gentle Puritan: A Life of Ezra Stiles, 1727–1795* (Chapel Hill: University of North Carolina Press, 1962), 59.

13. Cotton Mather, *Ratio Disciplinae Fratrum Nov Anglorum* (Bos-

ton, 1726), 118–21; Williston Walker, *The Creeds and Platforms of Congregationalism* (1893; reprint ed., Philadelphia: Pilgrim, 1960), 487; Gambrell, *Ministerial Training*, 53.

14. Donald M. Scott, *From Office to Profession: The New England Ministry, 1750–1850* (Philadelphia: University of Pennsylvania Press, 1978), 1–17; see also Edward M. Cook, *The Fathers of the Towns: Leadership and Community Structure in Eighteenth-Century New England* (Baltimore: Johns Hopkins University Press, 1976), 120, 133; Richard L. Bushman, *From Puritan to Yankee: Character and the Social Order in Connecticut, 1690–1750* (Cambridge: Harvard University Press, 1967), 13–14, 16.

15. Cf. Hans W. Frei, *The Eclipse of Biblical Narrative: A Study in Eighteenth and Nineteenth Century Hermeneutics* (New Haven: Yale University Press, 1974), 3.

16. Stout, *New England Soul*, 4–6, 13–14.

17. Kenneth Silverman, ed., *Selected Letters of Cotton Mather* (Baton Rouge: Louisiana State University Press, 1971), 19; Samuel Willard, *Brief Directions to a Young Scholar Designing the Ministry, for the Study of Divinity* (Boston, 1735).

18. Cotton Mather, *Manuductio ad Ministerium* (1726; reprint ed., New York: Columbia University Press, 1938), 5–7.

19. Ibid., 2.

20. Ibid., pp. 80–89; Willard, *Brief Directions*, 3–4.

21. Willard, *Brief Directions*, 3–4.

22. Mather, *Manuductio*, 7; William Ames, *The Marrow of Theology*, trans. John D. Eusden (Boston: Pilgrim, 1968), 77; Jonathan Edwards, *The Importance and Advantage of a Thorough Knowledge of Divine Truth*, in *The Works of President Edwards*, ed. Samuel Austin (Worcester, Mass., 1808), vol. 8: 6.

23. Edward Farley, *Theologia: The Fragmentation and Unity of Theological Education* (Philadelphia: Fortress, 1983), 31, 59–63.

24. Mather, *Manuductio*, 15–19 (emphasis added).

25. Ibid., 80–82.

26. Increase Mather, *David Serving His Generation* (Boston, 1698), 17–18, 21.

27. Solomon Stoddard, *A Guide to Christ* (Boston, 1714), title page and preface.

28. Edmund S. Morgan, *Visible Saints: The History of a Puritan Idea* (New York: New York University Press, 1963).

29. Mather, *Manuductio*, 104–5; Mather's discussion of preaching appears on 89–106.

30. Ibid., 89–115.

31. Ibid., 96.

32. Ibid., 24–25.

33. [Cotton Mather], "Important points, relating to the Education at

Harvard Colledge, needful to be Enquired into" (Mather Family Papers, American Antiquarian Society, Box 6, Folder 2).

34. For the extension of toleration in New England, see Bushman, *Puritan to Yankee*, 16, 167–68; Richard Hofstadter, *America at 1750: A Social Portrait* (London: Cape, 1972), 208–9.

35. Josiah Quincy, *The History of Harvard University* (Cambridge, 1840), 2: 534–36.

36. Norman Fiering, "The First American Enlightenment: Tillotson, Leverett, and Philosophical Anglicanism," *New England Quarterly* 54 (1981): 307–44.

37. Peter Gay, ed., *The Enlightenment: A Comprehensive Anthology* (New York: Simon and Schuster, 1973), 116.

38. Mead, "Evangelical Conception of the Ministry," 238–39.

39. This colonial revival was one wing of a transatlantic, interdenominational movement of piety that included the Methodists in England, Presbyterians in Scotland and Ireland, and the Moravian Brethren in Saxony. With variations, each of these evangelical groups emphasized that the essential index of true religion was an inward conversion wrought by the Holy Spirit. Correspondingly, they simplified theology to those doctrines most directly concerned with personal salvation and focused ethics on personal holiness as the fruit of conversion. Typically, the role of the laity was elevated and the authority of the ministerial office challenged. In New England, the religious force of the Awakening concentrated in the years 1740 to 1742. To the south, among Presbyterians, Baptists, and later Methodists in the Middle Colonies, Virginia, and the Carolinas, the excitement extended over a longer period.

40. For a summary of the complex theological divisions in New England during this period, see Edwin Scott Gaustad, *The Great Awakening in New England* (New York: Harper, 1957), 128.

41. Richard Warch, "The Shepherd's Tent: Education and Enthusiasm in the Great Awakening," *American Quarterly* 30 (1978): 177–98.

42. Ebenezer Pemberton, *The Knowledge of Christ Recommended* (New London, 1741), 4–6.

43. Ibid., 23–24.

44. Douglas Sloan, ed., *The Great Awakening and American Education: A Documentary History* (New York: Teachers College Press, 1973), 42–43, 47–48.

45. Howard Miller, "Evangelical Religion and Colonial Princeton," in *Schooling and Society: Studies in the History of Education*, ed. Lawrence Stone (Baltimore: Johns Hopkins University Press, 1976), 121.

46. Henry F. May, *The Enlightenment in America* (Oxford: Oxford University Press, 1976).

47. Norman S. Fiering, "Benjamin Franklin and the Way to Virtue," *American Quarterly* 30 (1978): 199–223.

48. Leonard J. Trinterud, *The Forming of an American Tradition: A*

Re-examination of Colonial Presbyterianism (Philadelphia: Westminster, 1949): 138–41.

49. William A. Clebsch, "William Smith on Education: Religion, 'The Soul of the Whole,'" *Historical Magazine of the Protestant Episcopal Church* 52 (1983): 369–90.

50. Douglas Sloan, *The Scottish Enlightenment and the American College Ideal* (New York: Teachers College Press, 1971), 88–98.

51. Thomas Clap, *The Religious Constitution of Colleges* (New London, 1754), 4–6, 14, 15–16.

52. John Corrigan, "'Habits from the Heart': The American Enlightenment and Religious Ideas about Emotion and Habit," *Journal of Religion* 73 (1993): 183–99; Mark A. Noll, "Jonathan Edwards and Nineteenth-Century Theology," in *Jonathan Edwards and the American Experience,* ed. Nathan O. Hatch and Harry S. Stout ((New York: Oxford University Press, 1988), 262–69.

53. Ezra Stiles, *A Discourse on the Christian Union* (Boston, 1761), 96–97.

54. Ibid., 96–97, 125–26.

55. Sidney E. Mead, *The Lively Experiment: The Shaping of Christianity in America* (New York: Harper and Row, 1963), 63.

56. Jonathan Edwards, *A Treatise concerning Religious Affections,* ed. John E. Smith, *The Works of Jonathan Edwards,* vol. 2 (New Haven: Yale University Press, 1959), 84.

57. Edwards, *Works of President Edwards* (Worcester), 8: 6–8, 10–11, 295–97, 301–2.

58. Samuel Hopkins, *The Life and Character of the Late Reverend Jonathan Edwards* (Boston, 1765), 24–28.

59. Conrad Cherry, *The Theology of Jonathan Edwards: A Reappraisal,* reprint ed. with new introduction and foreword by Stephen J. Stein (Bloomington: Indiana University Press, 1990), 31, 37.

60. Hopkins, *Jonathan Edwards,* 29–31, 35.

61. Cf. Irving Howe, *The American Newness: Culture and Politics in the Age of Emerson* (Cambridge: Harvard University Press, 1986), 29.

62. The phrase is borrowed from H. Richard Niebuhr, *The Kingdom of God in America* (New York: Harper, 1937), xvi.

63. Michael J. Crawford, *Seasons of Grace: Colonial New England's Revival Tradition in Its British Context* (New York: Oxford University Press, 1991), 180.

64. Edwards, *Religious Affections,* 101–02, 122.

65. Jonathan Edwards, *The Nature of True Virtue,* ed. William K. Frankena (Ann Arbor: University of Michigan Press, 1960), 1–4.

66. Ibid., 4, 18, 20–23.

67. Ibid., 4.

68. Ibid., 27–28, 30–35.

69. Jonathan Edwards, *Dissertation concerning the End for Which*

God Created the World, in *Works of President Edwards* (Worcester), 6: 23–24, 53.

70. *Minutes and Letters of the Coetus of the German Reformed Congregations in Pennsylvania, 1747–1792,* ed. J. I. Good and W. J. Hinke (Philadelphia: Reformed Church Publication Board, 1903), 392–93, 403–4, 409.

71. Abdel Ross Wentz, *History of the Gettysburg Theological Seminary* (Philadelphia: United Lutheran Publication House, 1926), 39–48.

72. Quincy, *History of Harvard,* 2: 259–60, 502–03.

73. A letter from Jacob Green to Joseph Bellamy in 1775, cited in Mark A. Noll, "Jacob Green's Proposal for Seminaries," *Journal of Presbyterian History* 58 (1980): 210–22.

74. James W. Alexander, *The Life of Archibald Alexander* (Philadelphia, 1855), 15–112.

75. Barton Warren Stone, *The Biography of Eld. Barton Warren Stone, Written by Himself,* ed. John Rogers, 5th ed. (Cincinnati, 1847), 6–13.

76. Alexander, *Archibald Alexander,* 34–36, 112–22; Stone, *Barton Warren Stone,* 4–11, 16.

77. Alexander, *Archibald Alexander,* 80–81.

78. Natalie A. Naylor, "'Holding High the Standard': The Influence of the American Education Society in Ante-Bellum Education," *History of Education Quarterly* 24 (1984): 479–97.

79. In Timothy Dwight, *A Sermon Preached at the Opening of the Theological Institution in Andover* (Boston, 1808), 37.

80. Ibid., 13–14.

81. [Eliphalet Pearson], "Thoughts on the Importance of a Theological Institution," *Panoplist* 3 (1807–8): 306–16.

82. Samuel S. Schmucker, *An Inaugural Address Delivered before the Directors of the Theological Seminary of the General Synod of the Evangelical Lutheran Church* (Carlisle, Penn., 1826), 31, 40.

83. Dwight, *Theological Institution in Andover,* 26–27.

84. Lefferts A. Loetscher, *Facing the Enlightenment and Pietism: Archibald Alexander and the Founding of Princeton Theological Seminary* (Westport, Conn.: Greenwood Press, 1983), 132.

85. Pearson, "Importance of a Theological Institution," 310–12; "List of Books Recommended by Dr. Tappan to Theological Students," *Panoplist* 2 (1806–7): 325–26; "Outlines of a Theological Institution," *Panoplist* 3 (1807–8): 345–48.

86. Walter Lippmann, *A Preface to Morals* (New York: Macmillan, 1929), 76.

Chapter Two

1. Edwards Amasa Park, "The Theology of the Intellect and That of the Feelings," *Bibliotheca Sacra* 7 (1850): 533–69.

2. Lawrence A. Cremin, *American Education: The National Experience, 1783–1876* (New York: Harper Colophon Books, 1982), 18.

3. A Society of Clergymen, "Thoughts on the State of Theological Science and Education in Our Country," *Bibliotheca Sacra* 1 (1844): 736–49, 757–63.

4. William Warren Sweet, "The Rise of Theological Schools in America," *Church History* 6 (1937): 271.

5. Douglas Sloan, "Harmony, Chaos, and Consensus: The American College Curriculum," *Teacher's College Record* 73 (1971–72): 232.

6. John W. Nevin, *My Own Life: The Earlier Years* (Lancaster, Penn.: Eastern Chapter, Historical Society of the Evangelical and Reformed Church, 1964), 8; see also, Louise L. Stevenson, *Scholarly Means to Evangelical Ends: The New Haven Scholars and the Transformation of Higher Learning in America, 1830–1890* (Baltimore: Johns Hopkins University Press, 1986), 57.

7. Lyman Beecher, *A Plea for Colleges*, 2d ed. (Cincinnati, 1836), 16.

8. Ibid., 15.

9. Ibid. 26–27.

10. Albert Barnes, *Home Missions* (New York, 1849), 8.

11. Horace Bushnell, *Barbarism the First Danger* (New York, 1847), 32.

12. Barnes, *Home Missions*, 37.

13. W. G. T. Shedd, "College Education," *Bibliotheca Sacra* 7 (1850): 132–34.

14. Ibid., 143.

15. Edwards Amasa Park, "The Utility of Collegiate and Professional Schools," *Bibliotheca Sacra* 7 (1850): 632–34.

16. Philip Schaff, "General Introduction to Church History," *Bibliotheca Sacra* 6 (1849): 409–10.

17. Philip Schaff, "The Progress of Church History as a Science," *Bibliotheca Sacra* 7 (1850): 75–76.

18. Stevenson, *Scholarly Means to Evangelical Ends*, 36, 139.

19. Park, "Utility of Collegiate and Professional Schools," 643.

20. Edward Farley, *Theologia: The Fragmentation and Unity of Theological Education* (Philadelphia: Fortress, 1983), 49–124.

21. Brian A. Gerrish, *Tradition and the Modern World: Reformed Theology in the Nineteenth Century* (Chicago: University of Chicago Press, 1978), 41.

22. H. George Anderson, "Challenge and Change within German Protestant Theological Education during the Nineteenth Century," *Church History* 39 (1970): 42–44.

23. Philip Schaff, *Germany: Its Universities, Theology, and Religion* (Philadelphia, 1857), 278–94.

24. Friedrich August Gottreu Tholuck, "Theological Encyclopedia and Methodology," *Bibliotheca Sacra* 1 (1844): 188–89.

25. Ibid., 569.

26. Ibid., 552–56.

27. Ibid., 338–40.

28. Ibid., 193–95.

29. Ibid., 561–66.

30. Ibid., 726 (emphasis added).

31. Gerrish, *Tradition and the Modern World,* 43.

32. Friedrich Schleiermacher, *Brief Outline on the Study of Theology,* trans. Terrence N. Tice (Atlanta: John Knox, 1966), 26.

33. The quotations, representative of many scholars, come from Bela Bates Edwards, "Present State of Biblical Science," *Bibliotheca Sacra* 7 (1850): 1–13.

34. Schaff, "Progress of Church History," 75.

35. Henry Boynton Smith, "The Nature and Worth of the Science of Church History," *Bibliotheca Sacra* 8 (1851): 415–26.

36. Schaff, "Introduction to Church History," 419.

37. Ibid., 434.

38. For examples of the experiences of nineteenth-century blacks with theological education, see John Mercer Langston, *From the Virginia Plantation to the National Capitol: An Autobiography* (1894; reprint, New York: Bergman, 1969), 111–16; Daniel Alexander Payne, *Recollections of Seventy Years* (1888; reprint, New York: Arno, 1968), 45, 56–64; Gregory U. Rigsby, *Alexander Crummell: Pioneer in Nineteenth-Century Pan-African Thought* (New York: Greenwood, 1987), 25–28.

39. Gilbert H. Barnes, *The Anti-Slavery Impulse, 1830–1844* (New York: Appleton-Century, 1933), 40–41, 44–46.

40. Ibid., 64–70.

41. Gilbert H. Barnes and Dwight L. Dumond, eds., *Letters of Theodore Dwight Weld, Angelina Grimke Weld and Sarah Grimke, 1822–1844,* 2 vols. (New York: Appleton-Century-Crofts, 1934), 1: 136–46.

42. Ibid., 70–77.

43. Robert Bruce Mullin, "Biblical Critics and the Battle over Slavery," *Journal of Presbyterian History* 61 (1983): 210–26.

44. Ibid., 213–14.

45. Nevin, *My Own Life,* 90–93.

46. Cf. Mullin, "Biblical Critics," 215; J. Earl Thompson, "Abolitionism and Theological Education at Andover," *New England Quarterly* 47 (1974): 251–56, 259.

47. Bliss Perry, "Emerson's Most Famous Speech," in *The Praise of Folly and Other Papers* (Boston: Houghton Mifflin, 1923), 97–101.

48. Ralph Waldo Emerson, "The American Scholar," in *Ralph Waldo Emerson: Essays and Lectures,* ed. Joel Porte (New York: Literary Classics of the United States, 1983), 53–56, 64.

49. Emerson the reader is vividly portrayed in the recent biography

by Robert D. Richardson, *Emerson: The Mind on Fire* (Berkeley: University of California Press, 1995).

50. Emerson, "American Scholar," 56.

51. Ibid., 57.

52. Richardson, *Emerson*, 90.

53. Emerson, "American Scholar," 58–59.

54. Ibid., 60, 62.

55. Ibid., 65.

56. Henry Nash Smith, "Emerson's Problem of Vocation: A Note on 'The American Scholar,'" *New England Quarterly* 12 (1939): 58–59, 67.

57. Emerson, "American Scholar," 63–64, 70–71.

58. F. O. Matthiessen, *American Renaissance: Art and Expression in the Age of Emerson and Whitman* (London: Oxford University Press, 1941), 51.

59. Cf. Lawrence Buell, *New England Literary Culture: From Revolution through Renaissance* (Cambridge: Cambridge University Press, 1986), 69.

60. Emerson, "American Scholar," 70–71.

61. See, in general, H. Jackson Forstman, *A Romantic Triangle: Schleiermacher and Early German Romanticism* (Missoula, Mont.: Scholars Press, 1977); James Hastings Nichols, *Romanticism in American Theology: Nevin and Schaff at Mercersburg* (Chicago: University of Chicago Press, 1961).

62. For a survey of these debates, see two essays by D. G. Hart, "Divided between Heart and Mind: The Critical Period for Protestant Thought in America," *Journal of Ecclesiastical History* 38 (1987): 254–70; and "Poems, Propositions, and Dogma: The Controversy over Religious Language and the Demise of Theology in American Learning," *Church History* 57 (1988): 310–21.

63. Henry Boynton Smith, "The Relations of Faith and Philosophy," *Bibliotheca Sacra* 6 (1849): 674.

64. Horace Bushnell, *Views of Christian Nurture, and of Subjects Adjacent Thereto* (Hartford, 1847), 21–22, 150, 173, 183–84.

65. Cited in Theodore Appel, *The Life and Work of John Williamson Nevin* (Philadelphia, 1889), 179–80 (emphasis added).

66. Horace Bushnell, *God in Christ* (Hartford, 1849), 38–40.

67. Ibid., 30.

68. Ibid., 46.

69. Ibid., 79–80.

70. Ibid., 46–47.

71. Ibid., 73–75, 93.

72. Ibid., 50–55, 67–70, 80–81.

73. Ibid., 67.

74. Ibid., 92, 302, 308.

75. Charles Hodge, Review of *God in Christ* by Horace Bushnell, *Biblical Repertory and Princeton Review* 21 (1849): 276–77.

76. Ibid., 277.

77. John W. Nevin, Review of *God in Christ* by Horace Bushnell, *Mercersburg Review* 1 (1849): 311–12.

78. John W. Nevin, *The Mystical Presence and Other Writings on the Eucharist*, ed. Bard Thompson and George W. Bricker (Philadelphia: United Church Press, 1966), 24.

79. Ibid., 255.

80. Bushnell, *God in Christ*, 294–300.

81. John W. Nevin, "Catholicism," *Mercersburg Review* 3 (1851): 9, 17.

82. Ibid., 5.

83. Sidney E. Mead, *The Nation with the Soul of a Church* (New York: Harper, 1975), pp. 48–77.

84. Walter Lippmann, *A Preface to Morals* (New York: Macmillan, 1929), 49–50.

85. Cf. Edward Shils, *The Calling of Sociology and Other Essays on the Pursuit of Learning* (Chicago: University of Chicago Press, 1980), 363–67.

Chapter Three

1. Francis L. Patton, "Christian Theology and Current Thought," in Addresses at the Induction of Rev. Francis L. Patton into the Cyrus H. McCormick Professorship of Didactic and Polemic Theology, in the Presbyterian Theological Seminary of the North-West (Chicago, 1872), 28, 58–59; Benjamin B. Warfield, "Inaugural Address," in Discourses Occasioned by the Inauguration of Benj. B. Warfield, D. D. to the Chair of New Testament Exegesis and Literature in Western Theological Seminary (Pittsburgh, 1880), 21, 44–45.

2. William R. Hutchison, *The Modernist Impulse in American Protestantism* (Cambridge: Harvard University Press, 1976), 105–10.

3. Josiah Royce, "Present Ideals of American University Life," *Scribner's Magazine* 10 (July-December, 1891): 383.

4. Daniel Coit Gilman, "The Idea of the University," *North American Review* 133 (October, 1881): 356.

5. Laurence R. Veysey, *The Emergence of the American University* (Chicago: University of Chicago Press, 1965).

6. Charles W. Eliot, "On the Education of Ministers," *Princeton Review* (May, 1883): 340–56.

7. Ibid., 346.

8. Ibid., 344–45.

9. Ibid., 343–44, 346.

10. Ibid., 349–54.

11. Francis L. Patton, "On the Education of Ministers: A Reply to President Eliot," *Princeton Review* (July, 1883): 48–66.

12. Ibid., 57.

13. Ibid., 53.

14. Ibid., 59.

15. Ibid.

16. Cf. Van Harvey, *The Historian and the Believer: The Morality of Historical Knowledge and Christian Belief* (New York: Macmillan, 1966).

17. William Rainey Harper, "Shall the Theological Curriculum Be Modified, and How?" *American Journal of Theology* 3 (1899): 46.

18. Ibid., 46–50.

19. Ibid., 47.

20. Ibid., 51, 56–63, 66.

21. George Harris et al., "Modifications in the Theological Curriculum," *American Journal of Theology* 3 (1899): 324–43.

22. Ibid., 336.

23. Ibid., 330.

24. Cf. Charles Wood, *Vision and Discernment: An Orientation to Theological Study* (Atlanta: Scholars Press, 1985), 3.

25. Benjamin W. Bacon, "The Problem of Religious Education and the Divinity School," *American Journal of Theology* 8 (1904): 686.

26. Charles A. Briggs, "A Plea for the Higher Study of Theology," *American Journal of Theology* 8 (1904): 436–38.

27. The history of the evangelical scholars in the century from 1880 to 1980 is set forth, with particular reference to biblical scholarship, by Mark A. Noll, *Between Faith and Criticism: Evangelicals, Scholarship, and the Bible in America* (San Francisco: Harper, 1986).

28. Hutchison, *Modernist Impulse*, 2–4; see also Kenneth W. Cauthen, *The Impact of American Religious Liberalism* (New York: Harper, 1962), 5–6.

29. Charles A. Briggs, "The Scope of Theology and Its Place in the University," *American Journal of Theology* 1 (1897): 38.

30. Shailer Mathews, *The Church and the Changing Order* (New York: Macmillan, 1907), 2. Concerning the rhetoric of social crisis, see Charles R. Strain, "Toward a Generic Analysis of a Classic of the Social Gospel: An Essay-Review of Walter Rauschenbusch, Christianity and the Social Crisis," *Journal of the American Academy of Religion* 46 (1978): 525–43.

31. Mathews, *Church and the Changing Order*, 3, 100–102.

32. Henry Churchill King, *Reconstruction in Theology* (New York: Macmillan, 1901).

33. Mathews, *Church and the Changing Order*, 13, 17.

34. Newman Smyth, *Passing Protestantism and Coming Catholicism* (New York: Scribner, 1908), 17–21.

35. Harry Emerson Fosdick, *The Living of These Days: An Autobiography* (New York: Harper, 1956), vii.

36. In addition to Fosdick's autobiography, see also William Jewett Tucker, *My Generation: An Autobiographical Interpretation* (Boston: Houghton, Mifflin, 1919), or Shailer Mathews, *New Faith for Old: An Autobiography* (New York: Macmillan, 1936).

37. Walter Rauschenbusch, *A Theology for the Social Gospel* (New York: Macmillan, 1918), 27.

38. William R. Hutchison, ed., *American Protestant Thought: The Liberal Era* (New York: Harper and Row, 1968), 79.

39. Harper, "Theological Curriculum," 46.

40. William Adams Brown, "A Century of Theological Education and After," *Journal of Religion* 6 (1926): 368.

41. Ibid., 373.

42. Shailer Mathews, *The Faith of Modernism* (New York: Macmillan, 1924), 2.

43. Rauschenbusch, *Theology for the Social Gospel*, 8.

44. Cf. Edward Shils, *Tradition* (Chicago: University of Chicago Press, 1981), 38–39, 40, 43.

45. Mathews, *Faith of Modernism*, 97–98.

46. Fosdick, *Living of These Days*, 164.

47. Walter Lippmann, *A Preface to Morals* (New York: Macmillan, 1929), 82.

48. Robert Wohl, *The Generation of 1914* (Cambridge: Harvard University Press, 1979), 5.

49. Mathews, *Church and the Changing Order*, 44–45.

50. Walter Rauschenbusch, *Christianizing the Social Order* (New York: Macmillan, 1912).

51. Cited in Veysey, *Emergence of the American University*, 117.

52. Shailer Mathews, "Vocational Efficiency and the Theological Curriculum," *American Journal of Theology* 16 (1912): 165–80.

53. Benjamin E. Mays, *The Negro's God as Reflected in His Literature* (1938; reprint New York: Russell and Russell, 1968), 23–24, 28–29, 80, 245–55.

54. William Adams Brown, *Christian Theology in Outline* (New York: Scribner, 1906), 57; cf. Hutchison, *Modernist Impulse*, 2.

55. Rauschenbusch, *Christianizing the Social Order*, 119–20.

56. Rauschenbusch, *Theology for the Social Gospel*, 7.

57. Ibid., 5, 14, 20.

58. Ibid., 97, 108–09.

59. Mathews, *Church and the Changing Order*, 11–13.

60. William James, *The Varieties of Religious Experience: A Study in Human Nature* (New York: Longmans, Green, 1902), 331.

61. Mathews, *Faith of Modernism*, 61.

62. James, *Varieties of Religious Experience*, 30, 431, 31 (italics deleted).

63. Shailer Mathews, *The Atonement and the Social Process* (New York: Macmillan, 1930), 9–13, 22–25, 37, 183–84.

64. Shailer Mathews, *The Growth of the Idea of God* (New York: Macmillan, 1931), vii, 3–4, 9, 14–15.

65. Shirley Jackson Case, "The Historical Study of Religion," *Journal of Religion* 1 (1921): 4–5, 11; Shirley Jackson Case, "The Rehabilitation of Church History in Ministerial Education," *Journal of Religion* 4 (1924): 242.

66. Mathews, *Faith of Modernism*, 48–49.

67. Shirley Jackson Case, "The Religious Meaning of the Past," *Journal of Religion* 4 (1924): 582, 589, 590; Case, "Historical Study of Religion," 16; see also Robert W. Funk, "The Watershed of the American Biblical Tradition: The Chicago School, First Phase, 1892–1920," *Journal of Biblical Literature* 95 (1976): 4–22.

68. Gerald Birney Smith, *Practical Theology: A Neglected Field in Theological Education* (Chicago: University of Chicago Press, 1903), 18–19.

69. Gerald Birney Smith, "The Task and Method of Systematic Theology," *American Journal of Theology* 14 (1910): 222–23.

70. Smith, *Practical Theology*, 12–13, 17.

71. Ibid., 3–4, 19.

72. Ibid., 6.

73. Ibid., 20–21.

74. Ibid., 21.

75. Benjamin B. Warfield, "The Task and Method of Systematic Theology," *American Journal of Theology* 14 (1910): 192–205.

76. George Burman Foster, "The Contribution of Critical Scholarship to Ministerial Efficiency," *American Journal of Theology* 20 (1916): 175; Smith, "Task and Method of Systematic Theology," 220; Gerald Birney Smith, *Social Idealism and the Changing Theology* (New York: Macmillan, 1913), 89.

77. William Adams Brown, "The Task and Method of Systematic Theology," *American Journal of Theology* 14 (1910): 208.

78. Ibid., 210, 211.

79. Ibid., 213, 215.

80. William Adams Brown, *The Case for Theology in the University* (Chicago: University of Chicago Press, 1938), 5, 10–14, 69–70, 95–96, 105.

81. Smith, "Task and Method of Systematic Theology," 217–24.

82. Brown, "Task and Method of Systematic Theology," 215.

83. Smith, "Task and Method of Systematic Theology," 226.

84. Ibid., 231.

85. Ibid., 215–16, 230.

86. Mathews, *Faith of Modernism*, 48–49.

87. Mathews, *Atonement*, 185, 187; Mathews, *Idea of God*, 5–6.

88. Rauschenbusch, *Christianizing the Social Order*, 121.

89. Foster, "Critical Scholarship," 168.

90. Ibid., 170.

91. Ibid., 171.

92. Ibid., 173.

93. Ibid., 176.

Chapter Four

1. Robert L. Kelly, *Theological Education in America: A Study of One Hundred Sixty-One Theological Schools in the United States and Canada* (New York: Doran, 1924); William A. Daniel, *The Education of Negro Ministers* (New York: Doran, 1925); William Adams Brown and Mark A. May, *The Education of American Ministers*, 4 vols. (New York: Institute of Social and Religious Research, 1934); H. Richard Niebuhr, Daniel Day Williams, and James M. Gustafson, *The Advancement of Theological Education* (New York: Harper, 1957).

2. Kelly, *Theological Education*, viii.

3. Brown and May, *Education of American Ministers*, 1: 82.

4. Benjamin E. Mays, "The Education of Negro Ministers," *Journal of Negro Education* 2 (1933): 342–51.

5. Niebuhr, Williams, and Gustafson, *Advancement of Theological Education*, 226, 231, 235–36.

6. Brown and May, *Education of American Ministers*, 1: 79–81.

7. Kelly, *Theological Education*, 271–77.

8. Niebuhr, Williams, and Gustafson, *Advancement of Theological Education*, 79, 89, 215.

9. Ibid., 17–19, 23.

10. William R. Hutchison, ed., *Between the Times: The Travail of the Protestant Establishment in America, 1900–1960* (Cambridge: Cambridge University Press, 1989), vii.

11. Brown and May, *Education of American Ministers*, 1: 6–15, 96, 220.

12. William Adams Brown, *Christian Theology in Outline* (New York: Scribner, 1906): 58.

13. William Adams Brown, "A Century of Theological Education and After," *Journal of Religion* 6 (1926): 383.

14. Brown and May, *Education of American Ministers*, 1: 11.

15. William Adams Brown, "The Seminary of Tomorrow," *Harvard Theological Review* 12 (1919): 167.

16. Ibid., 168–74.

17. Ibid., 174–78.

18. William Adams Brown, "The Common Problems of Theological Schools," *Journal of Religion* 1 (1921): 282, 288–89.

19. Ibid., 291–95.

20. William Adams Brown, *The Church in America: A Study of the Present Condition and Future Prospects of American Protestantism* (New York: Macmillan, 1922), vii–viii, 3–4.

21. For examples of the involvement of academic theologians in interdenominational church programs, see Eldon G. Ernst, *Moment of Truth for Protestant America: Interchurch Campaigns Following World War One* (Missoula, Mont.: Scholars Press, 1974).

22. Ronald C. White and C. Howard Hopkins, eds., *The Social Gospel: Religion and Reform in Changing America* (Philadelphia: Temple University Press, 1976), 72–79.

23. Herbert L. Willett, ed., *Progress: Anniversary Volume of the Campbell Institute on the Completion of Twenty Years of History* (Chicago: Christian Century Press, 1917).

24. Harry Emerson Fosdick, *The Living of These Days: An Autobiography* (New York: Harper, 1956), 66.

25. George Burman Foster, "The Contribution of Critical Scholarship to Ministerial Efficiency," *American Journal of Theology* 20 (1916): 178.

26. H. Richard Niebuhr et al., *The Church against the World* (Chicago: Willett, Clark and Company, 1935), 2.

27. H. Richard Niebuhr, "Religious Realism and the Twentieth Century," in *Religious Realism*, ed. Douglas Clyde Macintosh (New York: Macmillan, 1931), 413–14; and *Church against the World*, 135–36.

28. Niebuhr, "Religious Realism," 414–16.

29. Niebuhr et al., *Church against the World*, 17–18 (emphasis added).

30. Ibid., 8.

31. Ibid., 38–59, 102–11, for the views of Wilhelm Pauck and Francis Miller on this process of accommodation to culture.

32. Ibid., 137–38.

33. Ibid., 139 (emphasis added).

34. Ibid., 102–11.

35. Will Herberg, *Protestant, Catholic, Jew: An Essay in American Religious Sociology* (Garden City: Doubleday, 1955), 15.

36. Niebuhr et al., *Church against the World*, 126–27, 135–38.

37. Ibid., 2.

38. Ibid., 3–5.

39. Ibid., 12.

40. H. Richard Niebuhr, "Translator's Preface," in Paul Tillich, *The Religious Situation*, trans. H. Richard Niebuhr (New York: Henry Holt, 1932), xvi–xvii; see also Langdon Gilkey, *Gilkey on Tillich* (New York: Crossroad, 1990), 11–12, 62–63.

41. Niebuhr, "Translator's Preface," xviii–xix.

42. Niebuhr et al., *Church against the World,* 150.

43. H. Richard Niebuhr, *The Kingdom of God in America* (New York: Harper and Row, 1937), 26–27, 137; see also 30, 46–51.

44. H. Richard Niebuhr, *The Purpose of the Church and Its Ministry: Reflections on the Aims of Theological Education* (New York: Harper and Row, 1956), 36–37.

45. H. Richard Niebuhr, *The Meaning of Revelation* (New York: Macmillan, 1941), 5.

46. Ibid., 7.

47. Ibid., 13.

48. The phrase is from Niebuhr, *Kingdom of God in America,* 55.

49. Ibid., 2.

50. Niebuhr, *Meaning of Revelation,* 80 (emphasis added).

51. H. Richard Niebuhr, "The Idea of Covenant and American Democracy," *Church History* 23 (1954): 127.

52. Niebuhr, *Kingdom of God in America,* 2.

53. Niebuhr, "Idea of Covenant," 129–35 (emphasis added); *Kingdom of God in America,* 10.

54. Niebuhr, *Purpose of the Church,* 2–3.

55. For an analysis similar to that of the following paragraphs, see Jon Diefenthaler, "H. Richard Niebuhr: A Fresh Look at His Early Years," *Church History* 52 (1983): 172–85.

56. Brown, "Seminary of Tomorrow," 176.

57. H. Richard Niebuhr, *The Social Sources of Denominationalism* (New York: Henry Holt, 1929), vii, 6, 12.

58. Ibid., 25.

59. Ibid., 16, 21.

60. Ibid., 30–31, 54, 63–65, 72.

61. Ibid., 266.

62. Ibid., 279–80.

63. Ibid., 266.

64. Niebuhr et al., *Church against the World,* 123.

65. Ibid., 123–24.

66. Ibid., 153–55.

67. Niebuhr, *Kingdom of God in America,* xiv–xv.

68. Tillich, *Religious Situation,* 154–55.

69. Niebuhr, *Kingdom of God in America,* 30, 43.

70. Ibid., xiv, 98, 166–68; Niebuhr, *Meaning of Revelation,* x.

71. Niebuhr, *Kingdom of God in America,* 14–15; see also *Meaning of Revelation,* 40.

72. Ibid., 26–27.

73. John W. Nevin, *The Mystical Presence and Other Writings on the Eucharist,* ed. Bard Thompson and George W. Bricker (Philadelphia: United Church Press, 1966), 255.

74. Brown, *Christian Theology*, 58.

75. Niebuhr, *Purpose of the Church*, 26–27.

76. Ibid., 17–18.

77. Ibid., 6.

78. Herberg, *Protestant, Catholic, Jew*, 15, 52–53, 274–76, 284–85.

79. Niebuhr, *Purpose of the Church*, 11–12, 15.

80. Ibid., 87–88.

81. Ibid., 40–41.

82. Ibid., 41.

83. Ibid., 42.

84. Ibid., 43; for an historical interpretation of this same point with regard to American revivalism, see Niebuhr, *Kingdom of God*, 175–77.

85. For the situation of Roman Catholic academics, see John Tracy Ellis, "American Catholics and the Intellectual Life," *Thought* 30 (1955–56): 351–88; B. B. Edwards's comment of 1853 is cited in Sidney E. Mead, *The Lively Experiment: The Shaping of Christianity in America* (New York: Harper, 1963), 129.

86. Merle Curti, "Intellectuals and Other People," *American Historical Review* 60 (1954–55): 275.

87. Richard Hofstadter, *Anti-Intellectualism in American Life* (New York: Random House, 1963), 24–25.

88. Ibid., 26–30.

89. Ibid., 38–39.

90. Jacques Barzun, *The House of Intellect* (New York: Harper, 1949), 4–6.

91. Niebuhr, *Purpose of the Church*, 108 (emphasis added).

92. Ibid., 112.

93. Ibid., 112–13, 125.

94. Ibid., 20.

95. H. Richard Niebuhr, "What Are the Main Issues in Theological Education?" *Theological Education in America*, Bulletin 2 (September, 1954), 9.

96. H. Richard Niebuhr, *Radical Monotheism and Western Culture* (New York: Harper and Row, 1960), 15.

97. Ibid., 95–99.

98. Walter Lippmann, *A Preface to Morals* (New York: Macmillan, 1929), 112–13, 268–69.

99. Niebuhr, *Purpose of the Church*, 28–29; Niebuhr, *Radical Monotheism*, 95–96.

100. Niebuhr, *Meaning of Revelation*, 59.

Chapter Five

1. Daniel Day Williams, "Tradition and Experience in American Theology," in *The Shaping of American Religion*, ed. James Ward Smith and

A. Leland Jamison (Princeton: Princeton University Press, 1961), 443, 445 (emphasis added).

2. Ibid., 456–57.

3. Ibid., 449, 455, 464–68.

4. Ibid., 481.

5. Ibid., 473.

6. Sidney E. Mead, *The Nation with the Soul of a Church* (New York: Harper, 1975), 63, 76; Robert N. Bellah, "Civil Religion in America," in *American Civil Religion*, ed. Russell E. Richey and Donald G. Jones (New York: Harper, 1974), 33, 40.

7. I borrow the term from William R. Hutchison, ed., *Between the Times: the Travail of the Protestant Establishment, 1900–1960* (Cambridge: Cambridge University Press, 1989).

8. Langdon Gilkey, *Naming the Whirlwind: The Renewal of God-Language* (Indianapolis: Bobbs-Merrill, 1969), 9–10, 102–03.

9. John E. Smith, *The Analogy of Experience: An Approach to Understanding Religious Truth* (New York: Harper, 1973), xiv, 48, 63.

10. Gilkey, *Naming the Whirlwind*, 5, 9–10, 18, 39–71.

11. Ibid., 248–49, 297.

12. Smith, *Analogy of Experience*, xiv, 40–41.

13. Gilkey, *Naming the Whirlwind*, 296.

14. See, for example, John B. Cobb, "Claiming the Center," *Criterion* 25 (Winter, 1986): 2–8; Ronald F. Thiemann, "Making Theology Central in Theological Education," *Christian Century* 104 (February 4–11, 1987): 106–08; Van A. Harvey, "On the Intellectual Marginality of American Theology," in *Religion and Twentieth-Century American Intellectual Life*, ed. Michael J. Lacey (Cambridge: Cambridge University Press, 1989), 172–92.

15. Edward Farley, *Theologia: The Fragmentation and Unity of Theological Education* (Philadelphia: Fortress, 1983), 4.

16. Katie G. Cannon et al., *God's Fierce Whimsy: Christian Feminism and Theological Education* (New York: Pilgrim Press, 1985), 6–7.

17. Ibid., 140–41.

18. David A. Hollinger, "How Wide the Circle of the 'We'? American Intellectuals and the Problem of the Ethnos since World War II," *American Historical Review* 98 (1993): 318, 320, 322.

19. For examples of this relation between particularity and transcendence, see James H. Cone, "Black Theology in American Religion," *Journal of the American Academy of Religion* 53 (1985): 755–71; Jacquelyn Grant, "Womanist Theology: Black Women's Experience as a Source for Doing Theology, with Special Reference to Christology," in *African American Religious Studies: An Interdisciplinary Anthology*, ed. Gayraud S. Wilmore (Durham: Duke University Press, 1989), pp. 210, 213, 215, 221.

20. Martin Luther King, Jr., *Where Do We Go from Here: Chaos or Community?* (Boston: Beacon, 1968), 47, 48, 50, 54, 132.

21. Ibid., 133.

22. Cornel West, *Race Matters* (Boston: Beacon, 1993), 3–4.

23. David H. Kelsey, in *Between Athens and Berlin: The Theological Education Debate* (Grand Rapids: Eerdmans, 1993), 95–100, has suggested that contemporary debate over theological education can be organized around two questions of unity and pluralism. One asks whether the theological course of study "is adequate to the inherent unity (or 'integrity' or 'identity') of the 'Christian thing.'" Another asks whether the theological course of study "is adequate to the pluralistic world in which 'the Christian thing' is actually lived." Other critics have suggested that by connecting unity or identity with Christianity, on the one hand, and pluralism with the world, on the other hand, typologies such as Kelsey's themselves constrain the extent of diversity and possibility in the current situation. See, for example, Rebecca Chopp, "When the Center Cannot Contain the Margins," in *The Education of Practical Theologians: Responses to Joseph Hough and John Cobb's Christian Identity and Theological Education*, ed. Don S. Browning, David Polk, and Ian S. Evison (Atlanta: Scholars Press, 1989), 63–76.

24. Martin Luther, *The Large Catechism*, trans. Robert H. Fischer (Philadelphia: Fortress, 1959), 9.

25. It is an interesting case in the history of perceptions that contemporary complaints about the "marginalization" of theological scholarship in the life of churches can trace a lineage at least as old as Cotton Mather's lament of 1723 that before the "excellent young ministers" of Massachusetts "came to be what they are, they found it necessary to lay aside the learning which they brought from the college with them."

26. Jackson W. Carroll and Wade Clark Roof, eds., *Beyond Establishment: Protestant Identity in a Post-Protestant Age* (Louisville: Westminster/John Knox, 1993), 11–27; Robert Wuthnow, *The Restructuring of American Religion: Society and Faith since World War II* (Princeton: Princeton University Press, 1988), 71–99.

27. Joseph C. Hough and John B. Cobb, *Christian Identity and Theological Education* (Chico, Calif.: Scholars Press, 1985), 4, 20.

28. Joseph C. Hough and Barbara G. Wheeler, eds., *Beyond Clericalism: The Congregation as a Focus for Theological Education* (Atlanta: Scholars Press, 1988), 8.

29. Counterproposals to Hopewell's congregational paradigm are made by John B. Cobb, Letty M. Russell, and Beverly W. Harrison, in Ibid., 23–29, 31–35, 137–51.

30. Robert Wood Lynn, "Notes toward a History: Theological Encyclopedia and the Evolution of Protestant Seminary Curriculum, 1808–1968," *Theological Education* 17 (Spring, 1981): 137, 140.

31. Joseph C. Hough, "Reform in Theological Education as Political Task," *Theological Education* 17 (Spring, 1981): 152–66. I borrow the idea

of the theological seminary as a "hybrid creation," from Robert W. Lynn, "Why the Seminary: An Introduction to the Report of the Auburn History Project" (unpublished typescript, 1979), 2–4.

32. Gilkey, *Naming the Whirlwind*, 121–22.

33. Farley, *Theologia*, 35–37.

34. Edward Farley, "The Reform of Theological Education as a Theological Task," *Theological Education* 17 (Spring, 1981): 93–117.

35. These ventures to reform the theological encyclopedia as a critical inquiry receive their most thorough and closely reasoned revaluation from systematic theologian Charles M. Wood of Southern Methodist University in *Vision and Discernment: An Orientation in Theological Study* (Atlanta: Scholars Press, 1985). How, Wood asks, can the various inquiries of the theological curriculum be "ordered to a genuine theological purpose and contribute to one coherent process of reflection in the service of the church?" He recommends that theology is best thought of as a "critical inquiry," which aims to achieve reflective awareness about the standards of judgment appropriate to some prior, ongoing human activity. In the case of theology, that ongoing human activity is the activity of Christian communities, which Wood summarizes with the theological term *witness*. Hence, the comprehensive aim of Christian theology as a critical inquiry, in Wood's view, is "to test Christian witness by the criteria which pertain to its validity precisely as Christian witness." The disciplines of theological study properly represent a series of critical questions about any given instance of Christian witness and a parallel series of constructive questions about the nature of Christian witness per se. The discipline of *historical theology* asks the critical question of whether a given witness is genuinely Christian, thereby also raising the constructive question of the nature of genuine Christian witness. The discipline of *philosophical theology* asks the critical question of whether this witness is true, thereby raising the constructive question of the truth of Christian witness. The discipline of *practical theology* asks the critical question of whether a particular witness is fittingly enacted, thereby raising the constructive question of how Christian witness is fittingly enacted. Finally, systematic theology and moral theology have the comprehensive integrative task of ordering these three basic disciplines into a unified constructive interpretation of Christian teaching and conduct. Adequate theological reflection within this new version of theological encyclopedia, Wood proposes, requires cultivation of two capacities of critical judgment: vision, the capacity to grasp things in their relatedness, and discernment, the capacity to render discriminating assessment of a particular situation. As a specifically educational enterprise, theological study is the process of equipping persons to make these judgments of vision and discernment within the threefold inquiry into Christian witness.

36. Don S. Browning, ed., *Practical Theology: The Emerging Field in Theology, Church, and World* (San Francisco: Harper, 1983); Lewis S.

Mudge and James N. Poling, eds., *Formation and Reflection: the Promise of Practical Theology* (Philadelphia: Fortress, 1987).

37. Hough and Cobb, *Christian Identity and Theological Education*, 81–93.

38. Don S. Browning, *A Fundamental Practical Theology: Descriptive and Strategic Proposals* (Minneapolis: Fortress, 1991), 10–11.

39. Ronald F. Thiemann, *Constructing a Public Theology: The Church in a Pluralistic Culture* (Louisville: Westminster/John Knox, 1991), 154–55.

40. John Williamson Nevin, *The History and Genius of the Heidelberg Catechism* (Chalmersburg, Penn., 1847), 127–28.

41. Stephen L. Carter, *The Culture of Disbelief: How American Law and Politics Trivialize Religious Devotion* (New York: Basic Books, 1993), 8.

42. Robert Bellah, "Discerning Old and New Imperatives in Theological Education," *Theological Education* 19 (1982): 12.

43. Martin E. Marty, *The Public Church: Mainline, Evangelical, Catholic* (New York: Crossroad, 1981), 3–6, 16; Martin E. Marty, "Religious Power in America: A Contemporary Map," *Criterion* 21 (Winter, 1982): 28–29.

44. See, for example, Thiemann, *Constructing a Public Theology;* the statement of the task of public theology comes from Linell E. Cady, "H. Richard Niebuhr and the Task of a Public Theology," in *The Legacy of H. Richard Niebuhr*, ed. Ronald F. Thiemann (Minneapolis: Fortress, 1991), 119.

45. See, most recently, Douglas Sloan, *Faith and Knowledge: Mainline Protestantism and American Higher Education* (Louisville: Westminster/John Knox, 1994).

46. Stephen Crites et al., *Liberal Learning and the Religion Major* (Atlanta: American Academy of Religion, 1990), 3–5, 9–11, 16, 20–21. Although an adequate treatment of this extraordinarily important development is beyond the scope of this book, an invaluable recent guide is Walter H. Capps, *Religious Studies: The Making of a Discipline* (Minneapolis: Fortress, 1995).

47. Leon Pacala, "Reflection on the State of Theological Education in the 1980s," *Theological Education* 18 (Autumn, 1981): 9–43; Jackson W. Carroll, "Project Transition: An Assessment of ATS Programs and Services," *Theological Education* 18 (Autumn, 1981): 45–165.

48. Cf. George Lindbeck, *University Divinity Schools: A Report on Ecclesiastically Independent Theological Education* (New York: Rockefeller Foundation, 1976), v, 1–2, 26, 53–54.

49. Ray L. Hart, "Religious and Theological Studies in American Higher Education: A Pilot Study," *Journal of the American Academy of Religion* 59 (1991): 715–827.

50. For a lucid evaluation and response to this commonplace, see Schubert M. Ogden, "Theology and Religious Studies: Their Difference and the Difference It Makes," *Journal of the American Academy of Religion* 46 (1978): 3–17.

51. William F. May, "Why Theology and Religious Studies Need Each Other," *Journal of the American Academy of Religion* 52 (1984): 748–57.

52. George M. Marsden and Bradley J. Longfield, eds., *The Secularization of the Academy* (New York: Oxford University Press, 1992), pp. 5, 21–39.

53. Cf. James M. Gustafson, "The Sectarian Temptation: Reflections on Theology, the Church and the University," *Proceedings of the Catholic Theological Society of America* 40 (1985): 83–94.

54. I owe this point to Robin W. Lovin, "Faith Seeking Articulation: Doing Theology in Politics," in *Public Faith: Reflections on the Political Role of American Churches*, ed. W. Clark Gilpin (St. Louis: CBP Press, 1990), 7–24.

55. William James, *The Varieties of Religious Experience: A Study in Human Nature* (New York: Longmans, Green, 1902), 141.

56. Ibid.

57. Ibid., 122.

58. William James, *A Pluralistic Universe* (New York: Longmans, 1909), 8.

59. James, *Varieties of Religious Experience*, 122–23.

60. James, *Pluralistic Universe*, 282.

61. Cf. Edward Farley, "Interpreting Situations: An Inquiry into the Nature of Practical Theology," in Mudge and Poling, *Formation and Reflection*, pp. 1–26.

62. James, *Pluralistic Universe*, 212–13.

63. Walter Lippmann, *A Preface to Morals* (New York: Macmillan, 1929), 259.

64. John Dewey, *A Common Faith* (New Haven: Yale University Press, 1934), 18–19.

65. Ibid., 19.

66. Lippmann, *Preface to Morals*, 322.

67. The term "public intellectual" has become ubiquitous since the mid-eighties, not only in books but in popular magazines and professional journals from the *Christian Century* and the *New Yorker* to the *Journal of American History* and *American Literary History*. A provocative reading of the religious issues from a commentator thoroughly conversant with the traditions of American empiricism is William Dean, *The Religious Critic in American Culture* (Albany: State University of New York Press, 1994).

68. John Dewey, *The Public and Its Problems* (New York: Henry Holt, 1927), 12–13, 15, 126, 142.

69. Edward W. Said, *Representations of the Intellectual* (New York: Pantheon, 1994), xiv, xv–xvi, 11–12.

70. Cf. Said, *Representations of the Intellectual,* 44.

71. Vaclav Havel, "The Responsibility of Intellectuals," *New York Review of Books* 42 (June 22, 1995): 36–37.

72. Edward Shils, "The Intellectuals and the Powers: Some Perspectives for Comparative Analysis," in *On Intellectuals: Theoretical and Case Studies,* ed. Philip Rieff (Garden City: Doubleday, 1969), 41.

INDEX